ACCLAIM FOR
THE 5 PATHS TO PERSUASION

"Decoding your prospects is the critical first step in getting to yes, and [this book] offers solid tools for doing exactly that."
—*Fast Company*

"One of the critical challenges in managing a large number of key accounts is how to uniquely define what matters most to each one, yet have a consistent way to discuss and measure value. Miller and Williams's research provides a thorough understanding of each account's needs and a simple way to create and execute overall strategy."
—Tom Levenick, vice president of sales, Labatt USA

"Their research provides an excellent way to look at value from the respondent's point of view. The insights from their data clearly show where and how to focus resources to improve the customer's experience."
—Michael J. Jackson, general manager,
General Motors Western Region

"Miller and Williams tap into not only the rational aspects of the buying decision, but also the emotional drivers, which are recognized as being crucial to a full understanding of buyer behavior."
—Clive Chafer, director, vice president of marketing,
Master-McNeil Inc., Europe

"Will greatly improve high-level sales productivity by helping salespeople identify the five executive decision styles and showing them how to prepare for and present to each of these styles."
—Reed Hilliard, general manager (ret.), Agilent Corporation

THE 5 PATHS TO PERSUASION

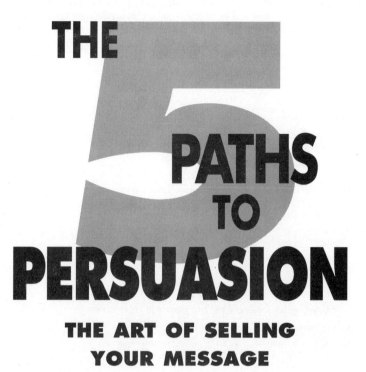

THE ART OF SELLING
YOUR MESSAGE

Robert B. Miller and Gary A. Williams

with Alden M. Hayashi

WARNER
BUSINESS
BOOKS™

NEW YORK   BOSTON

Copyright © 2004 by Robert B. Miller and Gary A. Williams
All rights reserved.

Warner Business Books / Warner Books

Time Warner Book Group
1271 Avenue of the Americas, New York, NY 10020.
Visit our Web site at www.twbookmark.com.

The Warner Business Books logo is a trademark of Warner Books.

Printed in the United States of America
Originally published in hardcover by Warner Books
First Trade Edition: September 2005

10 9 8 7 6 5 4 3 2 1

The Library of Congress has cataloged the hardcover edition as follows:

Miller, Robert B. (Robert Bruce)
      The five paths to persuasion : the art of selling your message /
Robert B. Miller and Gary A. Williams; with Alden Hayashi.   .
            p. cm.
Includes index.
      ISBN 0-446-53239-8
   1. Communication in management. 2. Persuasion (Psychology) 3. Influence (Psychology)
I. Williams, Gary A. II. Title.
      HD30.3.M553 2004
      658.4'5—dc22

                                                                        2003015786

ISBN 0-446-69590-4 (pbk.)

Book design and text composition by L&G McRee
Cover design by Brigid Pearson

Authors' Note

Throughout *The Five Paths to Persuasion*, our goal has been to present an open and candid discussion of the five styles of decision makers and the ways to influence each. To accomplish that—while also respecting the confidentiality of our many clients and colleagues—we have used pseudonyms for them and their companies, and we've also altered certain identifying details of their experiences. For the examples of prominent CEOs and other executives (Carly Fiorina of Hewlett-Packard, Bill Gates of Microsoft, Larry Ellison of Oracle, and so on), some of our classifications of their decision styles are based on our firsthand observations and dealings with them; other categorizations are based on secondary sources, including an extensive review of media accounts of how they've made business decisions. Lastly, for the sake of simplicity, we have used the word "we" loosely throughout this book to indicate both or just one of us.

—RBM and GAW

Acknowledgments

No book just gets written. The origins of this book began many years ago in questions raised by colleagues, friends, family, and clients. Over the years we have been very fortunate to have worked with literally hundreds, if not thousands, of people who not only encouraged us in the development of our ideas and methodologies but also felt strongly enough to coach and critique us. Too numerous to mention individually, we nonetheless acknowledge and are grateful to them all. Three individuals' contributions call for special recognition.

Our literary agent, Daniel Greenberg, and his firm, Levine & Greenberg, have proven themselves to be superb advocates for us to the publishing world, and a constant source of excellent coaching and support. Our abundant thanks.

Rick Wolff, our executive editor at Time Warner Business Books, is the best. His enthusiasm for this project has been contagious, and his encouragement along the path has been much appreciated. It is always great to be in the hands of a true professional.

Finally, our colleague and collaborator, Alden Hayashi, has made this project a joyous endeavor. Not only is he a truly gifted writer and wordsmith, his ability to probe and question us in depth about our research and its implications has produced a much better book than we could have completed by ourselves. Our gratitude is great.

ROBERT B. MILLER
GARY A. WILLIAMS
Spring 2003

Contents

List of Illustrations

Foreword

Ask yourself this question: Is it important to understand how the decisions that affect my company's success will be made? Information and ideas zip around faster than ever before. And while much has been written to help the members of the business community deal with an increasingly complex environment, surprisingly little attention goes toward understanding the fundamental building block of business: individual decision making.

About ten years ago, I had dinner in a small restaurant with Bob Miller. Bob was already a well-established authority on sales and marketing practice with his groundbreaking work represented in the *Strategic Selling*® and *Conceptual Selling*® books and seminars. Our organization was very interested in accelerating its growth, and Bob's guidance did much to help us understand an effective process for setting sales strategy and tactics. During dinner, our conversation turned to the notion of a "decoder ring," some way of interpreting the words, actions, and attitudes of decision makers. The value of the decoder ring is that the people representing a company would be more comfortable and effective in building relationships and exchanging information with the decision makers they wished to serve. You see, I had already experienced the unpleasant frustration of having the best solution to a customer's problem and still finishing in second place.

Fast-forward to about four years ago. Bob came by my office and introduced his partner, Gary Williams. I quickly came to respect Gary's intellect and enthusiasm. With his understanding of research methodology and his uncanny ability to interpret data, and Bob's knowledge of sales process and relationship dynamics, the two make a powerful team. We talked about a couple of projects Bob and Gary proposed tackling for our firm. As our meeting drew to a close, Bob made a reference to our dinner conversation years ago. "We have been working on that decoder ring," he said.

Most of us in business spend a lot of time, energy, and money on developing and delivering the right products and services in hopes of filling a customer's needs. But all of this effort amounts to nothing if the right decision makers don't feel compelled to buy. With *The Five Paths to Persuasion*, Bob and Gary articulate a fresh, straightforward viewpoint on understanding executive decision styles. This book will help you to translate your ideas into a more compelling case whether you are influencing an internal or external decision maker. Bob and Gary, thanks for the decoder ring!

JACK DONOVAN, President,
ARAMARK Education Services Group
May 4, 2003

PART 1

A NEW FRAMEWORK
FOR UNDERSTANDING
PERSUASION

Chapter 1

Introduction

It was a tense weekend. Jason Wheeler and Ed Reynolds, entrepreneurs in Los Angeles, kept on trying to reach their new business partner, Rick Pearson. They called frantically, first Pearson's office, next his home, and then his place in Palm Springs, hoping he might be spending the weekend there. But Pearson was nowhere to be found, and Wheeler and Reynolds had been counting on him for the $100,000 investment he had promised to give them that Friday.

Earlier, Pearson had been ecstatic about the deal. A self-made multimillionaire, he was bored and had been looking for new business opportunities. So when Wheeler and Reynolds told him about this new urban recording artist who had just broken from her recording company, Pearson was instantly enthralled with the idea of signing her up and launching a new label to advance her career. He had promised Wheeler and Reynolds the $100,000 as an initial investment—money that the two men were now counting on to finance some promotional work for her. But then Friday rolled around and Pearson had all but disappeared. What happened?

In today's tough business environment, deals are being lost, promotions are being scuttled, and raises are being denied because people lack the necessary skills to effectively persuade others. Even win-win proposals that should have been no-brainers are instead being tabled—the victims of intense scrutiny and skepticism. Indeed, especially in tough times, good ideas do not sell themselves; they need help.

In *The Five Paths to Persuasion*, we present a new framework for understanding how best to influence others. From our two-year study of nearly seventeen hundred executives, we have found that persuasion is most effective when it's tailored to one of five types of people:

- *Charismatics*, like Jack Welch and Oprah Winfrey, who are easily enthralled with new ideas, particularly bold and innovative ones, but will not make a move until they are sure that others have thought through the details
- *Thinkers*, like Bill Gates and Michael Dell, who need to cautiously and methodically work through each pro and con of every conceivable option before rendering a decision
- *Skeptics*, like Larry Ellison and Ted Turner, who are highly suspicious of every piece of information and will rarely trust anything that doesn't fit with their worldview
- *Followers*, like Carly Fiorina and Peter Coors, who make decisions based mainly on how other trusted people, including themselves, have made similar decisions in the past
- *Controllers*, like Martha Stewart and Ross Perot, who must be in charge of every aspect of the decision-making process and need to have some ownership of an idea before proceeding with it

The five styles of decision making span a wide range of behavioral characteristics. Controllers, for instance, shun risk, whereas Charismatics actively seek it out. But in spite of such differences, people often mistakenly use a one-size-fits-all approach when trying to persuade others, concentrating too much on the content of their argument and not enough on how the intended recipient wants to receive that information. In fact, we know of numerous companies that force their salespeople to use canned presentations, with the same format and order of information—down to the exact number of PowerPoint slides!—for different customers in diverse industries. Another common mistake is that people misapply the Golden Rule: They try to sway others as they themselves would like to be persuaded.

Such tactics simply don't work. In our research, we have found that far too many decisions have gone the wrong way because of a crucial mismatch in how information was presented versus how it *should* have been presented. An argument geared for a Follower, for instance, might easily flop when delivered to a Skeptic, no matter how terrific the ideas. Instead, people should tailor their presentations to the executives they are trying to persuade, using the best language to deliver the right information in the most effective sequence and format. After all, Bill Gates and Oprah Winfrey do not make important business decisions in the same way. Knowing the differences can dramatically improve your ability to sway executives like them.

Human behavior is far too complex for cookie-cutter approaches. But the breakthrough of our new framework is that you don't have to start from scratch every single time you're dealing with someone new. Our study shows that executives tend to make big decisions in one of five predictable ways, and through empirical research we have determined the strategies that are the most effective for influencing each. *Paths to Persuasion* helps you to understand—and adapt to—the different ways in which your colleagues, partners, bosses, and others make decisions. In particular, you will learn how the five types of executives prefer to hear (or see) specific types of information at different stages in their decision-making processes.

With this information, you can tap into the full power of persuasion. You will be both seen and heard, even by busy top executives. You will push through your initiatives and close deals. And you will successfully argue for the raises and promotions you deserve. In short, by learning how to make your arguments stick, you'll avoid the type of costly mistake that the entrepreneurs Wheeler and Reynolds committed, and you will get business done.

Chapter 2

How Does Persuasion Work?

The process of persuasion appears mysterious and inexplicable only when you don't understand the underlying principles. In fact, whether you're successful or not in influencing others is hardly a matter of luck or happenstance. To be effective, you first need to recognize that

1. **Proposals must be custom-tailored.** All too often, deals fall through because they aren't presented with arguments targeted specifically to the decision maker.
2. **The behavior of executives can be decoded.** People make important decisions by receiving and processing information in one of five styles: Charismatic, Thinker, Skeptic, Follower, or Controller.
3. **Persuasion requires an arsenal of tools.** To influence each of the five types of decision maker, you need to know what tools to use—and in what order.

PROPOSALS MUST BE CUSTOM-TAILORED

Executives succeed or fail largely on their ability to make good decisions—and to recognize and correct bad ones quickly. This is particularly true for crucial choices (whether to close a division, for instance) when the chips are down and the pressure's on. Learning mostly from experience, successful executives have built a complex and often subtle set of criteria that guides their thinking. Both logic and emotion play important roles, but how each of those is weighted during the decision-making process can vary greatly depending on the individual. Of course, some executives are much better skilled than others at making good decisions, and even though they strike out on occasion, their batting averages over time are exemplary. Especially in clutch situations, they hit their fair share of home runs and grand slams, earning them the top jobs.

We have long been intrigued by the decision-making processes of executives—and for good reason. For decades, we've taught the principles of *Strategic Selling*®, a best-selling book that one of us (Bob) coauthored, to myriad large corporations, including blue-chip corporations like ARAMARK, Coca-Cola, Bank of America, Hallmark, Hertz, Hewlett-Packard, Johnson & Johnson, and Rockwell International, to name just a handful. Specifically, we have helped implement at those companies a disciplined and proven approach for making important sales to other businesses. One of the key lessons of *Strategic Selling*® is that salespeople need to identify the key decision maker (called the Economic Buyer) who will give the final approval to buy a product or service. This key person has the power and authority to say yes when everybody else has said no, and he can also kill a deal by overriding the favorable recommendations of others.

Throughout the years, we have found that our clients would often do everything right—removing all the obstacles to a deal—but then their proposal would somehow get stuck with the key decision maker. Or, worse, that executive would kill a deal even when it should have been a slam dunk. What had happened in those situations? Why had the executive vetoed a proposal, even when his key lieutenants had been pushing for it to go forward?

That question has long troubled us because we have seen countless instances of decisions going the wrong way. The disappointment can be painfully perplexing, especially after you've expended considerable effort to identify the key decision maker, address her concerns, and get a meeting scheduled with her, only to find that the deal gets mysteriously scuttled in the final stage for unknown reasons. And therein lies the problem: If you don't understand how people make decisions—the kinds of information they need and the order in which they need it—how effective can you be in influencing their thinking, trying to get them to see your point of view? Without knowing how people think, you could very well be transmitting important information that the key decision maker is not receiving (or, worse, is receiving but is misinterpreting).

THE BEHAVIOR OF EXECUTIVES CAN BE DECODED

The study of persuasion dates back millennia. In ancient Greece, because citizens had to argue their own cases in the courts of law, they would seek the counsel of sophists, professionals skilled in the art of rhetoric. The Greek philosopher Aristotle contended that effective persuasive skills required three elements: *logos* (well-reasoned arguments), *ethos* (the speaker's credibility and trustworthiness), and *pathos* (the feelings and mind-set of the audience). In other words, Aristotle rightly understood that persuasion relies on both rational and emotional factors (winning both the minds *and* hearts of people) and that the process is a two-way street, relying not only on how information is transmitted but also in how it's received.

Nevertheless, subsequent research over the centuries has tended to assume that people are basically the same, that we, for example, are all swayed by bargains ("Act now and you'll get two for the price of one!"). But different individuals can have disparate reactions to the same circumstances. For instance, although many people will jump to take advantage of a bargain, others might be suspicious ("Why are they offering two for the price of one? Is something wrong?"). Such differences are what this book is all about.

To investigate them, we conducted a two-year study of 1,684 executives from a wide range of industries, including automotive, consulting, consumer durables and apparel, retail, services, software, and telecommunications. For the project, we interviewed the participants through e-mail, fax, in person, and over the phone. Roughly 70 percent of the interviews were done on-line, primarily because of time constraints on the part of the executives, another 10 percent were conducted through faxes, and the remainder were done in person or over the phone. (For additional details of the study, see appendix I.)

During the interviews, we asked the participants about the different facets of their decision-making processes. The executives described their various tendencies—for instance, how much time they typically needed to make a decision. That is, could they be comfortable making a big decision on the spot, or do they require at least overnight to sleep on it? Such characteristics and preferences are often set early in a businessperson's career, and they evolve based on experience. In short, people have natural tendencies toward decision making that get reinforced through repeated successes—or that are changed after multiple failures.

We then mapped the answers to those interview questions onto different components. From an extensive review of the psychological literature, we identified a total of twelve attributes that are important in how people make decisions:

1. *Risk:* the willingness to make decisions that might have large negative consequences
2. *Responsibility:* the desire for authority to make decisions *and* be held accountable for their outcome
3. *Competitiveness:* the drive (and ambition) to achieve more than others
4. *Rebellion:* the desire to move beyond the status quo and generally accepted alternatives
5. *Impulsiveness:* the urge to make attention-grabbing and thrilling final decisions, often very quickly
6. *Persistence:* the desire for others (and for oneself) to continually drive the decision-making process toward a final resolution

7. *Fear and uncertainty*: the tendency to become worried or concerned when making a particular decision
8. *Self-absorption*: the habit of becoming unduly concerned with one's own thoughts, interests, and activities
9. *Playfulness*: the desire for lively, spirited interactions with others in the decision-making process
10. *Education*: the need to learn and understand from others about the various issues involved in a decision
11. *Intelligence and facts*: the need for rational, highly accurate information
12. *Bargains*: the willingness to make spur-of-the-moment decisions provided the price is right

After we had compiled the data from the interviews, we performed a cluster analysis and found that the behavior of the executives fell into one of five groups, which we've labeled Charismatics, Thinkers, Skeptics, Followers, and Controllers. Each of them shares definite and distinct likes and dislikes with respect to the twelve components of decision making. Charismatics, for instance, seek responsibility in making big decisions, whereas Skeptics avoid it. The exhibit "Summary of the Five Styles of Decision Makers" contains a high-level description of the different categories. The accuracy of our survey results—for example, that 25 percent of the executives in our study were Charismatics—is plus or minus 2.9 percent. (For details of how each of the twelve components is related to the five styles of decision makers, see appendix II.)

In the May 2002 issue of the *Harvard Business Review*, we published the early results from our research, and in this book we present a comprehensive analysis and discussion, including our latest findings. Our study of executive decision making is ongoing. We are currently in the process of updating the data, and we plan to do so annually.

We should note that people in our study did not classify themselves into the five categories. The assessments were done automatically through a cluster and regression analysis based on how the participants answered the interview questions. Furthermore, our research should not be confused with standard tests and indicators like Myers-Briggs, which are skewed more toward a person's personality. Our

SUMMARY of the FIVE STYLES of DECISION MAKERS

	CHARISMATICS 25%	THINKERS 11%	SKEPTICS 19%	FOLLOWERS 36%	CONTROLLERS 9%
DESCRIPTION	Charismatics are always looking for the next big idea, and they are easily enthralled with bold, innovative approaches.	Thinkers need to cautiously and methodically work through each pro and con of every conceivable option before rendering a decision.	Skeptics are inherently suspicious of any information that doesn't fit with their worldview. They need to hear things from very credible sources.	Followers make decisions based on how other trusted executives (including themselves) have made them in the past.	Controllers must be in charge of every aspect of the decision-making process. They need to have some ownership of an idea before proceeding with it.
PROMINENT EXAMPLES	Richard Branson Lee Iacocca Herb Kelleher Jack Welch Oprah Winfrey	Warren Buffett Michael Dell Bill Gates Katharine Graham Alan Greenspan	Steve Case Larry Ellison Tom Siebel Ted Turner	Edgar Bronfman Jr. Peter Coors Carly Fiorina Bob Nardelli Jim Parker	Jacques Nasser Rosie O'Donnell Ross Perot Martha Stewart George Steinbrenner
CHARACTERISTICS	Enthusiastic imaginers, innovative risk seekers, proactive and decisive, responsible and accountable, bottom-liners, interactive	Methodical and process-oriented, information-driven, quantitative and precise, relentlessly thorough, guarded and cautious, balanced, intellectually fluid	Iconoclasts, brazenly outspoken, fearlessly confident, assertive and demanding, determined and driven, visionary	Devoted to the tried and the true, averse to the new, conscientious corporate citizens, deft people handlers, empathetic, difficult to identify	Driven by fear, proactive, fiercely self-reliant, absolute and resolute, meticulous, unyielding perfectionists

study focused specifically on how people make decisions (the amount of time they need, for instance) and not on their personalities.

Of course, people don't make decisions in exactly the same way every time; much depends on the circumstances. Nevertheless, we contend that when it comes to difficult, high-stakes choices that involve numerous complex issues and serious consequences, everyone has a style of decision making that they're most comfortable with and that they will use. Call it a default mode. It's what's worked for them in the past, and it's the style that they will use in the future, particularly when the pressure's on.

PERSUASION REQUIRES AN ARSENAL OF TOOLS

In the study, we also asked the participants to describe how others have been presenting information to them. Their responses confirmed much of what we have experienced in our combined sixty years in sales, marketing, and consulting for executives at a variety of companies. Specifically, we uncovered a staggering mismatch between how people want information presented to them and how others are actually presenting it. For example, close to 80 percent of sales presentations focus on Skeptics and Controllers, even though those two groups represent less than 30 percent of all executives. Furthermore, virtually no presentations are targeted at Charismatics, yet that group accounts for fully a quarter of the population. Followers are also underserved: Only 6 percent of presentations are geared toward them despite the fact that more than one of three executives is a Follower.

Our primary goal in *Paths to Persuasion* is to provide you with a new framework and the tools to prevent such mismatches. To persuade the five styles, each of which requires a different approach, we introduce the concept of a *persuasion toolkit*. The generic toolkit contains more than a dozen items, including assessments of risk, case studies of similar proposals, testimonials from key people, recommendations from experts, and so on. (See exhibit "The Persuasion

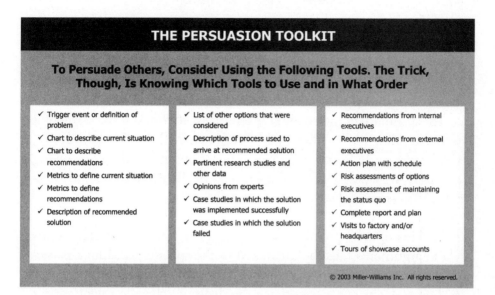

THE PERSUASION TOOLKIT

To Persuade Others, Consider Using the Following Tools. The Trick, Though, Is Knowing Which Tools to Use and in What Order

- ✓ Trigger event or definition of problem
- ✓ Chart to describe current situation
- ✓ Chart to describe recommendations
- ✓ Metrics to define current situation
- ✓ Metrics to define recommendations
- ✓ Description of recommended solution

- ✓ List of other options that were considered
- ✓ Description of process used to arrive at recommended solution
- ✓ Pertinent research studies and other data
- ✓ Opinions from experts
- ✓ Case studies in which the solution was implemented successfully
- ✓ Case studies in which the solution failed

- ✓ Recommendations from internal executives
- ✓ Recommendations from external executives
- ✓ Action plan with schedule
- ✓ Risk assessments of options
- ✓ Risk assessment of maintaining the status quo
- ✓ Complete report and plan
- ✓ Visits to factory and/or headquarters
- ✓ Tours of showcase accounts

Toolkit.") This array of tools can be customized to your particular company and job. In most situations, each of the items will be present (though not necessarily utilized) in one form or another.

A crucial item in the toolkit is the *trigger event*, defined as a change that spurs people to act. The classic example is an IRS audit that finally pushes someone to hire an accountant after months of procrastination. In business, examples of trigger events are a start-up entering the market with a new technology, a competitor slashing its prices, new governmental regulations, a defection of major customers, and so on. With some executives (specifically, Controllers), the trigger event must actually occur before they will respond. For other execs, a warning of an upcoming trigger event is often sufficient to provoke action.

Consider the persuasion toolkit to be the arsenal at your disposal. The trick, though, is knowing what tools to deploy and in what order (and whether to use some of the tools at all), because that knowledge will lead you down the right path to persuading others. A key thing to remember is that different types of people prefer hearing (or seeing) certain types of information at specific points in an argument. Thinkers, for instance, want all the details of a proposal presented to them in a logical fashion, whereas Charismatics are interested in just the bottom line. Using the wrong tools (or the right ones but in the wrong order) will likely lead you down dead ends that can be difficult, if not impossible, to escape from.

To summarize, persuading executives requires a fundamental understanding of how they make decisions. Without that knowledge, you could easily become your own worst enemy by doing or saying precisely the wrong thing at the wrong time. To avoid such costly mistakes, you should always keep in mind that

- Cookie-cutter approaches aren't effective. Instead, presentations and arguments must be organized in the specific way that a particular executive likes to receive information.
- How and why executives make the decisions they do might appear puzzling only when you don't understand the factors that are governing their behavior. In fact, executives make decisions in one of five predictable ways.
- There is no easy solution and no silver bullet. Persuasion requires an array of tools that must be used in a specific order, all targeted to the decision style of the person you're trying to sway.

Before we begin our journey down the different paths of persuasion, there are a few points worth discussing. First, we would like to emphasize that our categorizations of executives are meant only to describe their decision-making processes. Some people might view some of our labels as pejorative, particularly the words "Follower" and "Controller," but our intention was not to judge any of the five decision-making styles or to imply that one might be inferior to another. We selected our labels merely as brief descriptors of the primary way in which each group tends to make decisions. As you will learn in chapters 3 through 12, each style can be very effective in certain organizations and situations. Followers, for instance, tend to be highly responsible decision makers who can excel at large, established corporations. Controllers, too, can be among the best type of executive when a company is undergoing dramatic transformations to its business. In other words, no decision-making style is inherently better than another, and each of them has proven highly effective for countless successful executives.

Recently, we received an e-mail from the COO of a telecom company in the Netherlands who wondered if we had any conclusions about which style of decision making tends to lead to better choices. The short answer is that we have not investigated that issue in any quantitative way. That is, we haven't tried to determine what percentage of Charismatics are good decision makers and then compared that with the percentage of Thinkers (or Skeptics, Followers, or Controllers) who also happen to be exemplary in that regard. Empirically, though, we can definitely say that we've observed good decision making in all five styles. We've observed bad decision making in all of them, too. Each style has its distinct strengths and weaknesses, and under different circumstances a strength can easily become a weakness (and vice versa).

Throughout this book, we describe the five decision-making styles in detail, but we are fully aware that this information is neither exhaustive nor definitive. In many respects, one Controller can be very different from another, for instance, and they both might exhibit only some of the traits we list. Nevertheless, the general characteristics that we discuss will help you to distinguish among the five types. To help in that process, chapters 3 through 12 present *approach profiles* that highlight the likes and dislikes of Charismatics, Thinkers, Skeptics, Followers, and Controllers. (In those chapters, we also describe specific tactics for influencing each of the styles.)

Interestingly, we have found that the demands of a particular job will sometimes accentuate or attenuate certain aspects of a person's natural style. For example, a Thinker in a small start-up might have to speed up his decision making. But the default mode will always still be there. That is, a Thinker might be able to emulate the decision-making process of a Charismatic when he absolutely has to, but the change will be uncomfortable and very likely not as effective. In chapter 13, we discuss the situational aspects of decision making in greater detail, and we provide useful tools and tips that can help to identify people's true default modes of decision making. Specifically, we introduce the *behavioral dial*, which helps to explain how the five styles are related.

We should also note that our categorizations are based solely on how people make decisions—and not necessarily on their personalities. Someone with a charismatic personality, for instance, can easily have a Follower style of decision making. That said, people in a grouping do tend to share similar characteristics; for example, Skeptics tend to be somewhat antisocial. In chapter 14, we address this issue in detail, and we talk about how confusion between personality and decision-making style can lead to bad mistakes.

Lastly, we want to emphasize that our intention is not to trivialize the intricate and subtle ways in which people analyze situations to arrive at their conclusions. Without question, scientists may never fully understand the myriad complexities of that process. But our research shows that executives do tend to behave in certain predictable ways when they need to make big decisions. They prefer, for example, to receive specific information in a certain order, and if you understand those tendencies, you can substantially increase the impact of your arguments.

Such knowledge can also be invaluable in various other business situations. In chapter 15, we describe how you can assemble better teams by considering each potential member's decision-making style, and we also discuss the most effective ways to persuade small groups as well as large audiences. More important, chapter 15 explains in detail the underlying principle that we hope you'll learn from this book. That take-home message is this: It's not about you. Persuasion is all about the other person—his needs, his concerns, and his issues. More to the point, persuasion is all about how the other person processes information to make crucial decisions. To be effective in swaying someone, you first have to put yourself in that person's place and understand his style of making decisions, whether he's a Charismatic, Thinker, Skeptic, Follower, or Controller. Only then can you begin to tailor your message for maximum impact. With that basic principle in mind, let's begin our journey down the different paths to persuasion.

PART 2

THE FIVE STYLES OF
DECISION MAKING—AND
HOW TO INFLUENCE EACH

Chapter 3

The Charismatic Decision Maker

EXAMPLES	**Herb Kelleher, Jack Welch, Richard Branson, Lee Iacocca, and Oprah Winfrey**

Charismatics are always looking for the next big idea. When something strikes their fancy, they quickly embrace it, showing intense emotion and enthusiasm. In particular, they love innovative approaches and are not threatened by bold, revolutionary thinking. Yet although Charismatics are easily enthralled with new ideas, they make their final decision based on a balanced set of information because they've been burned by their impulsiveness too many times in the past. In essence, Charismatics are

1. **Enthusiastic imaginers.** They are passionate about new ideas and can easily envision the exciting possibilities of a proposal without getting prematurely bogged down in the messy details.
2. **Innovative risk seekers.** They embrace out-of-the-box thinking and are often entrepreneurs and mavericks in their industry.
3. **Proactive and decisive.** They make bold decisions quickly— but only when they are sure that others have thought through all the issues.

4. **Responsible and accountable.** They seldom pass the buck, and they readily take the blame for their mistakes.
5. **Bottom-liners.** They cut to the chase quickly, demanding to know the headlines and bulleted items.
6. **Interactive.** They think aloud, openly communicating their thoughts with others in efforts to stimulate the discussion.

ENTHUSIASTIC IMAGINERS

When Herb Kelleher and Rollin King founded Southwest Airlines in 1971, they broke all the rules. Drawing up their basic business plan on a cocktail napkin in a bar, they decided to concentrate on short-haul markets—Dallas to Houston, for instance—and compete against ground transportation. To do that, they had to slash costs, so they decided to do away with assigned seats for passengers so that employees could turn planes around quickly at the gate. The cut-rate, no-frills airline became a dazzling success—a multibillion-dollar operation that has been the subject of many a glowing case study on how to run a business.

Kelleher's penchant for embracing out-of-the-box thinking has become the stuff of legend. When someone pointed out to him that many mechanics couldn't attend company picnics because they had to work the graveyard shift, Kelleher decided to have a barbecue at 2:00 A.M., with him and several pilots doing duty as the chefs.[1] When a potentially messy and expensive legal battle loomed over another firm's use of Southwest's slogan, Kelleher contacted the CEO of the other company and suggested they settle their dispute quick and easy by arm wrestling. (Kelleher won.) To ease tensions between flight attendants and their schedulers, Southwest had the two sides switch jobs for a day so that each could gain a better grasp of the other's perspective.[2]

Kelleher, who chain-smokes and is particularly fond of bourbon, has woven his passion for good ideas into the very fabric of the Southwest Airlines culture. "The rule at Southwest is, if somebody has an idea, you read it quickly and you respond instantaneously," says Kelleher. "I think showing respect for people's ideas is very, very important because as soon as you stop doing that, you stop getting ideas . . . You ought to be with your people enough that they are comfortable to just pop on in and give you their ideas."[3]

Reverence for ideas is common among Charismatics. "You have to encourage all your people to make a contribution to the common good and to come up with better ways of doing things," says Lee Iacocca, former head of Chrysler. "You don't have to accept every single suggestion, but if you don't get back to the guy and say, 'Hey, that idea was terrific,' and pat him on the back, he'll never give you another one."[4]

Jack Welch, the renowned former CEO of General Electric, operates in a similar vein. "Business isn't all about creativity. It's about seeing the value of an idea—sometimes having it, sometimes seeing it, but expanding it," he says. "Seeing an idea is as valuable as having it. Using it, and sharing it, bringing it to life, is as valuable as generating it."[5] When Welch was asked what kept him from becoming bored even after running GE for seventeen years, his response revealed the classic restlessness that a Charismatic feels. "We get a great kick out of the fact that we have made this company think outside itself," he said. "We want people who get up every morning with a passion about finding a better way: finding from their associate in the office, finding from another company. We're constantly on the search."[6]

Likewise, Richard Branson, the founder of Virgin Group, is always on the hunt. Over the years, he has owned stakes in hundreds of businesses, spanning a dizzying array: airlines, cosmetics, trains, soft drinks, financial services, music stores, cinemas, mobile phones, and bridal services. Described as a "classic throw-it-against-the-wall guy," Branson keeps a notebook with him just to keep track of his myriad business ideas.

Known as "big picture" people, Charismatics can't be bothered with number crunching. In fact, they might even pride themselves on that. Oprah Winfrey, for instance, readily admits that she can't read a balance sheet even though she runs a multimillion-dollar empire that encompasses her talk show, her magazine, Harpo Films, and a stake in Oxygen Media, the women's cable company.[7] Similarly, Branson admits, "It took me years to work out the difference between net and gross."[8] In his autobiography, Branson talks about how his dyslexia, which plagued him in his school years, made him more intuitive. "When someone sends me a written proposal," he says, "rather than dwelling on detailed facts and figures I find that my imagination grasps and expands on what I read."[9]

Charismatics see the world in pictures, images, diagrams, and charts. Jack Welch says that to prepare for analyst meetings, he would often sit for hours with his finance and investor relations teams, working on figure after figure. "I've always thought that chart-making clarified my thinking better than anything else," he notes. "Reducing a complex problem to a simple chart excited the hell out of me."[10] Charismatics are fond of using visual metaphors in their speaking and writing, and they can be particularly concerned with visual appearances. Not surprisingly, they are usually impeccably dressed—and they frequently expect everyone around them to be, too.

INNOVATIVE RISK SEEKERS

In conjunction with their passion for new ideas, Charismatics are not afraid of risk. In fact, they actively court it. Richard Branson, who once crash-landed in a hot-air balloon attempting to circle the globe, gets a rush from taking on the big guys. After starting Virgin Atlantic Airways to compete against the well-entrenched British Airways, he had the sheer audacity to launch Virgin Cola, going head-to-head against Coca-Cola and PepsiCo in one of the toughest markets to crack.

At General Electric, Jack Welch worked hard to keep the multinational corporation as adventurous and entrepreneurial as possible. "One of the real advantages of a big company," he says, "is the ability to take on big projects with huge potential. The quickest way to neutralize that advantage is to go after the scalps of those who dare to dream and reach—but fail. That just reinforces a risk-averse culture."[11] As an example, he relates the story of GE's attempt in the late 1970s to develop Halarc, a lightbulb that would last ten times longer than a conventional bulb and use less energy. The $50-million project ultimately failed. "Instead of 'punishing' those involved in the Halarc effort," Welch says, "we celebrated their great try. We handed out cash management awards and promoted several Halarc players to new jobs . . . We wanted everyone in the company to know that taking a big swing and missing was okay."[12]

Welch certainly lived that philosophy himself when he postponed his retirement in 2001 to try to pull off what would have been the biggest deal in GE's history—the proposed merger with Honeywell— a move that ultimately flopped. When asked whether he regretted that decision, his response was that of a dyed-in-the-wool Charismatic: "When the chance to do this deal came along . . . , I had two choices—take a swing or not. It was a no-brainer. Why would the last act of my corporate life be to play it safe?"[13]

Branson, who has experienced his fair share of business flops, has a similar perspective. "Most of our businesses do succeed," he says, "but if something completely fails, as long as we bow out gracefully and pay off all our debts, and nobody gets hurts, then I don't think people disrespect Virgin for trying."[14]

That's why many successful Charismatic executives have strong number two people—to help them kill the bad ideas. For Lee Iacocca when he was at the helm of Chrysler, that person was Tom Denomme, then vice president of corporate strategy. This is how Iacocca describes Denomme: "His real title should be devil's advo- cate. He tosses out an idea a minute, some of them a bit off the wall."[15] The standing joke among Branson's key lieutenants is that one of their jobs is to keep the boss grounded. "Richard comes up with ideas, and we say: 'Down, Richard,'" notes Virgin Atlantic CEO Steve Ridgway.[16]

PROACTIVE AND DECISIVE

Charismatics have no trouble pulling the trigger when the timing is right; they do not suffer from "analysis paralysis." "I was never one of those guys who could just sit around and strategize endlessly," says

Lee Iacocca. "Unfortunately, the world doesn't always wait for you while you try to anticipate your losses. Sometimes you just have to take a chance—and correct your mistakes as you go along."[17] Iacocca, who was famous for his bold decision making, explains his philosophy for action: "At some point you've got to take that leap of faith. First, because even the right decision is wrong if it's made too late. Second, because in most cases there's no such thing as certainty."[18]

Indeed, Charismatics are decisive, take-charge people who loathe wasting time in consensus management. A favorite hobbyhorse of Bob Lutz, the former president of Chrysler and now the chairman of GM North America, is the dangers of *not* ruffling feathers. "The ability to compromise is, of course, a wonderful thing," he says. "And the promotion of team members' self-esteem is, of course, a noble goal. But neither is an end in itself. We're not running major corporations in order to perform social experiments. We are attempting to get work done."[19] For Southwest's Kelleher, the mantra of "ready, fire, aim" works fine for him. "If you take too much time aiming," he explains, "you never get to fire. You have to strike quickly with blinding speed . . . If you don't do it, someone else is going to."[20]

In their daily lives, Charismatics have little time for self-absorption and introspection. Hamlet was definitely not a Charismatic; Jack Welch most certainly is. When Welch was told that some critics of his best-selling autobiography, *Jack: Straight from the Gut*, contended that the book failed to reveal the inner man, he replied tersely, "I wrote the book I wanted to write. I may not have written the book that they wanted me to write."[21] Later, when asked in an interview whether he, like many heroes, had tragic flaws, he said, "That's something I've never thought about. I don't think that much about myself."[22]

Richard Branson exudes a similar impatience for looking inward. "Some people say that my vision for Virgin breaks all the rules and is too wildly kaleidoscopic," he says. "Others say that Virgin is set to become one of the leading brand names of the next century; others analyze it down to the last degree and then write academic papers on it. As for me, I just pick up the phone and get on with it."[23]

This is not to say that Charismatics are reckless gunslingers. They are not. They avoid acting rashly, continually fighting their urge to make spur-of-the-moment decisions. When Welch was asked what his biggest weakness was, he replied, "I may be too impulsive . . . I'll get into a deal too fast sometimes. Or I'll take a shine to someone and immediately give him or her a battlefield promotion. That wasn't such a great formula early in my life. My success rate was 50-50 at best."[24]

This explains why Charismatics often show great exuberance for a new idea and then defer in giving their final commitment. In fact, the emotions of Charismatics are only the first step in their decision-making. Through their experience (typically from the bad decisions they've made), they have learned to temper their initial enthusiasm by checking into the rational measures for moving forward. They seek out facts to support their emotions, and if such data can't be found, they quickly lose enthusiasm for an idea. Charismatics may not seem to want all the details of each bulleted item, but they need to know that there's a well-developed plan to back up each of those items. In other words, they must know that others have thought through everything, and unless they are secure in that knowledge, they won't take action because they've been burned too many times in the past.

One of the strongest dislikes for a Charismatic is when people don't have the complete answers or they haven't done the necessary work to be confident that they do. Charismatics respect those who have done their homework and can stand up to aggressive interrogation. "Self-confident people aren't afraid to have their views challenged," says Welch. "They relish the intellectual combat that enriches ideas."[25] In short, Charismatics need to know that everything's been analyzed thoroughly. When something is questionable, *everything* becomes suspect. A single red flag will raise countless others, and soon the Charismatic has lost all confidence and trust in a person's proposal.

RESPONSIBLE AND ACCOUNTABLE

To be sure, successful Charismatics are responsible decision makers who only take *educated* risks. "In the press, I'm sometimes described as a flamboyant leader and a hip-shooter, a kind of fly-by-the-seat-of-the-pants operator," says Lee Iacocca. "But if that image were really true, I could never have been successful . . . Whenever I've taken risks, it's been after satisfying myself that the research and the market studies supported my instincts. I may act on my intuition—but only if my hunches are supported by the facts."[26]

From their past mistakes, Charismatics have learned to keep their intense emotions and passions in check. "You have to look at things the way a scientist would: This experiment didn't work out; it's over," says Herb Kelleher, the former Southwest CEO. "You can't get emotional about it. That's the key as far as I'm concerned: There's no ego involved. You can't keep something on life support for years and years because you've let your self-esteem get tied up in things."[27]

This keen sense of responsibility in Charismatics is underscored by internal and external congruity of how they act and what they say. In other words, they walk the talk, and what they say is what they do. Think of John Wayne's character in the movie *True Grit*. Yes, Charismatics can talk a good game, but they will also get the results to back them up. The caveat here is that with Charismatics the thought is the deed. After they have given their initial approval, they expect you to do the necessary follow-up work because, quite frankly, they will be too busy moving on to the next big idea. Charismatics can't understand why, if they've expressed their initial enthusiasm, others haven't followed through to investigate the idea thoroughly and confirm its merits. With a Charismatic, the ball is always in someone else's court for follow-through.

While Charismatics are risk takers, they are totally willing to be held accountable for their decisions and will take responsibility when they've messed up. In his autobiography, Jack Welch readily takes his lumps for GE's ill-advised acquisition of Kidder, Peabody, a merger that several GE board members had expressed their reservations about. "It was a classic case of hubris," admits Welch. "Frankly, I was just full of myself . . . I thought I could make anything work."[28]

After the acquisition, Welch learned that GE would have to take a $350-million charge against its earnings because one of Kidder's traders had made numerous fictitious trades. Welch blames himself for not personally investigating that trader, who had just netted a $9-million cash bonus. "Normally . . . I would have dug into how one person could be so successful, and I would have insisted on meeting him. I didn't," Welch says. "It was my fault because I didn't ask the 'why' questions I normally did."[29] Later Welch called each of the fourteen business leaders at GE to apologize for the debacle.

BOTTOM-LINERS

Charismatics concern themselves with tangible issues and are impressed with intelligence and facts. They can absorb huge amounts of information rapidly and want to move quickly from a big idea to the details, especially those relating to implementation. The bottom line is that Charismatics are bottom-line people. They are looking for immediate results; they want to know what the payback is. But they also want that information in headlines and bulleted items. They don't want to hear tortured details about the problem; they want to know about the solution.

Therein lies the challenge: Charismatics have little patience for long meetings chock-full of PowerPoint slides. The last thing they want is to get bogged down in detail after detail. This was a lesson that was learned by Tim Bennett soon after Oprah Winfrey had hired him to be her chief operations officer in 1994. Bennett wanted to set up a meeting with Oprah to discuss capital planning, and perhaps sensing that she was less than enthusiastic about the subject, he requested just fifteen minutes of her time. Her response: "I'll give you five."[30]

In their constant quest for bottom-line results, Charismatics do not tie themselves to any ideas, approaches, or strategies. They are very adaptive to change and will continually modify plans in search of better results. They disdain rigidity and prefer the freedom of making and adjusting decisions as they go along. According to Herb Kelleher, such flexibility has been one of the secrets of Southwest's success. "One way we avoid complacency—and this may just be because I don't have a long attention span—is that we reject the idea of long-range planning," he asserts. "We say, do strategic planning, define what you are, and then get back together soon to define whether you need to change that. And have the alacrity of a puma. Because this plan about what we're going to do ten years from now will almost certainly be invalidated in the next six months."[31]

INTERACTIVE

When making decisions, Charismatics need to talk things through, and they prefer spirited interaction with others. They want to play with a proposal and brainstorm with it, throwing and batting ideas around. They'll scribble things on a white board or sheet of paper with the expectation that others will hammer out the details later. When confronted with tough decisions, Jack Welch says that he often used a favorite phrase—"Let's wallow in this"—to signify to others his desire to meet and think through the difficult issues.[32]

In person, Charismatics are enthusiastic, captivating, and talkative. They can easily dominate a conversation, speaking quickly and animatedly. In meetings, they have great difficulty sitting quietly and will frequently interrupt others. Many Charismatics like Herb Kelleher seem to have unlimited energy. "When I first met Herb," recalls Ron Kirk, then mayor of Dallas, "I thought the guy would just spontaneously combust. I just didn't see how anybody—certainly not anyone that much older than me—could play as hard, work as hard, drink as hard, smoke as hard . . . The man is just inexhaustible."[33]

At the root of this need for interaction is the strong desire for education: Charismatics want to understand the impact of any change and are very open to learning what they need to know. When Jack Welch was at the helm of GE, a multibillion-dollar international conglomerate, he proclaimed, "I have the greatest job in the world. We go from broadcasting, engines, plastics, the power system—anything you want, we've got a game going. So from an intellectual standpoint, you're learning every day."[34]

An interesting trait of Charismatics is that even though they might be in leadership roles, they are very willing to ask for help. They may say, "Correct me if I'm wrong here" or "I don't have any experience with this" or "I don't pretend to be an expert" or "Help me understand this" or "Am I the only one who doesn't get this?" or "Tell me what's wrong with this idea." Such comments might at first seem self-effacing and even ingratiating, but they are genuine attempts to open a discussion to encourage people to give their honest opinions.

Charismatics are not afraid of admitting their limitations. "Throughout my life," says Richard Branson, the founder of Virgin,

"I've always needed somebody as a counterbalance, to compensate for my weaknesses and to work off my strengths."[35] Indeed, Charismatics are great at surrounding themselves with the people they need, and they are adept at delegating. Oprah Winfrey, for instance, used to routinely rely on her longtime lieutenant Jeff Jacobs, then president of Harpo, to help her with her deficiency in strategic thinking. "If I called a strategic-planning meeting," she says, "there would be dead silence, and then people would fall out of their chairs laughing."[36] She has also delegated operational issues to other key people, freeing herself to concentrate on the content of her products.

WHAT CHARISMATICS SEEK—AND WHAT THEY AVOID

Charismatics like Oprah Winfrey and Richard Branson raise a crucial point. In our work with clients, we have found that people often mistake personality traits for styles of decision making. Some of the confusion arises from the fact that certain Charismatic decision makers do have tremendously charismatic personalities. But that is not always the case. Simply put, people with charismatic personalities do not necessarily use a Charismatic style of decision making, and we can think of countless examples. Perhaps the most striking was John F. Kennedy. President Kennedy had tremendous charisma; he charmed everyone with his good looks, dynamic personality, and reassuring confidence. But make no mistake: When it came to decision making, Kennedy was a Thinker. His thorough, detailed analysis of the Cuban Missile Crisis—for example, his extrapolating ways that the United States could allow Soviet premier Nikita Khrushchev to save face in the heated standoff—reveals the mind of a calculating chess master.

To avoid this trap of mistaking people's personalities for their style of decision making, our survey of nearly seventeen hundred business executives looked specifically at those people's behaviors when they made decisions. We asked them how long it took them to make important decisions, their willingness to make a choice that might have negative consequences, their desire for others to educate them about the issues involved, and so on. We found that a quarter of the participants were Charismatics, and our results provide hard, quantitative data of the specific likes and dislikes of those people in terms of their decision making.

A summary of that information is contained in the exhibit "Approach Profile for Charismatics." In the figure, note that of the twelve components we surveyed, Charismatics have the strongest need for education, responsibility, persistence, risk, and intelligence and facts when making a decision. Of their aversions, they most dislike fear and uncertainty in others and self-absorption in themselves.

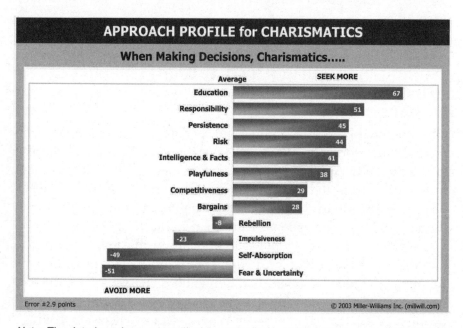

Note: The data have been normalized to range from −100 (maximum aversion) to +100 (maximum desire).

Also note that cost is not a huge factor with Charismatics, as they have just a moderate desire for bargains. If you are trying to sell something to someone who gets wrapped up in the benefits and features of the product without once asking about the cost, you can be sure the person is a Charismatic.

• • •

Highlights of our survey are that Charismatics

- Are passionate about new ideas, especially those that demonstrate bold, innovative thinking.
- Seek risk and are easily enthralled with out-of-the-box approaches.
- Make decisions quickly—but they will not act until enough pieces are in place, even though their initial enthusiasm might have led you to believe otherwise.
- Take responsibility for their decisions and will accept the blame for their mistakes.
- Focus on the bottom line, particularly on anything that will make their organizations more competitive.
- Prefer interacting with others to brainstorm and fine-tune ideas in an effort to understand the full impact of any proposed change.

In a nutshell, Charismatics use a very methodical approach, and their final choice will be based on a balanced set of information. They want the full proposal and report, which they themselves might not read but will certainly have someone else look at later. After that information has been analyzed and confirmed, Charismatics have no trouble pulling the trigger. Before that, though, they restrain themselves, knowing full well that their impulsiveness has led to costly mistakes in the past.

Chapter 4

Persuading the
Charismatic Decision Maker

Charismatics are the easiest of the decision-making styles to persuade when you use the right approach. All too often, though, people bungle a deal with a Charismatic because they don't fully understand several basic principles. To win over Charismatics, you must

1. **Give the headlines first.** Get to the point quickly, highlighting important information in bulleted items, and present the solution before describing the problem in detail.
2. **Stay grounded no matter what.** Fight the urge to join in their excitement; instead, remain focused on the bottom line.
3. **Address risks up front.** Openly discuss any potential downsides but also delineate the measures that can help minimize them.
4. **Follow through, follow through, and follow through.** Always assume the ball is in your court until the final decision is made.

GIVE THE HEADLINES FIRST

All business executives are busy people, but the attention span of a Charismatic decision maker is particularly brief. For example, Charismatics have already read as much from this chapter as they care to know, because we started off by presenting a list of the four main points. Likewise, in a meeting with a Charismatic, you need to start off with your most critical information. Otherwise, if you try to lead up to a crucial point, you risk losing the Charismatic's attention. Even if you have an hour scheduled for your meeting, don't assume that you'll be able to run through your entire presentation, logically building up to your conclusions. With a Charismatic, the conclusions must come first, and you need to deliver them in headlines and bulleted items.

Also remember that Charismatics are easily bored with canned presentations. They much prefer the rough-and-tumble of spontaneous discussion. In a meeting with them, the interruptions come early as they try to quickly assimilate your argument and move to its conclusions. After they've grasped the big picture, they want to immediately talk about implementation. Often Charismatics will jump into implementation issues when you're still giving the overview. They won't hesitate to interrupt you to get to the bottom line of how the information being discussed can best be used in their organization. They might even get up to move around the room and take control of the discussion. At the core of that behavior is a keen desire for interaction with others: Charismatics think aloud; they want to play with ideas; they love brainstorming.

Those characteristics can work to your advantage, especially when you're inadvertently caught off guard. In business, few things are more excruciatingly painful than when you need to deliver a proposal at an important meeting without being properly prepared. We found ourselves in that unenviable position recently, but because the decision maker was a Charismatic, all was not lost.

Kevin Capelli, the senior vice president of marketing and programs at Wenger Medical Instruments (WMI), the operating company of a Fortune 500 corporation, is a classic Charismatic—always restless to find new ways of doing things better. (Note: To respect the confidentiality of our clients, we have used pseudonyms and have altered identifying details of the examples in this chapter.) He has little patience for hearing excruciating details about a problem; he just wants to know about the solution. Or, as he himself puts it, "Just give me the frigging answers and then explain why."

When Capelli moved from a competitor to WMI, he asked us to meet with him and Lane Kline, his sales manager, to talk about how we might do business together. Capelli made it sound like the meeting would be purely informational, an informal sit-down-and-talk type of discussion. If anything, we thought he would be doing most of the talking, educating us about WMI's business and his plans for it.

We flew to the East Coast for the meeting, and when we walked into the conference room, our hearts stopped. In addition to Capelli and Kline, more than a dozen people were sitting around a U-shaped conference table. Through our surprise, we heard someone politely ask, "Do you want to connect your computer somewhere?"

Apparently, the group was expecting a formal presentation. But Charismatics like Capelli don't care about slide shows. They prefer lively, spontaneous interaction. Fortunately, the room contained a large white board, which covered almost an entire wall. So we began writing down the highlights of what we did for clients, and then we said, "Tell us about one of your potential customers and let's walk through what we could do to help you with that account." And for the next forty-five minutes, we did just that, essentially developing a blueprint of how WMI should handle that prospective client. Throughout the discussion, Capelli was continually jumping in, left and right, with incisive questions that helped everyone focus on the pertinent issues.

After that on-the-fly analysis, Capelli said he wanted to talk with his team about whether our sales process, which we had just described, would work at WMI, so we offered to leave the conference room to allow for free discussion. Within ten minutes, we were called back, and Capelli said, "Okay, we're ready to go, and we need to start thinking about dates when we can get our people here for training." We were pleasantly surprised because we hadn't even considered that Capelli would make a decision on the spot—let alone without even discussing the pricing of our seminars first!

Even then, we didn't assume that we had his business locked up just because he told us so. When we returned to our office in San Diego, we promptly followed up with Kline, the sales manager, sending him a detailed report of our proposal, and we copied Capelli on that correspondence. Interestingly, we got WMI's business even though it was considering another consulting firm that hadn't even had the chance to present its proposal. Therein lies another important lesson: When Charismatics are considering several options, be sure that you're among the first to be discussed and considered, because when Charismatics see something they like, they could jump the gun and make a decision before investigating the remaining choices. The attention span of Charismatics is short: They want to solve problems quickly and move on.

The take-home message of our experience at WMI is not that it's okay to wing it when you're dealing with a Charismatic. Fortunately for us, everything worked out well, and we got the company's business. But we could have easily botched it if we hadn't been quick on our feet. The lesson is this: The way to make your point with a Charismatic is through freewheeling, open discussion. Even though you still need to do your homework and prepare extensively for your meetings with them, you must also allow and encourage spontaneity and interaction.

An effective tactic to accomplish that is to prepare just a few charts for your meeting. This will aid you in clarifying your own thinking and help you to focus on the main points that you need to make. But don't count on using those exact figures in your meeting. Instead, plan on modifying them in your head (according to the way in which the Charismatic has steered the discussion) and then redrawing the information on a white board. This will encourage greater interaction among those in the meeting—and it will also add to the impromptu atmosphere.

To hold a Charismatic's attention, your arguments must be simple and straightforward, and your overall presentation should be logical and systematic. But don't become rigidly attached to what you've prepared. During your meeting, be ready to bypass key sections of your argument to react to a Charismatic's needs. Charismatics will take you down the paths they desire. Your job is to keep them on track in spite of all the detours. To do that, keep a mental or written checklist of all the important points you need to make. Then toward the end of your meeting, do a quick review of those items and bring up any key information you missed. Throughout the discussion, use the following buzzwords to maintain a Charismatic's interest: *results, proven, actions, show, watch, look, bright, easy, clear, focus, perception, quick, instant, creative, imagine.*

STAY GROUNDED NO MATTER WHAT

The biggest mistake that people make when trying to persuade a Charismatic is that they get swept up in the Charismatic's enthusiasm. Remember that Charismatics seldom make snap judgments that are truly final decisions. Instead, they fight their impulsiveness, and their approach to decision making is very methodical, even though their initial exuberance might have led you to believe otherwise.

Remember Jason Wheeler and Ed Reynolds from chapter 1, the entrepreneurs in Los Angeles who were looking for investor capital to launch the career of an urban recording artist? They made the cardinal mistake of feeding into the enthusiasm of Rick Pearson, the multimillion-dollar businessman who is a Charismatic decision maker. In hindsight, it's easy to understand why Wheeler and Reynolds made that blunder.

Before their big meeting, Wheeler and Reynolds knew that Pearson, who had invested in numerous ventures in the past, was the type of person who was always on the lookout for a deal. The owner of several companies, including a real estate franchise, Pearson considered himself to be a business visionary, and he was growing restless for new challenges.

When Wheeler and Reynolds arrived at Pearson's office promptly at 7:00 A.M. for their meeting, Pearson greeted them with a huge grin. He couldn't wait to tell Wheeler and Reynolds that he had just sold a chunk of his company for an eight-figure sum. "He didn't want to brag, but he wanted to brag," recalls Wheeler. "He was so excited because this was a dream of his. He was just thirty-nine and was already a multi-multimillionaire." At the same time, Pearson was hardly about to rest on his laurels. "I'm always looking for other opportunities," he told Wheeler and Reynolds. "Anything that would make more money I'd always be interested in."

Wheeler and Reynolds seized the opportunity and launched into their pitch, and Pearson was immediately hooked. "His eyes lit up," recalls Wheeler, "and he said, 'I don't know anything about the music industry, but I'm looking for new challenges. This is great.'" Quickly, the three men were feeding off one another's enthusiasm. Literally sitting on the edge of their chairs, they talked about what a fantastic opportunity this was—the chance to launch a new record label—and about how exciting working together would be. Soon the meeting, which Pearson had scheduled for just fifteen minutes, had stretched into an hour.

And the signs only got better. It just so happened that one of Pearson's key employees had been in the music industry in a previous job, so Pearson gave her a sample CD of the artist. After listening to the recording, she called Reynolds and raved, "This is fantastic. This girl is hot! This is a can't-miss opportunity." She also mentioned how she had been dying to get back into the music industry and was thrilled at the prospect that Pearson, her boss, was considering doing just that.

In a subsequent phone conversation, Pearson asked Reynolds, "How much money do you need?" Reynolds explained that for an equity stake in the new recording label, they were looking at an investment of $500,000. Shorter term, they needed $100,000 to finance some of the early promotion work to help bring the artist to market quickly. "Okay, I'm in," Pearson said. "It's a done deal. I'll have a check for you on Friday."

When Reynolds hung up the phone, he did a high five with his partner, Wheeler. "We were really excited," recalls Wheeler. "We thought it was a no-miss deal. I mean, $100,000 was peanuts to this guy, and he had one of his key employees telling us that the artist was absolutely the hottest thing. We thought for sure the deal was going to happen."

But it didn't. The check never arrived, and Wheeler and Reynolds spent a frantic weekend trying to get in touch with Pearson.

Later they learned what had happened. At home, Pearson was literally sitting down to write the $100,000 check when his wife asked, "What are you doing?" When Pearson told her about the venture, she weighed in. "What do you know about the music industry? Do you have any statistics? Who are these people you're dealing with? Do you have anything except this CD?!" Pearson's wife put the kibosh on the deal as her questions triggered doubts in his mind that grew faster than weeds.

At that point, Wheeler and Reynolds could do little to correct the situation. Pearson had made his decision. "If we had to do it over again," says Wheeler, "we definitely would have given him an extensive, detailed business plan." The document would have addressed the concerns of Pearson's wife with all the necessary data, market statistics, and other information.

Why hadn't Wheeler and Reynolds done that in the first place? Part of the problem was that in their past dealings with Pearson he had never once asked for such documentation. Wheeler recalls another meeting for a separate business deal in which he had spent hours preparing a PowerPoint presentation of his proposal, but when Wheeler got to the meeting, Pearson told him to put away his laptop. "Just tell me what you've got," said Pearson. At a different meeting, Pearson tossed aside and completely ignored a twelve-page report that Wheeler had given him.

Another part of the problem was Pearson's tremendous enthusiasm for Wheeler and Reynolds's proposal, which lulled them into a false sense of security. "We didn't even think to give Pearson a detailed report or business plan," admits Wheeler. "After all, he was so enthusiastic, and he already had a key employee giving the deal a green light all the way."

The painful ordeal taught Wheeler and Reynolds a valuable lesson: When trying to persuade Charismatics, you need to fight the urge to join in their excitement. Charismatics don't necessarily want you to share in their enthusiasm; they know that they have enough enthusiasm for everyone else. What they're really looking for is someone to think through the details for them and have the persistence to carry things out and get them done. At the end of the day, what really drives Charismatics are bottom-line results. They're never satisfied. They're always looking to improve performance by increasing quality or by doing more with less. In other words, Charismatics need to know what's in it for them, but they also need to know that you've thought through all the necessary details. Remember that with a Charismatic, one red flag raises countless others.

ADDRESS RISKS UP FRONT

When a Charismatic becomes enthralled with your proposal, an effective tactic is to slightly undersell things that pique her interest. In other words, you should be prepared to merely acknowledge the items that she greets with enthusiasm and discuss the risks of each of those things. You should be very honest and up-front about the potential downsides of your proposal, while also delineating the measures that can help minimize those risks. If you try to conceal that information, you can be sure that the Charismatic will discover it later—when you're not around to talk her through it. By openly discussing any risks and by helping to keep the Charismatic grounded, you will convey a sense of realism to her and strengthen her confidence and trust in you. Remember that Charismatics are risk seeking, so they're not going to be threatened or frightened by the possibility that something might go wrong. Even when a Charismatic would rather gloss over or ignore the risks involved, the much better tactic is to deal with them up front.

Consider our experience several years ago with Chris Tyler, who was then the vice president of corporate market development at a multibillion-dollar beverage company. Tyler had just taken charge of the firm's on-premise national accounts, including customers like Ground Round, Outback Steakhouse, and other restaurant chains. Soon after he was given this new responsibility, Tyler called us to ask if we'd be interested in helping him to set up a new system for his sales professionals. The system would provide a uniform structure and process so that people wouldn't have to reinvent the wheel every time they approached new potential customers.

At the time, Tyler was at a conference in Miami, so we flew there to meet with him in his hotel suite. We talked him through our system and explained how we could profile his customers to obtain data about what they *really* wanted from his company, and not what they just said they wanted. That information would then help his people to develop blueprints of specific sales strategies tailored for different customers. "That's exactly what I need," said Tyler. "I need this kind of information on every single one of my accounts, and then I'll understand what's going on with my team. Right now there's no information I can get out of them."

Tyler had made up his mind, then and there, that he wanted to hire us. But we wanted to know more first. We asked him about his people and whether they would be receptive to a new system and the training that it would require. During the conversation, Tyler told us that John Maya, his director of national accounts, could be a problem. Maya had been passed over for a promotion several times because he wasn't getting results, which is why Tyler had been tapped to take over the operation.

We probed Tyler about Maya because not only did we want Tyler to appreciate fully any potential problems, we also wanted to know for ourselves what we were getting into. But Tyler pooh-poohed any risks. "Maya really doesn't have a choice because I'm his boss and this is what he's going to do," said Tyler. Still, we probed for more information. "If Maya's not on board, what kind of problems would that present?" we asked.

Throughout the meeting, it became clear to us that Tyler saw us as the solution for his company's lack of a uniform sales system. With Charismatics, the thought is the deed, and Tyler had the attitude of "Okay, I'll hire you, and that will solve my problem." What he was really doing, though, was not solving his problem, but transferring it to us, and we wanted to make sure that we had a fighting chance. We told Tyler that we were trying to figure out how to make him successful with the new system and that's why we were asking all these questions. Clearly, though, he was much more interested in talking about an implementation schedule and rollout dates than he was in discussing potential problems with Maya.

We did get the project, and Maya indeed was a major obstacle to our efforts. For two years, he fought us and tried to undermine our efforts with his passive-aggressive tactics. But the system was eventually successful—and both Tyler and Maya have since moved on to other jobs. As tough as that project was, we would have had an even more difficult time had we not made Tyler more aware of the potential downsides. And even with all the questions we asked and the probing we did, we actually *underestimated* the effort necessary to implement the system.

FOLLOW THROUGH, FOLLOW THROUGH, AND FOLLOW THROUGH

Charismatics will often give you their decision on the spot. But be forewarned: Even though this initial feedback might be favorable and stated with great enthusiasm, it is just their *preliminary* decision. To close the deal, you need to stay grounded in the tangible results and bottom-line impact of your proposal. And, most important, you need to follow through—even when you don't think it's necessary.

At our meeting with Kevin Capelli of Wenger Medical Instruments, he was already talking about a schedule for us to begin training his people. Nevertheless, after we had returned to our office in San Diego, we followed up with one of Capelli's key people, sending him a detailed report of our proposal and copying Capelli on that correspondence, to ensure that nothing fell through the cracks. In contrast, the crucial mistake that entrepreneurs Wheeler and Reynolds made in their dealings with Rick Pearson, the multimillionaire businessman, was that they were lulled into a false sense of security by Pearson's enthusiasm for their deal. Wheeler and Reynolds should have given Pearson a written report of their proposal in two versions: an executive summary (for Pearson to read) and an in-depth analysis (for him to use as a reference). The report should have included visual information—charts, figures, diagrams—to stress the major points of the proposal.

With a Charismatic, the ball is always in someone else's court (usually yours) for follow-through. Even if you've done all the work requested and turned it over to the right people, you still need to stay on top of things. At the very least, you need to follow up with the Charismatic's key lieutenants, and this is where most people fail. Although Charismatics might appear to be independent thinkers, they often rely on others—especially those with clout—for making major decisions. The Charismatic might have a CFO who has to look at every line item, or he might have a strategy expert who needs to go over your business proposal with a fine-tooth comb to make sure that everything's in place. By ignoring these people or trying to do an end run around them, you could easily sabotage yourself. On the other hand, when those people are satisfied, the Charismatic will sign off quickly, as Capelli at WMI did after our meeting with him and his team.

Recently, we faced a similar situation with Trent Dawson, the CEO of a national restaurant chain. Dawson had been a client of ours for a couple years when we proposed a new project: surveying customers at each of his hundreds of restaurants to determine what they truly wanted from their dining experience versus what they were getting.

Dawson was all for the project, but he first wanted us to make a formal pitch to his executive team, which included his COO, CFO, a representative from the IT department, and a marketing executive. When Dawson requested that meeting, he told us, "You know how it is. You know how we work around here. This is something that you have to do."

We indeed knew exactly what Dawson meant. His executive team wasn't going to rubber-stamp our proposal just because Dawson wanted to proceed and because we had already done other work for his company. The team's role was to play devil's advocate. Everyone would pepper us with questions, raise important issues, and do the necessary due diligence to ensure that our proposal really did pass the muster. In essence, their function was to protect Dawson from making a bad decision. So even though we had his support, the meeting was potentially dangerous for us. We couldn't move forward without it, and someone could raise a red flag that might shake Dawson's confidence and trust in us.

During the meeting, we got the distinct impression that people were placing hoops in front of us just to see whether we could jump through them. The COO, for instance, talked about a past project that we had done for the company and asked when he could expect some updated information from that work. We assured him that we would get that done promptly, regardless of whether we were awarded the current project. Being responsive to his request was essential for us to maintain our credibility with him. Had we failed to pass that test, he might have vetoed working with us in the future. The absolute wrong thing for us to do would have been to assume that we had Dawson, the CEO, in our pocket and could therefore be cavalier about the concerns of his executive team.

After the meeting, we followed up with the attendees, essentially telling them, "We just presented a pretty big proposal to you. Now that you've had a chance to think about it, tell us what your concerns are, and tell us how we need to adjust the project to make sure it fits your needs." That kind of follow-up helped us to seal the deal quickly. We were awarded the formal contract within just sixty days of the initial meeting—a pretty fast turnaround, considering we were negotiating with a billion-dollar corporation.

Although we were able to sign a contract with Dawson's company relatively quickly, dealing with a Charismatic decision maker isn't always that expeditious. Often the process requires no small amount of quiet perseverance: Charismatics expect you to wait patiently for them to make a final decision while they have others pore over the details of your proposal. That process could take some time, even though the Charismatic's initial enthusiasm may have led you to believe that the go-ahead was imminent.

KNOWING WHAT TO DO—AND WHEN TO DO IT

The key to getting the green light on your proposal is knowing what to do and when to do it. The exhibit "The Charismatic Plan" contains a chronological list of important to-do items. Note that the crucial items that you will use from your persuasion toolkit (discussed in chapter 2) are the trigger event or problem definition and the recommended solution. Of secondary importance are the risk assessments and high-level action plans. Of lesser importance—but still necessary—are the complete report and detailed plan, which you should provide to Charismatics for their future reference.

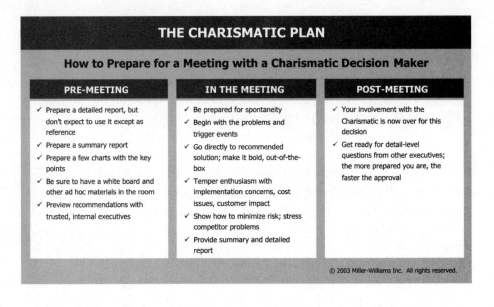

To summarize, the trick in persuading Charismatics is that you must

- Refrain from delivering your standard presentation. Instead, give the presentation that will hold their interest. Avoid staged deliveries and limit yourself to just a few PowerPoint slides. Throughout the meeting, be prepared for numerous interruptions as the Charismatic becomes engaged with the ideas being discussed. Whenever possible, draw diagrams and charts on a white board to convey important information visually.

- Fight the urge to join in their excitement. Stick with the bottom-line results, even if they don't. The key here is not to be deadpan or unemotional, but to slightly undersell everything that seems to make them excited. In other words, be prepared to merely acknowledge those items, features, or benefits and be sure to discuss the risks of each. This will convey a sense of realism to them and strengthen their confidence and trust in you.

- Have a frank and open discussion about risks. Charismatics might downplay those risks, but don't let that deter you. Continue pushing them until you are satisfied that they are well aware of any potential downsides. But also be sure to discuss the measures that will help minimize those risks.

- After the meeting, the ball is in your court for follow-through. Even though Charismatics love new ideas, getting their official commitment can be elusive. They might say, "This is exactly what we need," but then they'll delay the decision to proceed. For them to give their final approval, they need to know that you or others have thought things through and that everything is backed up by a thorough analysis. They might not look at that analysis, but they still need to know that it exists.

Chapter 5

The Thinker Decision Maker

EXAMPLES	BILL GATES, MICHAEL DELL, ALAN GREENSPAN, ROBERTO GOIZUETA, WARREN BUFFETT, AND KATHARINE GRAHAM

Thinkers need to cautiously and methodically work through the pros and cons of each option before rendering a decision. They are often described as cerebral, intelligent, logical, and academic, and they pride themselves on their ability to outsmart and outmaneuver the competition. They are voracious readers, especially in their field of expertise, and are usually seen as the experts or advisers in their organizations. Above all, Thinkers are

1. **Methodical and process-oriented.** They concern themselves with the details of how things work and are skilled at picking apart a problem and logically working through it to arrive at the optimum solution.
2. **Information-driven.** They have an insatiable need for all kinds of information, including customer surveys, market research, case studies, cost-benefit analyses, and so on.
3. **Quantitative and precise.** They are particularly swayed by arguments and information based on hard data.

4. **Relentlessly thorough.** They need to exhaustively explore every pro and con of all options before moving forward.
5. **Guarded and cautious.** They play their cards close to the chest as they carefully and meticulously process all pertinent information.
6. **Balanced.** They keep their emotions in check by relying heavily on rational thinking.
7. **Intellectually fluid.** They are open to new ideas and ways of thinking, even those that contradict their existing beliefs.

METHODICAL AND PROCESS-ORIENTED

When Michael Dell was fifteen, he bought himself his first computer, an Apple II, which he then promptly took apart. Why? Just to see how it worked. Dell was able to reassemble the computer into working order—a routine task for a youngster who had become adept at building radios from kits. Years later, when asked whether he had been worried that he might not be able to put the Apple II back together, he replied, "No, those were the days when you could go get all the data books about something, take the top off, and it was all simple. You could look inside and look at the data books and figure out what each of the components did."[1]

That type of methodical thinking enabled Dell to analyze the computer market and put together a brilliant business model for selling PCs directly to customers. Making that approach work required a thorough understanding of various complex processes. Take supply-chain management. Thanks to sophisticated software, Dell Computer factories can continually order parts throughout the day, so that the company needs to stock just a few hours' worth of such inventory. And because Dell Computer sells directly to customers, the company can keep just several days' worth of product in warehouses, compared to the industry norm of weeks. This kind of hyperefficiency has enabled Dell Computer to wage brutal price wars that have bloodied many a competitor.

Roberto Goizueta, former CEO of Coca-Cola, had a similar analytical brilliance. When Goizueta took the reins of Coca-Cola in the early 1980s, the company was headed for trouble as Pepsi, with its "Pepsi Challenge" ad campaign, had been steadily winning market share. Goizueta took a hard look at Coca-Cola's operations from top to bottom and realized that the company was essentially a syrup maker and advertiser that was at the mercy of its independent bottlers, many of which had not invested to modernize their operations. Because of such inefficiencies, Coca-Cola was hamstrung in its battle against Pepsi. Thus, Goizueta concluded that even though independent bottlers were a century-old tradition of the company, the system had to go. To that end, he began purchasing stakes in the bottlers to gain greater control over that part of Coca-Cola's business. The drawback to that strategy, though, was that it added substantial assets to Coca-Cola's balance sheet, which would result in lower returns for stockholders. Again, Goizueta's solution was masterful: He created Coca-Cola Enterprises, a holding company for the bottlers, and spun that off but retained a 49 percent stake to exert some control over those operations. In essence, what Goizueta did was to transform Coca-Cola from merely a syrup maker and marketer to becoming a manager over its value chain—from syrup manufacturing to bottling to distribution.[2]

A key strength of Thinkers is their ability to take apart a business or problem and logically analyze it by using a clear methodology. That kind of rational reasoning is so prized at Dell Computer that Michael Dell has made it a core part of his hiring process. "When I interview people, the first thing I do is find out how they process information," he says. "Do they really understand the strategy of the business they're involved in today? Do they understand ours? It's surprising how many people already in the workforce contribute in some way to their company's strategy but don't really understand it that well."[3]

On the other hand, Thinkers become lost when they don't understand a process or system and have no methodology to help them analyze it. That's why Warren Buffett, one of the best stock pickers in history, invests only in businesses that he thoroughly understands. Specifically, he needs to feel reasonably sure that he knows what the cash flow of the company will be at least twenty years out. If he can't determine that, he will not invest, even if the potential upside is huge. Consequently, Buffett avoided the Internet companies, and he has even shied away from making investments in high-tech veterans like Hewlett-Packard and Microsoft, his close friendship with Bill Gates notwithstanding. Instead, Buffett has thrown his money behind companies like Coca-Cola, See's Candies, and Gillette. "With Coke," says Buffett, "I can come up with a very rational figure for the cash it will generate in the future . . . I do admire the management of Intel and Microsoft, but I don't have a fix on where they will be in ten years . . . And if I started playing around without knowing how to value a company, I might as well buy lottery tickets."[4]

INFORMATION-DRIVEN

To help them understand all steps or unknown quantities in a process, Thinkers have a strong need for copious information. They need as much data as possible, including all pertinent market research, customer surveys, case studies, cost-benefit analyses, and so on, because they strive to understand all perspectives of a given situation. Not surprisingly, they are usually insatiable readers, especially in their field of expertise. Other types of decision makers might also have a passion for reading but for different reasons. Charismatics, for instance, tend to skim to get the main ideas quickly, and they would be perfectly content with a Cliffs Notes summary. Thinkers, on the other hand, want to read the original material thoroughly for a comprehensive understanding.

As a young adult, Federal Reserve chairman Alan Greenspan played the clarinet, tenor saxophone, and flute in a professional jazz band in New York City. During breaks, while the other members of the group went off to smoke joints, Greenspan passed the time by reading economics books he had borrowed from the public library. "Alan was in the books all the time," recalls a fellow musician.[5] That passion for reading has never left Greenspan and has even become a joke among those who know him well. Several years ago, when he was being honored at a ceremony hosted by a firm that had employed him decades earlier, he was told that he now owed considerable fines for the books that he had borrowed but not returned to the company's library—a sum that, with interest, had accrued to a modest percentage of the national debt.[6]

Some Thinkers are so addicted to information that they almost need daily fixes. Roberto Goizueta used to check Coke's stock price several times a day and would closely monitor theater box-office results after Coca-Cola had purchased Columbia Pictures. Of his school days, Goizueta once recalled, "I could memorize whole pages of history books."[7] Katharine Graham, legendary publisher and CEO of the Washington Post Co., routinely read the *Post* from start to finish, including all the classified ads and even the Sears, Roebuck supplements. When she was on the road, she would have the paper sent to her so that she wouldn't miss an issue.[8]

For Thinkers, two things underlie their thirst for information: an innate curiosity and the need to understand things. When Graham first took the reins of the *Post*, she asked questions about every facet of the publishing business. According to a colleague, she was never "too proud to ask what's an agate line, why is this press better than that one, what do these really mean?"[9] Roberto Goizueta had the same propensity. "I tend to be very open, to pick people's brains," he once remarked.[10] When Goizueta rightly realized that any CEO of a major corporation in the 1980s had to have a thorough understanding of business finance, he threw himself into the study of accounting, foreign currencies, and economics. "He used to come into my office fifteen or twenty times a day," recalls Sam Ayoub, who was then Coca-Cola's assistant financial officer. "He didn't know a word about accounting or finance, but he just asked questions and questions and questions."[11] Eventually, that knowledge came in handy as Coca-Cola pulled off several brilliant financial maneuvers, including its spin-off of Coca-Cola Enterprises.

With Thinkers, there seems to be no such thing as too much data. Michael Dell routinely surfs the Internet, even entering chat rooms and Usenet forums, to uncover as much as he can about what his customers are thinking. "I learn about things we are doing well. I learn when we screw up," he notes.[12] In fact, Dell Computer has teams that monitor those Internet sites to gather customer feedback.

QUANTITATIVE AND PRECISE

Thinkers are particularly impressed with information and arguments that are quantitative and metric-driven. They prefer—and are even fascinated with—the absolute precision of numerical data. Warren Buffett has long had an uncanny facility with numbers. As a youngster, he and a friend developed a mathematical system for picking winners at the racetrack, and they began selling that information in a tip sheet. Much later, after Buffett had established Berkshire Hathaway as a financial powerhouse, a colleague recalls that when he and Buffett were driving by a See's Candies store, one of the companies in Berkshire's portfolio, Buffett was able to rattle off sales numbers for that particular location. The incident made the colleague remember what someone had once warned him about Buffett: "Don't show him any number you don't want him to see, because he'll remember it."[13] Buffett is an avid bridge player. Someone who frequently plays with him has these observations about the man: "He knows all the odds in the game, and both bids and plays his hands with them in mind. He is analytical and focused when playing, and he keeps getting better."[14]

But Thinkers are not just automaton number crunchers. They also have the keen ability for finding patterns and trends in those numbers. A big reason for Alan Greenspan's success is that he can separate meaning from the surrounding noise. "It's not just a tremendous interest in the data for its own sake but, rather, he draws conclusions from the data which are insightful and unique," says William McDonough, president of the Federal Reserve Bank of New York.[15] Furthermore, Thinkers do not limit themselves to numbers. They are also precise and selective about the words they use. For instance, when speaking, they will pause as they search for just the right word, or they will correct themselves in midsentence when they realize that a word or phrase they've just spoken isn't exactly right. In general, they have a measured way of talking, their speech frequently alternating between a slow, rhythmic cadence and rapid conversation.

RELENTLESSLY THOROUGH

A Thinker's insatiable appetite for information comes from an incessant desire to be thorough. Thinkers want to be sure that all the facts are in place and that they understand every pro and con of all options before they feel comfortable in making a decision. They are sticklers for details, even minute ones. Roberto Goizueta was well known for his meticulous and thorough style of management. "He knew where every grain of sand was in the office," recalls a former colleague.[16]

Before making an important decision, Thinkers will often ask the opinions of everyone involved. On the surface, they might look as if they want to establish a consensus and make people feel that they have a say. But they also want to be thorough: Tapping into diverse views helps to ensure that they have left no stone unturned.

Alan Greenspan uses such an approach for meetings of the Federal Open Market Committee. Those meetings, attended by the Federal Reserve's governors, typically commence with a presentation by the Fed's staff economists, after which Greenspan asks each of the committee members for feedback. When everyone is done, Greenspan states his own opinions. "He produces consensus in the same way other good leaders do: by listening extremely closely to what others have to say, by synthesizing that very well, and by sensing the broad middle," says Roger Ferguson, member of the Fed Board of Governors.[17] Bob Woodward, the noted reporter of Watergate fame and author of a book about Greenspan called *Maestro*, agrees: "Greenspan . . . could have been a great intelligence officer or a great journalist because he knows how to listen."[18] Woodward asserts that Greenspan is far more inclusive than his predecessor, Paul Volcker. "[Greenspan] dominates the institution in a way that everyone agrees on. It's not with a heavy hand. He listens. He incorporates people's views. It's consensus leadership. But some consensus counts more than others. He decides."[19]

At Microsoft, important decisions are often made in long discussions that last from six to eight hours.[20] Known as marathons, the meetings are a striking reflection of the Thinker decision-making style of company founder Bill Gates. He, like all Thinkers, insists that issues be analyzed thoroughly to ensure that nothing is missed. In fact, one of his sayings is that he pays his people to "sit and think."[21] Similarly, Roberto Goizueta would probe his top managers at Coca-Cola so thoroughly about their businesses that the interlocutory sessions became known as the Spanish Inquisition.

Katharine Graham had a softer touch for prodding others to expand their thinking. Instead of issuing orders, she framed her requests by asking incisive questions along the lines of "Do you think it would be a good idea to . . . ?" and "Have you considered . . . ?"[22] A former colleague of hers says she had the "uncanny knack . . . for asking you the one question about your operation you weren't prepared to answer."[23]

GUARDED AND CAUTIOUS

Not usually known for their social skills, Thinkers tend to guard their feelings, emotions, and passions. That quality can make Thinkers tough to read because they will rarely show their cards up front. In a meeting, they will take contradictory points of view, asking a battery of questions in order to explore and understand all of the risks associated with an option, all without revealing whether their inclination is favorable or not. They might make a pointed comment and, after a response has been given, sit silently to digest that information—a habit that borders on self-absorption. Consequently, meetings with Thinkers can be nerve-racking because of the uncomfortably long stretches of dead airtime. Even the body language of Thinkers seldom betrays their feelings. In fact, Thinkers often conceal their intentions until they render their final decision. After they've heard everyone's arguments for and against a proposal, a common practice is for them to say, "Okay, I'll give you my decision tomorrow morning." It's not that Thinkers are slow—in actuality their minds are quite agile—it's just that they need ample time to process information thoroughly.

Not surprisingly, Thinkers tend to do their best thinking alone, not through interacting with others. On a typical day, Alan Greenspan wakes around 5:30 in the morning and spends an hour or two soaking in the bathtub—time he uses to read, think, and write. (He has written some of his important speeches there.) Later, at the office, he spends an additional couple hours reading reports, including those from his staff, and another two or three hours doing research for himself.[24]

But Thinkers can move fast, especially when they must and when they have the information they need. Effective Thinkers like Katharine Graham may be thorough, but they do not suffer from "analysis paralysis." Arthur Schlesinger Jr., the noted historian, summed it up best when he described Graham as someone who "listens long and makes reasonably quick decisions."[25] That quality was an invaluable asset when in 1971 Graham confronted perhaps the biggest decision in her professional life: whether to publish excerpts from the Pentagon Papers, the U.S. government's secret history of the Vietnam War. Her decision was a particularly precarious one because a federal court had just issued an injunction preventing the *New York Times* from publishing this material.

Ben Bradlee, then the executive editor of the *Post*, and members of his editorial staff had spent a tense day at his house in Georgetown, arguing with lawyers retained by the newspaper. The attorneys were strenuously against publication, citing various legal arguments. Finally, Bradlee called Graham to get her answer, and he knew that he needed her decision on the spot. Graham was at her home, hosting a party, and was just about to give a toast when the call came through. Fritz Beebe, the chairman of the board of the Washington Post Co., started off by summarizing the various arguments, both pro and con. "I asked about fifty questions," Graham would later recall of the conversation.[26] One of those questions was directed squarely at Beebe, whom she trusted. When she asked him point-blank whether he would publish the documents, Beebe paused and then replied, "Well, I probably wouldn't."[27]

Graham was astonished by Beebe's response because he was usually pro-editorial. Caught off guard, she requested some time to think things over. "Can't we talk about this?" she asked. "Why do we have to make up our minds in such haste . . . ?"[28] But Bradlee and the other editors who were on the call insisted that any delay would make the *Post* look like it had cowered to the government, a perception that would destroy staff morale. When Graham countered that publishing the Pentagon Papers might well result in litigation that would ruin the

Post, Phil Geyelin, an editor, replied, "Yes, but there's more than one way to destroy a newspaper." After hearing the different points of view, Graham braced herself and said, "Let's go. Let's publish."[29]

In her autobiography, Graham explains why she made that decision even after Beebe, one of her most trusted advisers, had recommended against it. Her description reveals that although she was under tremendous pressure that day, her acute, logical mind did not fail her: "I was extremely torn by Fritz's saying that he wouldn't publish . . . But I also heard *how* he said it: he didn't hammer at me . . . and he didn't say the obvious thing—that I would be risking the whole company on this decision . . . I felt that, despite his stated opinion, he had somehow left the door open for me to decide on a different course."[30]

In other situations, Thinkers are not afraid to sit by the sidelines when their analysis has determined that inaction is the best course of action. Part of Michael Dell's genius, say many observers, is his willingness to do nothing, even as others stampede. Years ago, he resisted the rush by competitors to offer handheld computing devices like PalmPilots. Instead, he cautiously waited, at one point saying he hadn't yet figured out a way to make any money in that market. Warren Buffett has a similar take on investing. "The nature of markets," he says, "is that at times they offer extraordinary values and at other times you have to have the discipline to wait."[31]

BALANCED

Buffett's advice reveals another characteristic of Thinkers: They rely on logic to check and restrain their emotions. If they do become emotional about something, they will do so only in small amounts and only for brief periods of time. Of the five decision-making styles, Thinkers come the closest to a totally rational decision maker—a trait that they often pride themselves on. Of course, people are human beings and are always influenced to some degree by their emotions. With Thinkers, though, emotional factors have far less power to sway. In fact, Thinkers like Buffett would contend that emotions tend to obscure what might otherwise be clear business decisions.

Buffett certainly makes a strong point. A $10,000 investment in Berkshire Hathaway in 1965, when he took over the firm, would have soared to more than $50 million in 1999, far outpacing the S&P 500. That kind of impressive return, claims Buffett, is less the product of a genius mind than the result of using willpower to temper one's emotions. "Success in investing doesn't correlate with IQ once you're above the level of 25," he asserts. "Once you have ordinary intelligence, what you need is the temperament to control the urges that get other people into trouble in investing."[32]

Thinkers do an exhaustive rational analysis, and then they let the chips fall where they may. Roberto Goizueta had that kind of vigorous thought process, so much so that he once remarked how he loved the times when "you can think through a problem so hard you can develop a sweat."[33] And Goizueta's thinking was clear, organized, precise, and unclouded by messy emotions. "His mind is like a piece of crystal," remarked a former colleague. "He sees through issues and gets right to the heart of the matter."[34]

The capacity for objective, logical analysis is one reason Thinkers are usually well respected, even when their decisions are unfavorable. Sometimes, though, Thinkers rely *too* heavily on the rational, giving short shrift to the emotional. Perhaps the greatest mistake of Goizueta's illustrious career was his introduction of New Coke in 1985. The decision seemed logical enough because the new soda had outperformed the original Coke in repeated taste tests. Nevertheless, tampering with the fabled secret formula of Coke, later dubbed the "marketing blunder of the decade," led to a groundswell of outrage from customers who felt betrayed. "We knew some people were going to be unhappy, but we could never have predicted the depth of their unhappiness," said Goizueta. "You cannot quantify emotion."[35]

Thinkers may be extremely rational, but that's not to say that they have no buttons to push. Their two strongest visceral desires in business are to be proactive and to win. Simply put, they love to compete, and they take great pleasure in outsmarting and outmaneuvering others. Bill Gates is a classic example. Years ago, when Microsoft was just another fledgling software start-up, Gates brilliantly outwitted executives at IBM who completely underestimated his ability to think several steps ahead. Like a chess master, Gates shrewdly outflanked the competition to establish Microsoft as the dominant force in the industry.

For all her grace, dignity, and refined restraint, Katharine Graham, too, had a competitive streak. As the CEO of the Washington Post Co., which owns *Newsweek,* she hated being scooped. A friend of her son's who was a reporter for *Life* recalls the following: "If we'd both hear some nugget of gossip at the same time and I'd mention reporting it to the *Life* bureau, she'd say, 'Oh, no, you don't, that's for *Newsweek*,' and [she'd] get right on the phone."[36] After Graham and Ben Bradlee had both published their memoirs, she would ask him how many copies his book had sold. After the veteran editor had told her, she would triumphantly exclaim, "I've sold more!"[37]

INTELLECTUALLY FLUID

Thinkers have an intellectual honesty and openness that is a hallmark of the way they process information, always updating their views with whatever makes the most logical sense. Alan Greenspan is not locked into any ideologies or theories; he will use bits and pieces of each to arrive at solutions that work. "He's not a monetarist, he's not a Keynesian—he's himself," says William McDonough.[38] Thinkers are not academic purists. Rather, successful Thinkers might best be described as intellectual pragmatists. To explain that philosophy, Roberto Goizueta liked to quote one of his grandfather's proverbs: "The quality of one's compromises is much more important than the correctness of one's position."[39]

This intellectual fluidity enables Thinkers to realize when they're wrong, and they are perfectly willing to reverse their decisions when that happens. In other words, their egos and emotions don't overwhelm their capacity to be swayed by a solid argument, even when their initial position was contrary. A classic example here is Bill Gates and his belated endorsement of the Internet. Initially, Gates poohpoohed the Internet as an unimportant technology. Later, though, after much lobbying by others at Microsoft, he changed his mind and threw his company's full weight behind it, saying, "The Internet is not a fad in any way. It is a fantastic thing; it makes software and computers more relevant."[40]

A healthy attitude toward mistakes has become an essential ingredient in the corporate culture of Dell Computer. "One of the first things I learned . . . was that there was a relationship between screwing up and learning: The more mistakes I made the faster I learned," says Michael Dell. "We've always seen mistakes as learning opportunities. The key is to learn well from mistakes that you make so that you don't repeat them."[41] Dell Computer even has a saying to reinforce that attitude: "Don't perfume the pig." By that, the company means that employees should never try to dress up a bad situation to make it look better; instead, they should admit their mistake, learn from it, and move on.

To be sure, Thinkers are lifelong students, and it is their constant thirst for learning that keeps them alert and active. Andrea Mitchell, the NBC News correspondent whose husband is Alan Greenspan, sums up that part of her spouse best: "Alan's curiosity is such an important part of his makeup. He's wide open to possibilities."[42] And as far as Mitchell is concerned, Greenspan, who is in his seventies, isn't about to slow down anytime soon. "This is not a man who will ever retire," she says. "He is too alive and too interested."[43]

WHAT THINKERS SEEK—AND WHAT THEY AVOID

Not every Thinker will have all the characteristic qualities of the archetypal Thinker. Katharine Graham was never known as a numbers person. But she did have a balanced and thorough way of making decisions that espoused the hallmark characteristics of a Thinker. Roberto Goizueta was hardly the awkward introvert. He had an engaging, charming personality and was an impeccable dresser, but his meticulous and intensely methodical way of solving problems revealed a decision-making style that was pure Thinker.

Thinkers are multifaceted decision makers, and to capture that complexity, our survey of nearly seventeen hundred business executives looked specifically at a range of those people's behaviors when they made important decisions. We studied how much time they needed to make those decisions, how much risk they could tolerate, and so on. Through such probing, we determined that 11 percent of the participants were Thinkers, and our results provide detailed data on their specific likes and dislikes.

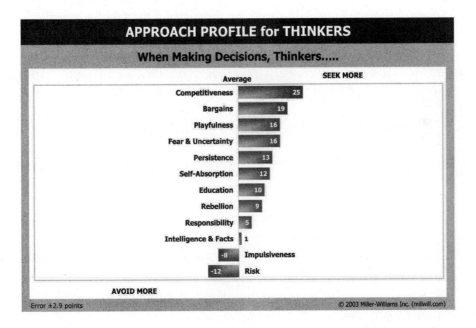

Note: The data have been normalized to range from −100 (maximum aversion) to +100 (maximum desire).

The exhibit "Approach Profile for Thinkers" contains a summary of that information. Perhaps the most striking characteristic is how even-keeled Thinkers are: They do not possess any extreme desires or aversions. Their strongest desire (and it is relatively moderate compared to the desires of the other decision-making styles) was to be competitive. What ultimately drives the business decisions of Thinkers is whether a proposal will make their company better than the competition, especially when the price is right (note that Thinkers also have a moderate desire for bargains). On the other hand, the strongest aversions were to risk and impulsiveness, which is why Thinkers often need a considerable amount of time to make decisions. They want to make sure that they understand the risks involved and that the appropriate measures will be in place to minimize them.

Our study also revealed some surprising things about Thinkers. Interestingly, the thought process of Thinkers is very selective but not always completely methodical. For instance, they will sometimes circumvent their own decision-making processes if they feel a bargain is in their best interest. In addition, Thinkers seek out some degree of playfulness in the decision-making process. They might ask a salesperson, "You can give me a good deal on this, can't you?" And Thinkers tend to be more control-driven than innovative-driven.

The major findings of our survey are that Thinkers

- Need to have a detailed understanding of the process used to arrive at a solution.
- Have an insatiable appetite for information.
- Prefer hard data, especially research that has been conducted using a rigorous methodology.
- Must analyze a problem thoroughly, exploring all the pros and cons of each potential solution.
- Proceed cautiously, guarding their feelings throughout the decision-making process.
- Resist being swayed by emotional arguments, preferring instead to rely on cold logic.
- Keep their minds flexible and open to new ways of doing things more effectively.

In short, Thinkers need to be sure for themselves that all the facts are in place—and that the processes used to analyze that information are error free. They must exhaustively explore all options, including every pro and con of each alternative. They need to know that every *t* has been crossed and every *i* has been dotted in whatever methodology was used to arrive at the optimum solution to a problem. Only after they've had the time to digest all that information will they be comfortable in rendering a decision.

Chapter 6

Persuading the
Thinker Decision Maker

Thinkers are difficult to persuade because of their strong desire for comparative information. Moreover, their cautious and guarded behavior makes it tough to know whether you are heading down the right path with them. Nevertheless, Thinkers can be swayed with the right approach, which requires that you

1. **Tell your story chronologically.** Never begin in the middle or the end of your story. Thinkers want to hear things from start to finish.
2. **Involve the Thinker in your process.** Give all details of the steps you used to arrive at your conclusions, and ask for help to fill any holes that you might have in your data or methodology.
3. **Be exhaustive but patient.** Provide all relevant data, including pertinent market research, customer surveys, case studies, cost-benefit analyses, and so on. After that, give the Thinker ample time to digest the material.
4. **Allow (and encourage) others to join the thinking.** Thinkers need others to think things through with them. This is their way to ensure that they haven't overlooked anything important.

TELL YOUR STORY CHRONOLOGICALLY

Thinkers can be swayed with logical arguments that appeal directly to their intelligence, and they much prefer presentations that are chronological. Thus, it is crucial that you tell your story from start to finish—with all the intermediate steps intact. Thinkers want to know exactly how you got from A to Z so that if they disagree with your reasoning from step F to G, they can question you on that. If you can't defend the reasoning behind that step, you'll need to make the necessary revisions and logically follow those changes throughout the rest of your argument. For Thinkers, a flaw in any step raises doubts about the entire process and its conclusions. Therefore, to be comfortable about any decision, Thinkers need to verify for themselves that all steps are error free. Consequently, never start in the middle or the end of your story. Or, as the legal saying goes, never assume facts not in evidence. Doing so is a recipe for sure disaster.

A few years ago, we unwittingly played a role in such a debacle with VeriTabs, a billion-dollar financial information company headquartered in Memphis. (Note: To respect the confidentiality of our clients and colleagues, we have used pseudonyms for them and their companies, and we have altered identifying details of the examples in this chapter.) At the time, VeriTabs was investigating whether to launch a dot-com firm that would offer a number of the company's services on-line, similar to the way in which the Barnes & Noble spin-off www.bn.com is the Web incarnation of the bookseller. VeriTabs hired an ad agency to determine whether an Internet spin-off would be viable and, if so, how it should be launched. The ad agency, in turn, hired us to assess whether VeriTabs had enough brand equity to establish itself quickly within the on-line community.

To answer that, we conducted a large-scale survey of VeriTabs's customers, developing extensive profiles of them, and found that the company's brand wasn't going to translate easily to a Web spin-off. But that didn't necessarily mean that such a maneuver would fail, just that it would require a considerable investment, particularly in marketing and advertising, to establish the company's brand with an on-line spin-off. Ralph Bedosian, a managing partner at the ad agency that retained us to conduct the brand survey, was in charge of developing the marketing campaign. When that work was completed, we would jointly present our results to VeriTabs's top brass.

Before the big meeting, we talked with Bedosian about the best approach for the presentation. We suggested that we commence with a discussion of the survey results, after which he could then unveil the new marketing campaign. But Bedosian wanted the order reversed: He would lead with the marketing campaign and then present our research results to explain the reasoning behind the campaign. His strategy was to get the VeriTabs execs so excited about the catchy marketing campaign that their enthusiasm would overshadow the discussion of why, because of what our survey results revealed, they would need to spend more money than they had originally anticipated. We disagreed with Bedosian, but because his agency (and not VeriTabs) had hired us, we had to follow his lead. Unfortunately for him, Arthur Rickman, the VeriTabs CEO, is a classic Thinker.

The meeting was held in the VeriTabs boardroom at the company's headquarters building in Memphis. About a dozen people were present: three from the ad agency, including Bedosian, and various VeriTabs executives, including Rickman, the chief marketing officer, the chief operations officer, a couple of marketing directors, and a vice president. We were sitting around a long conference table, with Rickman in the middle on one side and Bedosian and his colleagues from the ad agency directly across. Bedosian used storyboards for his presentation, and the first one showed the current status of VeriTabs products. The next storyboard showed what VeriTabs was hoping to accomplish with an on-line spin-off. Then Bedosian launched into the slogans that his agency had developed for the Web start-up. The catchphrases were vague, along the lines of "Stay in Power," and Bedosian didn't explain how his agency had come up with them or why they might work or how they would supposedly connect with customers.

Throughout the presentation, Rickman just sat there, trying to absorb everything. At one point, he flipped through a two-page handout that the ad agency had given him, but the skimpy document was just a very high-level summary with no details. Essentially, it showed no more than what the storyboards were going to portray. As Rickman looked back and forth between the handout and the storyboards, trying to find information that wasn't there, his frustration grew. He didn't even understand enough to ask any questions, so he sat there silently. In Thinkers, silence is a bad sign: It shows that they don't have the necessary background information to ask questions. Otherwise, they would jump right in with an intense series of queries about this particular option or that piece of data or that step in a process.

By the time Bedosian and his colleagues had gotten to the fifth storyboard, Rickman had had enough. "Hold on," he said. "I'm lost. Where are we in the process? I'm not sure where we are in trying to figure out what we're going to do." Bedosian then tried to explain that his agency had followed the progression of VeriTabs products to see how the new product line would fit in. "Wait a minute," said Rickman. "You guys are already talking about slogans and product launches when I don't even know if I want to do this yet. I'm still trying to figure that out. I would love to move forward with this but only if it makes sense for our company to do so. And I don't know whether we want to do this or not. I'm looking for some data, something to show me that this is the type of thing that we should be doing."

At this point, Rickman was out of his chair, pacing the room. In his fifties, Rickman is not a large man, but when he is agitated, his voice can boom, and this was one of those occasions. He walked over to the storyboards, flipped through them, picked them up, and tossed them over to a nearby credenza. "I don't need to see any of this stuff right now," he said. "We're way ahead of ourselves. I don't even know if I want to go into this business yet. I need to see some data."

Bedosian then turned to us, trying to salvage the situation, and told Rickman that we had some pertinent market research to present about the VeriTabs brand. But it was too late for that. "I want to see it," said Rickman, "but now I'm not in the right frame of mind. So here's what I want you to do: I want you to regroup and figure out what you're doing on this project. And then come back to re-present the information to me." With that, Rickman left the room.

Everyone was nonplussed. We were barely ten or fifteen minutes into the meeting, which had been scheduled for an hour, and Rickman had walked out. We had never seen a CEO take someone to task like that. People in the room couldn't help feeling sorry for Bedosian. He had made a serious miscalculation about the structure of his presentation, and he paid the price. When we gathered our belongings and headed out the room, his one remark was, "Well, that was interesting."

Two weeks later we flew back to Memphis for the do-over meeting, but this time the ad agency sent another executive instead of Bedosian. Together, we made a three-hour presentation to a team of VeriTabs people, which did not include Rickman but did include an executive VP who was present at the first meeting. This time we gave people a detailed report that included our survey results as well as an analysis of what it would cost for VeriTabs to transfer its brand equity to the on-line community.

In the end, Rickman scuttled his plans for launching VeriTabs.com. We realize that even if our initial meeting with him had gone without a hitch, he still might have made the decision he did because our data showed that the spin-off would have required a substantial investment. But Bedosian certainly didn't help his chances because his presentation was geared more for a Charismatic than a Thinker. Even if Rickman had been a Charismatic, Bedosian still should have described the problem in greater detail (that is, explained why VeriTabs would have difficulty establishing its brand on-line) *before* launching into the marketing slogans. Of course, hindsight is twenty-twenty, but the ideal presentation for Rickman would have first defined the problem thoroughly, listed the different options, discussed the pros and cons of each of those options, explained how risks would be minimized, and then arrived at the optimum solution. An unfortunate epilogue to this story is that the ad agency lost the VeriTabs account—more than a million dollars of business—and Bedosian was fired a few months later.

INVOLVE THE THINKER IN YOUR PROCESS

The reason Thinkers prefer a chronological presentation is that it enables them to easily follow someone else's logic. This in turn allows them to ask questions along the way to thoroughly understand that person's decision-making process. Such a presentation should include the following steps: (1) define the problem, (2) describe and evaluate the different options, (3) explain why a particular option is best, (4) assess the value of that option, and (5) evaluate the potential problems with that option.

In any meeting with a Thinker, you should not only plan a systematic presentation but also be prepared to answer numerous queries throughout the discussion. An important thing to remember is that the battery of questions is not personal, even though it might seem like an intense interrogation. Instead, it is simply the Thinker's attempt to gain an in-depth understanding of your methodology. Remember that Thinkers usually need to fully comprehend something before they will truly trust it. In fact, they are often more interested in the process that was used to obtain an answer than they are in the answer itself. So you need to fully explain your methodology and flow of logic and be prepared for Thinkers to challenge you whenever something is unclear. During a meeting, they may even take contradictory points of view, but don't be confused when that happens. They are merely trying to understand a situation from all perspectives. Playing devil's advocate helps Thinkers to make sure that they have left no stone unturned, so don't let that approach throw you off your game and don't take it personally.

Thinkers are most persuaded by logical arguments that incorporate an explanation of best practices and procedures, information and methods endorsed by experts, clever and unique approaches, extensive data analysis, and a discussion of future results. Furthermore, to hold a Thinker's attention, consider using the following buzzwords: *quality, academic, think, numbers, makes sense, intelligent, plan, expert, competition, proof, hear, tell, talk, future, risk free.*

Perhaps the best overall strategy is to focus on open communications. The ideal way to accomplish that is by involving Thinkers as much as possible in the process that you are using to arrive at a solution. This will engage them, and a side benefit is that they will begin to take ownership of your process, which will only help you in the long run in getting their ultimate buy-in. So don't hesitate to openly discuss your worries and concerns about the shortcomings of your proposal, and continually ask the Thinker for suggestions. Specifically, be candid about where your data are inconclusive or conflicting, where you've made assumptions (especially ones that you're unsure of), where your arguments are based on gut feelings, and so on. Thinkers won't hold that information against you; in fact, it's likely to increase your credibility with them.

This is why we recommend that the optimum approach for dealing with Thinkers is to schedule two presentations, perhaps a week apart. In the first meeting, show your process and the progress you've made in solving a problem. Get a clear understanding of any additional options or other information that the Thinker deems important. The most crucial thing to remember is that, as much as possible, you want to obtain the Thinker's input about your process. In the second meeting, highlight any revisions you've made to your process since the earlier presentation and then follow those changes through to their logical conclusions to make your recommendations. The two-meeting approach might seem inefficient, but it helps Thinkers to become familiar and comfortable with your process.

To understand why, consider Kevin McLaughlin, who is the deputy director of a state agency with a $40-million budget. In his mid-fifties, McLaughlin is intelligent and well read. He is also a classic Thinker: thorough and methodical. One thing his staff has learned is that, particularly for any major decision, they need to keep him informed of the process they are using to arrive at a solution. "I would always try to send Kevin a report before a meeting, so that he'd have the chance to review it. And then during the meeting I could talk him through the details," recalls Eric Vieau, who was the chief financial officer of the agency. The bigger the decision, says Vieau, the more important it was to involve McLaughlin in the different steps along the way.

Vieau recalls such a situation in the mid-1990s when he proposed that the agency upgrade its computer systems. At the time, only a quarter of the staff had desktop personal computers, and those were a hodgepodge of incompatible hardware and software. Worse, the PCs weren't networked, which aggravated the inefficiencies. McLaughlin was all in favor of investing in standardized and networked PCs, and he asked Vieau to investigate how to accomplish that.

One of the issues was whether to buy or lease the PCs. Another matter was the type of arrangement for the maintenance and servicing of the equipment. Vieau explored those and other issues and prepared a report for McLaughlin with details of the different alternatives.

Regarding the buy-or-lease decision, for instance, the report showed that although buying PCs would be cheaper, that option had various hidden costs. If the agency bought the equipment, it would have to do so in piecemeal fashion, perhaps purchasing fifteen PCs the first year, fifteen the next year, and so on. During this transition time, the new PCs wouldn't be compatible with the older, existing machines, thus aggravating the inefficiencies. By leasing the equipment instead, the agency could install everything at once, and everyone would be using the same software.

McLaughlin reviewed the report and asked Vieau to investigate various other issues: How would the costs fit into our budget? What impact might it have on other areas of the budget? Who would get what kind of PC? How would we train everyone, particularly those who weren't familiar with e-mail, word processors, Web browsers, and other software? What would be the best timing for the implementation? What brands should we go with?

Sometimes the answer to one of those questions would lead to another issue that would then need to be resolved. To determine who would get what kind of PC, for instance, Vieau had to come up with a position-by-position analysis to ensure that staff members didn't feel that any favoritism was involved. All administrative assistants, for example, would get a certain type of CPU and monitor. Those and other issues were worked through in numerous back-and-forth exchanges, until Vieau had provided McLaughlin with all the information he needed. After that, McLaughlin gave the project the green light.

McLaughlin's other managers have also adapted to his style of decision making. Mary Flood, the agency's director of finance and administration, recalls that she learned to accept the fact that decisions wouldn't usually be made in a single meeting. "Kevin would always ask, 'Have you looked at that?' or 'Have you considered this?' " she says of her boss. "His points were usually very good ones—you'd frequently say to yourself, 'Why didn't I think of that?'—but then you'd leave the meeting without a decision."

For smaller matters, Flood learned to copy McLaughlin on e-mails and memos to inform him on how she was handling them and to give him the opportunity to add his input. That way he wouldn't be blind-sided by any decision. So, for example, if Flood were handling a personnel problem with one of her staff, she would copy him on certain correspondence she might be having with someone from human resources so that McLaughlin would know what steps she was taking to address the problem. Usually he wouldn't comment, but occasionally he would have a suggestion.

BE EXHAUSTIVE BUT PATIENT

Thinkers like McLaughlin thrive on information. They have a strong need for data, facts, and figures, and this makes it difficult to persuade them. One effective tactic is to deliver that information in huge chunks interspersed with enough time for them to make sense of the material. You can almost never provide Thinkers with too much information. Even when you think you have, they will ask you for something that you hadn't even thought of. So expect that even when you're confident that you've exhausted all avenues, they will find other pathways to explore.

In Flood's meetings with McLaughlin, he would frequently ask her for some piece of information that she hadn't anticipated. When she first started working for him, she would leave those meetings thinking, "Why didn't I cover that base myself?" But as their working relationship evolved, she realized something important. Thinkers like McLaughlin don't necessarily expect you to have all your ducks in a row when you make a proposal. They believe that part of their job is to help their staffers clarify and fine-tune their thinking processes. And although Thinkers don't expect you to have all the answers at the outset, they do expect you to eventually locate and properly position your ducks after they've given you the necessary guidance.

If Thinkers want information that is proprietary or is otherwise difficult for you to provide, the best solution is to point them toward where they might get that information for themselves. Thinkers don't expect you to breach your or anyone else's code of ethics or privacy, but they do appreciate any guidance they can get.

After Thinkers have all the data they need, you should give them ample time and space to come to their own conclusions. Remember that Thinkers are less innovative-driven than they are control-driven, so it's important to give them some ownership of the decision-making process. After you've provided all the information they need, don't crowd them or you'll very likely annoy and irritate, rather than help.

Sometimes the wait can be unsettling. You might have struggled to painstakingly address every detail, dotting each *i* and crossing every *t*. After all that, you might feel that a decision should be imminent. But the truth is that Thinkers still need ample time to process information on their own terms. And if they say they'll make a decision at the end of the week, then they will make a decision at that time. In other words, you can take them at face value.

That point brings to mind an interesting dealing we had with James Gonon, the president and COO of Optektrix, a leading supplier of semiconductor manufacturing equipment. We've known Gonon for years. He's a Thinker: process-oriented and very much a numbers person. We had worked with him in the past, but we hadn't talked to him in about a year. So we thought long and hard about how we might get our feet through his door again. At the time, we were repositioning our firm to specialize in customer-value research, and we had a strong feeling that our methodology and hard data would appeal to Gonon. But we waited until we had something tangible that would demonstrate exactly what we were capable of doing.

In late 2001, we finished two major studies: one that covered the personal computer industry (detailing who bought PCs and why) and the other on how executives make decisions (that research was the basis of this book, *Paths to Persuasion*). We then knew we had something very powerful for Gonon to see. We didn't know what his exact needs were, and we didn't know which of the two studies might catch his eye. But we were hoping that our recent research might somehow be related to a project he had in mind, and at the very least we could show him our methodology, which we thought would interest him. So we called Gonon and scheduled thirty minutes of his time.

At the meeting, we presented him with the full reports of both studies; each document was more than fifty pages long. We also brought copies for his key people. Gonon was particularly interested in our research on decision making, especially our breakdown of the five executive styles. As he looked through that data, he said, "This is perfect timing because we have an executive call program that we want to put together for our sales professionals. Maybe you can help us out with that."

We were excited because we knew that executive call programs are extensive projects. They typically consist of two-to-three-year plans for sales professionals to strategize how best to cultivate relationships with key executives at major accounts. Gonon was considering our research as a tool that would enable his sales staff to make more effective presentations to Optektrix's clients. Our timing was indeed fortuitous in that we might be able to be a part of the company's executive call program from the ground level.

At the conclusion of our meeting with Gonon, he asked us to call him on his cell phone on February 27 at 6:30 in the morning. He was going to be touring a plant that day (thus the early time) and would then have a decision whether Optektrix would want to use us in the company's executive call program.

Three weeks later, on February 27, we called Gonon promptly at 6:30 A.M. "Thanks for calling me," he said. "I had a meeting about this yesterday, and we do want to go ahead. The person you need to talk with is John Switzler, so please give him a call. He's in China right now, but he'll be back on Thursday of next week." Gonon had the details in his head, and our phone call took no more than two minutes. When we later met with Switzler, an executive vice president with Optektrix, he had a copy of our report and had marked it up, so Gonon had obviously forwarded it to him to bring him up to speed.

Certainly, we were fortunate that we had caught Gonon at the perfect time, right when he was starting the planning for his executive call program. But we had bided our time until we had the kind of data that would appeal to him and so were ready when the opportunity presented itself. And, just as important, we were careful not to blow that opportunity.

During the three-week interlude between our initial meeting with Gonon and the subsequent phone call, he probably scrutinized our data and methodology and processed all that information. When everything passed muster, he had a meeting with other Optektrix executives to obtain their buy-in for including us in the company's executive call program.

The important point is this: During the three-week period, we had zero contact with Gonon. We took him at face value: If he said to phone him on a particular day, there was no reason to have any contact with him before that unless he requested it. If he had trouble understanding our research methodology, for instance, he might ask us for additional details, and we would obviously respond promptly to that request. But we didn't hear anything from him during those three weeks, so we assumed that everything was in order. In contrast, if Gonon had been a Charismatic, we might have called or written him just to stay in contact and to ensure that he hadn't dropped the ball.

Remember that Thinkers like to process information by themselves, and during that time you need to back off; otherwise, you're likely to annoy rather than help. Once Thinkers have all the information they need, they don't require additional assistance. What they prefer is that you give them the space they need to do their thorough analysis.

A primary caution with Thinkers is that they will never forget a bad experience, so you must be absolutely positive that any recommendation you make is truly the best option. Of course, you should do this for any of the five types of decision makers, but particularly so with Thinkers. And, anyway, Thinkers will eventually figure out for themselves whether something was truly the best alternative.

ALLOW (AND ENCOURAGE) OTHERS TO JOIN THE THINKING

Patience is particularly necessary when Thinkers need others to do some thinking, too. Thinkers like nothing more than when their colleagues and staff are analyzing a problem with them. They don't want yes-people. They want to know that everyone's done their homework. They want to know that others are being just as thorough as they are. And they will tell someone who hasn't been: They will request more data, or they will ask pointed questions along the lines of "Have you thought about this?" or "Have you considered that this might happen?" At the same time, Thinkers would be perfectly willing to listen to anyone who has uncovered a flaw in their logic, an inaccuracy in their data, or some other hidden problem with a process.

We certainly learned that lesson in dealing with a major client of ours in the food industry. Barry Clifton, the company's president, has eleven large divisions reporting to him, and each is a multimillion-dollar business. Clifton is a true Thinker—very process-oriented and methodical. Whenever he hears a promising proposal, he's likely to say, "Now, that's a good idea, but let's back off a little and consider all the ramifications."

Over the past several years, we have been working closely with one of Clifton's key lieutenants—Bill Seymore, who heads up an important division of the company. We conducted a survey of Seymore's customers, asking them to rank various value drivers, such as innovative menus, the variety and prices of dishes, restaurant decor, and so on. Using that data, Seymore was able to devise certain strategic initiatives to address each of those value drivers, and the payoffs have been substantial: Ever since he took over the division, it has become the leading business unit of the company.

Recently, we performed an extensive study of Seymore's customers to develop detailed behavioral profiles of them. Our approach to customer segmentation provided a quality of data that Seymore hadn't had before, enabling him to think outside the proverbial box to come up with a new, innovative strategic plan that he presented to Clifton and other top executives. This type of creative but process-oriented thinking, based on hard customer data, appealed to Clifton, and he requested a meeting with us to learn more about the kind of research we were capable of conducting.

At the meeting, we showed Clifton that our research wasn't the traditional type of customer-satisfaction survey in which consumers are asked to fill out questionnaires to rank the service they've just received. Instead, our research delves deeper into the behavior of those people, specifically their wants and desires and whether a particular company is fulfilling them. Clifton was impressed with the rigor of our research methodology, and it became clear to us that he was considering using our firm to conduct studies for several of his eleven divisions.

But Clifton was not going to impose anything. He was not going to tell his individual presidents how to run their business units, because he ultimately holds them responsible for their results. This is very much like a Thinker, to delegate and leave an important decision with the people who will be responsible for it. (In contrast, a Controller would have little compunction about issuing edicts.) Typically, Thinkers like Clifton are more likely to suggest something by saying, "I think this is of value." But Clifton would also be quick to point out that Seymore's division was the only unit to beat its financial numbers, and one of the distinctions is that Seymore had better data about his clients and customers—information that came from our research. So we had Clifton's imprimatur, although we knew he wouldn't be making the final decisions.

After our meeting with him, Clifton put us in touch with the presidents of two of his other divisions, and we have been in close contact with them to thoroughly explain how our customer research might help their businesses. We've had a number of conversations with these two executives, and, in fact, over the course of a month we were flying weekly to the East Coast to meet with them. Our goal was to keep the momentum going from our earlier meeting with Clifton. The process has taken time, but we know it's essential.

The point of this story is that Clifton wants all his top lieutenants to go through the thinking process that he went through to arrive at the conclusions that he did. He will continue to drive their reasoning of why they need to be using better customer data. If they don't come up with the answer that he did, he will tell them where their thought process was flawed and what they need to do to revise it. But if one of his division presidents can make a good case for taking an alternative approach, Clifton would be willing to hear that out. In fact, he'd be very interested in a strong counterargument because that would then help him to revise his own reasoning. This is why Thinkers need others to think things through with them: They want to ensure that they haven't overlooked anything important, that they haven't left any stone unturned. Using others in this way helps Thinkers to be thorough. So we need to be extremely responsive to Clifton's two presidents. We need to follow their reasoning and resolve any issues that they have because at some point Clifton will check his analysis with theirs. Of course, this process will be long and time-consuming, but it is crucial.

KNOWING WHAT TO DO—AND WHEN TO DO IT

Thinkers can be difficult to persuade because of their compelling desire for exhaustive information. You can greatly improve your odds with them by using a systematic approach. The accompanying exhibit "The Thinker Plan" contains a chronology of important to-do tasks. The most crucial item that you will use from your persuasion toolkit (as discussed in chapter 2) is your decision-making methodology itself. If that process is solid, you'll be on solid ground to persuade any Thinker. But expect that Thinkers will somehow find holes in your logic, information that is inconsistent or ambiguous, or other flaws in your argument. This is why we recommend a two-meeting approach. The first meeting will help you to involve the Thinker in your decision-making process, and you'll quickly learn the areas where you'll need to do some additional homework to address issues that you hadn't anticipated. Be sure to resolve all of those before your second meeting, which should then run more smoothly.

THE THINKER PLAN

How to Prepare for a Meeting with a Thinker Decision Maker

PRE-MEETING	IN THE MEETING	POST-MEETING
✓ Prepare to deliver the message in two meetings, showing process and progress in the first and recommendations in the second	✓ Stress competitor problems and the risk of the status quo	✓ Revise your methodology per the Thinker's suggestions and corrections
✓ Collect as much relevant data, facts, and figures as possible	✓ Show your process/methodology for deciding what to do	✓ During the second meeting, point out any changes in data or process in order to minimize surprises
✓ Perform detailed risk assessments of each option	✓ Examine the options available, highlighting their upsides and downsides	✓ Note the risk levels, cost projections, and revenue benefits
✓ Make sure a white board is available for the meeting	✓ Assemble lists of do's and don'ts on the white board	
	✓ Prep for a second meeting to more thoroughly discuss recommendations	

To summarize, the key to persuading Thinkers is that you must

- Make your case by telling your story from start to finish. Avoid presentations that focus on the bottom line without first laying the necessary groundwork. Thinkers don't necessarily want to know the ending of your story until they can understand the events that led up to that conclusion. In other words, Thinkers need to know the *how* and *why* before they can accept the *what*.
- Allow the Thinker to participate in your decision-making process. Remember that Thinkers won't fully trust anything that they don't first comprehend. In order for them to accept your recommendation, they need to thoroughly understand how you arrived at it. Until then, expect that you may be fighting a steep uphill battle.
- Supply the Thinker with all pertinent information. Remember that Thinkers are seldom bored with details; in fact, they relish them. Be prepared that even when you think you've been thorough, a Thinker will ask for additional data. It is crucial for you to remain patient, particularly as the Thinker processes the copious information.
- Expect that Thinkers might require others to think everything through with them. As important as it is for Thinkers to understand *your* decision-making methodology, they also sometimes need others to understand *their* thought processes as well. This step might appear to slow things down, but it's often necessary for Thinkers to ensure that they haven't overlooked anything important.

Chapter 7

The Skeptic Decision Maker

EXAMPLES	TED TURNER, STEVE CASE, LARRY ELLISON, AND TOM SIEBEL

Skeptics are inherently suspicious and will rarely trust information that doesn't fit with their worldview. They need to hear things from sources they deem to be credible; otherwise, they will aggressively challenge and usually discount the information, even when it's accurate. At their very core, Skeptics are

1. **Iconoclasts.** They constantly question the status quo and will vigorously attack anything that runs contrary to their worldview, especially if the source of that information has yet to earn their trust.
2. **Brazenly outspoken.** They are nonconformists who often have little regard for social propriety. They will say exactly what they think and let the chips fall where they may.
3. **Fearlessly confident.** They are unafraid of being wrong and will often make bold, risky decisions based purely on their gut feelings.
4. **Assertive and demanding.** They have strong personalities and will aggressively do what needs to be done—and they expect their staff to do the same.

5. Determined and driven. They are intensely focused and will stick to something until they succeed. Failure is not an option.

6. Visionary. They are not bogged down by the here and now. Instead, they easily envision the possibilities of what might be.

ICONOCLASTS

When Larry Ellison, cofounder of Oracle Corp., was growing up on the South Side of Chicago, he continually questioned everything. "I had a habit of asking questions that irritated my teachers," he recalls. "I was a little bit disruptive. I just didn't believe what they were saying."[1]

That attitude defines who Skeptics are. To them, virtually everything and everyone are suspect. They will question every single data point, especially any information that challenges their view of the world. And they will often pride themselves in being contrarians. "You can't win without being completely different," asserts Ellison. "When everyone else says we are crazy, I say, 'Gee, we must really be on to something.' The louder they say it, the more excited I get."[2]

Skeptics march to their own drummers, and that often accounts for their success (or failure) in business. "I've always been an iconoclast," says Ellison. "It has helped me make out like a bandit in technology, where conventional wisdom changes every five years."[3] Ellison knows from where he speaks. He has grown Oracle into a multibillion-dollar software behemoth, second only to Microsoft, and in the process he has become one of the richest men in the world.

For Skeptics like Ellison, trust simply doesn't come easily. They have difficulty believing others, particularly strangers, not necessarily because those people are untrustworthy, but because that is how Skeptics define themselves. By nature, Skeptics are suspicious, and they often pride themselves on being that way. It's almost a badge they wear: Nobody's going to pull anything over on them, because they're Skeptics.

Not surprisingly, Skeptics do not like being helped; they prefer having people think they know something already. If they do need help, they want it only from certain people. Their attitude is this: "If you're not my equal, then I can't accept what you're saying at its face value. Instead, I will have to hear what you're saying from a credible source who is my peer." In other words, Skeptics do want your input as long as you're credible with them. If you're not, you could have the best idea in the world and it will fall on deaf ears.

Skeptics run hot and cold with people. Breaking into their inner circle of trust is not easy, but when you're in, you are definitely in (and when you're out, you are painfully out). Skeptics tend to trust people who are similar to them: for instance, people who come from the same part of the country or went to the same college or worked for the same companies—in other words, people who have similar perspectives.

Perhaps because of their inherent distrust of others, Skeptics are often aloof. They can be emotionally detached, making it difficult to connect and engage with them on a personal level, even in one-on-one situations. Case in point: Tom Siebel, the CEO of Siebel Systems, the San Mateo, California, software giant that sells programs for managing customer relationships. Patricia House, who cofounded the company with Siebel, has known surprisingly little of the personal life of her close business partner. She did not know, for instance, whether Siebel's parents were still alive, even after having worked closely with him for years. Says Siebel, "On a professional level, we're as close as colleagues can get, but we're not involved in each other's personal or social lives."[4] Another Siebel exec sums it up best: "You don't come in and swap stories with Tom about your vacation."[5]

With Skeptics, there are no touchy feelings, no group hugs. They do not waste their time stroking others' egos, and they are not known as nurturers, comforters, or hand-holders. They do not like to be mentored, nor do they like to mentor others, which can make them poor at succession planning. Who will run Oracle after Larry Ellison leaves, or Siebel Systems after Tom Siebel calls it quits? Sometimes Skeptics can even isolate themselves from colleagues and staff, disappearing for long stretches of time.

BRAZENLY OUTSPOKEN

Nonconformist and unconventional, Skeptics do not easily yield to authority. In fact, they often resist it strenuously. Some of the great revolutionists in history were Skeptics (think of Napoleon Bonaparte). They are the rebels of industry because of their independent, iconoclastic attitudes. They break the rules and much prefer coloring outside the lines. Not surprisingly, Skeptics are both direct and forthright with their opinions. They say what they think, and they let the chips fall where they may. In doing so, they can be painfully blunt, alienating others. Diplomacy is not a strength.

Ted Turner, the founder of CNN and former vice chairman of Time Warner, has become so infamous for his brazen remarks that he has earned the nickname Captain Outrageous. "It's as if a child were speaking, without any social inhibitions,"[6] says Gerald Levin, the former head of Time Warner. Turner, who dislikes reading from prepared speeches, admits, "I don't have any idea what I'm going to say. I say what comes to my mind."[7]

In business meetings, Skeptics will often be disruptive and disagreeable—even rebellious and antisocial. During someone's presentation, they will think nothing of getting up and leaving temporarily. They will take phone calls and even carry on side conversations for extended periods of time. They might even lock heads with others whenever the opportunity arises. A senior executive at AOL describes how unpredictable—and disruptive—Ted Turner could be. "In meetings I've been in with him," the exec says, "he just sits there and in a piercing voice—louder than you would expect someone to talk—he interrupts or conveys a sense of 'Hurry up! Why am I here?' He gives off a feeling that he's in a rush, even if he's not doing anything."[8]

Skeptics appear to have little compunction about running roughshod over the unspoken rules of etiquette. They might arrive a half hour late for a meeting, saunter into the room, and then leave early—all without offering any apologies or explanations. They take great license with social conventions, and their lack of decorum can be stunning, their behavior even bordering on the obnoxious. Larry Ellison has often unabashedly transgressed the borders of social propriety, and stories about him have become the stuff of legend. After winning a sailboat race from Miami to Montego Bay, he got into his private jet and flew back over the course to taunt the other competitors. "It was an incredibly adolescent and immature thing to do," he says, "and I highly recommend it."[9]

Call them the bad boys of industry, but Skeptics simply don't care. Their attitude is this: "I am who I am, and you can take it or leave it." At their worst, Skeptics can be disdainful of others, even of potential allies, and their "I don't give a damn" attitude can lead to bad business decisions. For instance, they might ignore important feedback from employees and customers, thinking that those opinions don't really matter.

FEARLESSLY CONFIDENT

One of the most defining traits of Skeptics is that they are supremely confident and tend to have very strong personalities. Whenever you're in the presence of a Skeptic, you will know it. The reason is simple: They will absolutely make sure that you know it. Furthermore, you will know almost immediately where you stand with them. You can depend on them to tell you what they are thinking because their strong personalities and supreme confidence make them unafraid of being wrong. In this sense, dealing with Skeptics can be straightforward, if difficult, because you can usually take what they say at face value.

Many top executives have larger-than-life personas, but Skeptics seem to have cornered the market on that. The classic joke about Larry Ellison goes like this: What is the difference between Ellison and God? The answer: God doesn't think he's Larry Ellison. But therein lies one of the better qualities of Skeptics: They are seldom hamstrung by self-doubt. You might dislike their tactics and argue with their methods, but the bottom line is that Skeptics get results. Moreover, they are unafraid of making tough, even unpopular, calls. They might even feed off those big moments, and they can act quickly and decisively.

When the U.S. economy began to soften early in 2001, Tom Siebel took swift action, firing eight hundred employees, postponing bonuses, slashing travel and recruiting budgets, and shoring up the sales staff to close important deals. The speed with which Siebel brought the company's finances under control, keeping costs in line with revenues, was breathtaking (even if the company did underestimate the full extent of the downturn, forcing it to do additional belt-tightening the following year). Just a day after the September 11 terrorist attack, Siebel was using the company's internal Web site to assure people that all Siebel employees around the world had been accounted for and were safe. He then quickly set up the Siebel America Fund, which enabled employees to overcome their feelings of helplessness (and to channel their grief) by making contributions to those in need.

The supreme confidence of Skeptics makes them fearless risk takers. When Ted Turner was forming the Turner Broadcasting System (TBS) network, he had to borrow heavily. The risks were daunting because he still needed approval from the Federal Communications Commission, and he was being opposed by huge forces, including the major broadcast networks (ABC, CBS, and NBC), numerous local TV stations, the Hollywood studios, and professional sports organizations. But somehow Turner prevailed, winning FCC approval that paved the way for future growth in the cable industry.

Without a doubt, Skeptics have made some of the boldest, riskiest—and perhaps most impulsive—decisions in business. When Turner bought MGM for $1.5 billion in the mid-1980s, he assumed huge debts and reportedly made the decision without fully consulting his board.[10] The deal was arranged by Michael Milken, the infamous king of junk bonds. Just months later Turner had to sell back the MGM studio and other parts of the company for only $300 million.

Typically, Skeptics make decisions quickly, within days if not right on the spot. If their gut feelings are with them, they don't need any sort of heavy-duty quantitative analyses to back them up. But that's not to say that Skeptics have no use for market surveys, cost-benefit analyses, and other quantitative information. Like Thinkers, Skeptics love data, but the two types of decision makers process information very differently. Thinkers will take all of the data elements into consideration, whereas Skeptics typically already have a solution in mind, and they pore through the data to find things that will support them, often dismissing those pieces that don't.

ASSERTIVE AND DEMANDING

Skeptics are usually described as take-charge people. They do not excel at consensus managing, nor do they run democratic organizations. They can even be imperial taskmasters, calling on the phone at inconvenient times and expecting people to respond to their requests immediately. They often have an aggressive, almost combative style, and they favor a no-holds-barred approach to business. In meetings, they will frequently hijack the agenda, taking complete control of the discussion. And they will aggressively challenge what they don't believe, almost with the intensity of a pit bull.

When talking about Cuba and its leader, Ted Turner once remarked to a colleague, "Fidel ain't a Communist. He's a dictator, just like me."[11] That statement might be less of an exaggeration than one might think. Turner has refused to hire smokers, even though he himself once smoked. "I figured any young person who's dumb enough to smoke is too dumb to work at CNN or TBS," he explained.[12]

That aspect of Skeptics can often rub people the wrong way. Take Tom Siebel, who has been called a "tiger in the tie"[13] and who is well known throughout the computer industry as an autocratic, tough businessman. "The 'a' word comes up a lot when people bring up Tom," says Gary Kennedy, who hired Siebel years ago to work at Oracle.[14] Siebel himself admits, "There are people who think I'm God's gift to technology, and then there are people who think I'm the world's biggest S.O.B."[15]

To be sure, Skeptics can be excruciatingly demanding of people's energy and time. At Oracle, where Larry Ellison drives his managers hard, burnout is commonplace. "For most people, there really are only a certain number of years they can take," says a former Oracle executive.[16] On the other hand, the intense drive of Skeptics like Ellison is what pushes others to excel. "His great strength is to make exceptional employees do the impossible," notes a past colleague of Ellison's.[17]

Indeed, it must be noted that the very qualities that others find disagreeable in Skeptics often enable them to become very successful in business. Without Turner's demanding nature, CNN might never have become the network it is. During the Gulf War in 1990 to 1991, for instance, CNN continued its dogged coverage while the other networks pulled out. At the time, Tom Johnson, then president of CNN, received a number of calls from various government officials, including President Bush, pleading with him to vacate Baghdad.[18] But Turner insisted otherwise, and the round-the-clock coverage of that war cemented CNN's place as *the* source for important breaking news.

All that said, the aggressive, hypercompetitive nature of Skeptics can frequently be cranked up a few notches too high. Steve Case's combative style of management was well known throughout AOL when he was CEO there. According to those who worked with him, he liked to play devil's advocate to keep people off guard so that no one knew where he truly stood on an issue. In doing so, he would aggressively challenge people, and those who backed down were discounted. One AOL executive used the term "Darwinian management" to describe Case's approach of survival of the fittest.[19]

Case had little use for sycophants. "If you say yes all the time to him, he'll stop working with you," says an AOL executive. "If you are a peer, you have to tell him that he's wrong—if you think he's wrong."[20] The key word there is "peer." You would do well to remember that you should never challenge Skeptics unless you have established sufficient credibility with them.

The bottom line is that Skeptics like Ellison do want good, informed advice. As one Oracle exec puts it, "Larry will say, 'If I know more about your business than you do, we have a problem.'"[21] Essentially, Skeptics want to arrive at the right decision. They truly do want to make the best choice, even if it means that they will need to alter their viewpoint about something. But at the same time, they will be fiercely resistant to that change, and their ego and aggressive nature might make them insufferable throughout the process.

DETERMINED AND DRIVEN

If nothing else, Skeptics are intensely determined and driven. Since the early 1990s, for instance, former AOL Time Warner chairman Steve Case was almost obsessed with the idea that the Internet would one day become a universal tool that everyone would use. "That belief of his burns inside of him like radioactive uranium. It's ever present—it's the drive that propels him,"[22] noted an AOL executive.

That determination—along with the feeling that failure was not an option—was why AOL became the company that it did. Back in the mid-1980s, when AOL was just a tiny, unknown company called Quantum Computer Services, Case pulled off a major coup. To close a deal with Apple Computer, he rented an apartment in Cupertino, California, near Apple's headquarters building, and then proceeded to dog the company relentlessly for three months until he had a signed contract. "The deals he did—there was no logical reason for them to be done," says Marc Seriff, who helped found Quantum. "Apple, Tandy, IBM. None of them should have happened. We were a nobody."[23]

All successful executives are driven people, but the internal fires of Skeptics seem to burn brightest. They can be unbelievable workaholics, routinely logging in twelve-hour days, even on weekends. They are passionate and zealous, even manic. Simply put, they are out to prove something. Larry Ellison is driven by the words he continually heard as a youngster—his father's regular refrain of "You'll never amount to anything."[24] Indeed, with many Skeptics, an almost pathological aversion to failure has been baked into their psyches. Says Tom Siebel, "My father was supportive of anything we wanted to do, as long as we were good at whatever it was."[25]

The intense drive of Skeptics is usually accompanied by a laserlike focus. Much of Siebel's success can be attributed to his single-minded approach to business: Always think of the customer first. That edict is nonnegotiable, and every Siebel employee is constantly reminded of it. The artwork displayed on the walls at Siebel facilities comes from customer publications, and the conference rooms are named after major clients. Twice a year Siebel has an outside firm conduct extensive customer surveys, and compensation for all employees, even engineers, is tied to those surveys.

Once Skeptics have made a decision, they stay the course. Case, for instance, is well known for his steely resolve. "He doesn't second-guess himself or have regrets," says a senior AOL staffer.[26] The determination and tenacity of Skeptics can be a double-edged sword: They are able to exploit opportunities but might become blind to the risks involved. Indeed, the intense determination of Skeptics can make them unnecessarily intransigent. It can be painfully difficult to change their minds, and their stubbornness can prevent them from receiving valuable information. They might tune out someone who isn't on their wavelength, even if that person has useful insights, and might even isolate themselves from their colleagues and staff. They might brush off helpful criticism and cling to their own ideas, even as the contradictory evidence mounts.

Eventually, though, in such situations Skeptics *will* change their minds because, as noted earlier, they truly do want to arrive at the best solution. But when they do backpedal, they might easily blame someone else for their original decision. Case has been reluctant to accept full responsibility for the rocky merger between AOL and Time Warner. A major stockholder says that Case's explanation of what happened was something along these lines: "He had this vision. They did this grand deal. Then the guys running it screwed it up."[27] In fact, Skeptics are often unrepentant, and they can be notorious blamers. Worse, they might take more than their fair share of credit for successes.

VISIONARY

When Ted Turner created CNN, many scoffed at the idea of an around-the-clock cable network. Moreover, they pooh-poohed his philosophy of making the news the star. At CNN, anchors and corre-spondents were fairly anonymous, in striking contrast to the networks, which relied on broadcasting luminaries like Dan Rather and Walter Cronkite. But over the years, CNN has firmly established itself as a prime source of news, forever changing the television industry and becoming one of the best-known brands in the world.

Entire industries have been founded thanks to the visionary acumen of Skeptics. Tom Siebel rightly foresaw the market for software that would help companies coordinate their marketing, sales, and customer service more efficiently. "There had been successful applications of IT and computer technology to change the way we manage accounting, personnel, manufacturing, shopping and a host of other business activities," he recalls. "Yet in the last decade, the problems of sales and customer service had been largely untouched by computer technology . . . It seemed to me there would be an opportunity to build a pretty nice little business here."[28]

Siebel was right, and customer relationship management (CRM) software has grown to become a multibillion-dollar business. Today other software companies have seen the light of Siebel's vision, and the CRM market is being infiltrated by a host of competitors, including Oracle (which specializes in relational databases). Ironically, Siebel used to work at Oracle but left, in part, because he couldn't convince people there of the future potential of CRM. On his part, Larry Ellison of Oracle foresaw the huge potential for relational databases way back in the 1970s, when such software was in its infancy. Today relational databases help countless businesses to run by keeping tabs on everything from direct marketing to customer orders and fulfillment to inventory tracking.

Similarly, Steve Case was often admired as a prophet of the Internet, a digital seer of the new economy. Even back in the early 1980s, he foresaw the power of computers linked to each other over a vast global network. Skeptics seem to have a preternatural ability to foresee the future, and their prescience can be uncanny. They can see what will only later become obvious to others. They can be inspiring preachers of their vision, articulate and persuasive at rallying the troops. At AOL, staffers thought of Case as a technological messiah of the future. To those at CNN, Ted Turner was a folk hero of sorts.

On a related note, Skeptics sometimes see their lives as part of a larger cause, and they will often relate to historical or fictional figures, drawing heavily from metaphors. Larry Ellison, for instance, seems to have fashioned his life after that of a samurai. He derives inspiration from Musashi Miyamoto, the seventeenth-century samurai, and has named his champion sailboat *Sayonara*. He collects antique Japanese artwork and weaponry and hosts an annual cherry-blossom dinner. He is also building a multimillion-dollar estate near San Francisco in the style of a medieval Japanese village. When completed, the grounds will contain a teahouse and acres of gardens.

WHAT SKEPTICS SEEK—AND WHAT THEY AVOID

Tom Siebel is widely known throughout the computer industry as an authoritarian leader with a "my way or the highway" style of management. In the laid-back culture of Silicon Valley, he has decreed a dress code at his company that hearkens back to the old IBM of decades ago: no khaki pants or casual garb for employees who deal

APPROACH PROFILE for SKEPTICS

When Making Decisions, Skeptics.....

	Average	SEEK MORE
Self-Absorption		44
Rebellion		38
Risk	12	
Competitiveness	10	
Education	4	
Impulsiveness	2	
Fear & Uncertainty	-2	
Intelligence & Facts	-3	
Bargains	-5	
Playfulness	-9	
Persistence	-13	
Responsibility	-33	

AVOID MORE

Error ±2.9 points   © 2003 Miller-Williams Inc. (millwill.com)

Note: The data have been normalized to range from -100 (maximum aversion) to +100 (maximum desire).

with customers. At Siebel Systems, the men wear suits and ties and the women don pants or skirt suits. But his personality aside, when it comes to making important decisions, Siebel is a classic Skeptic, not a Controller.

To separate people's personality traits from their decision-making styles, our survey of nearly seventeen hundred business executives investigated various characteristics of those people, such as their desire for (or aversion toward) having outside help when they had to make an important decision with serious consequences. Through such probing, we found that nearly one out of five executives is a Skeptic. The exhibit "Approach Profile for Skeptics" contains an overview of that category of decision maker.

Our results show that the strongest desire of Skeptics is for self-absorption. When confronted with an important choice, they do not particularly need the input of others, and they are not big supporters of consensus management. They much prefer—and may even insist on—making decisions that are theirs alone to make. Note also that Skeptics desire rebellion and risk. This is why they have little fear in taking the road not taken. In fact, such untrodden routes may even be inherently more alluring to them.

Our survey also revealed that Skeptics have a strong aversion toward responsibility. At first, this can seem paradoxical: Although Skeptics desire authority and will quickly step up to the plate at important moments, they can be quick to make excuses when they strike out. And they may take more than their fair share of credit for any home runs. Call it the window-mirror syndrome:[29] When things go wrong, they peer out the window to apportion blame; when things go right, they gaze into the mirror and take credit.

Note also that Skeptics have an aversion toward others who are persistent. They loathe when colleagues and staff members prod them for a decision, and even gentle reminders are likely to do more harm than good. Nobody likes being rushed, but this is especially true for Skeptics because of their defiant nature. Pressure tactics can easily backfire, provoking them to prolong the time they need to make their decision.

Interestingly, Skeptics have just a moderate desire to be competitive. In our research, we have found that Skeptics will frequently claim that their primary goal is to better their companies with respect to rival firms, but that objective is actually secondary to their greater desires for self-absorption and rebellion. When push comes to shove, Skeptics will make decisions essentially for themselves, based on how they feel and on their need to choose a course of action that is contrary to what others are doing.

In summary, we have found that Skeptics

- March to their own drummer, making decisions that go against the grain of conventional wisdom.
- Tell you exactly what they think, leaving little doubt as to how they feel.
- Make bold, risky decisions often by pure gut, because they are unafraid of being wrong.
- Do what it takes to get the job done, even if they need to step on numerous toes.
- Ignore distractions and focus single-mindedly on the task at hand.
- Have little regard for what is or what *should* be, preferring to concentrate on what *could* be.

Skeptics are the lone wolves of the business world. They are headstrong and fiercely independent. They might not be the best team players—in fact, they can be aggravating (even infuriating) to work with—and their strong, aggressive personalities can border on the abrasive. At the same time, their restless impatience and determined nature often enable them to accomplish the impossible. Moreover, their propensity to think outside the proverbial box can lead to gutsy, brilliant decisions that are truly inspired.

Chapter 8

Persuading the Skeptic Decision Maker

Because Skeptics rarely trust anything that doesn't fit with their worldview, persuading them might sound like a daunting task. But the process is actually straightforward. Skeptics do want to move forward with good proposals, but they first need to make sure that they have full confidence in the source of those ideas. When they do, they can make decisions quickly, within days if not right on the spot. For that to happen, you need to

1. **Above all, establish your credibility.** Before doing anything else, you need to gain the Skeptic's confidence. To help build the necessary credibility, consider gaining the endorsement from someone the Skeptic trusts.
2. **Hold your ground, but find the middle ground.** Be prepared that the Skeptic might vigorously challenge you. Stand firm in your ideas, but also avoid putting the Skeptic on the defensive.
3. **Keep your emotions—and your ego—in check.** Do not take personally anything that the Skeptic says or does. Instead, maintain a calm confidence as you respond rationally and patiently to each of the Skeptic's concerns.
4. **Go to the source of credibility.** When presenting data to back you up, don't rely on secondary information. Use the primary source whenever possible.

ABOVE ALL, ESTABLISH YOUR CREDIBILITY

Skeptics are defined by their highly suspicious nature. Because they have great trouble accepting anything at face value, they distrust nearly everything and everyone. Whereas most people tend to operate with the attitude of "innocent until proven guilty," Skeptics have the reverse belief of "guilty until proven innocent." To persuade Skeptics, then, you first need to establish your credibility. Otherwise, your ideas, however brilliant, will fall on deaf ears.

Skeptics tend to trust people who are similar to them—people who, for instance, went to the same college or worked for the same previous company. They are also impressed with reputations and name brands, particularly those institutions with long, solid histories. Universities like Harvard and Stanford and blue-chip leaders like BMW, Microsoft, and Coca-Cola carry a lot of weight. Skeptics also value expertise in any specific area, such as in marketing or finance.

If you are somewhat unknown to a Skeptic, you need to find a way to have credibility transferred to you prior to or during a meeting. An effective tactic is to gain the endorsement from someone the Skeptic trusts. If, for instance, you're trying to win the approval from the president of your company who's a Skeptic, you might first float your proposal by one of his trusted lieutenants. After gaining her buy-in, you might then consider having her jointly pitch the idea with you. Moreover, you could strategize and have her present any data or information that might be controversial.

Credibility can be transferred, but ultimately it must be earned. And for that to happen, you might have to go through some very aggressive questioning as the Skeptic challenges you and your proposal. In effect, Skeptics conduct tests of whether they should believe you or not. But it's a reverse kind of exam: They are looking for reasons to distrust you, and only if they fail to find them will they begin to deem you credible. Think of it this way: With Skeptics, you start with an empty glass, and if you hold up to their scrutiny, they begin to fill the container with their trust. With other people, you might start with a full glass, and only after betraying their trust does your glass get emptied. In other words, Skeptics do not give the benefit of the doubt to anyone who is unproven. And they might aggressively challenge you, shooting countless arrows your way, to see whether you can stand up to the onslaught. If you wither, then Skeptics will write you off as somebody they don't want to do business with.

Although establishing credibility with a Skeptic can be a long, uphill effort, once you've accomplished it the rest of the journey can be surprisingly easy. After gaining the trust of Skeptics, you will then be able to openly discuss issues on their level. And when Skeptics have full confidence in the person who has proposed something, they can make decisions quickly, sometimes even on the spot.

We experienced many of these issues in our dealings with Darren Taber, the CEO of a multibillion-dollar high-tech company. (Note: To respect the confidentiality of our clients and colleagues, we have used pseudonyms and have altered identifying details of the examples in this chapter.) Taber is a shrewd, brilliant businessman who is known throughout the industry for his tough, aggressive style of management. He is also a classic Skeptic.

Recently, Taber became interested in a study that we had done on his industry. Our research, which included data about his company, investigated the juxtaposition of customer loyalty and satisfaction, and it showed that the two qualities do not always track with each other. Specifically, customer loyalty does not necessarily reflect customer satisfaction. In certain markets and for various reasons, customers are sometimes loyal to a vendor (perhaps they feel a sense of obligation) even though they aren't satisfied. After hearing about this research, Taber called to invite us to meet with him and several of his senior execs at his headquarters building.

We were excited that Taber was interested in our work, because we were hoping that his company might become a client of ours. And we were certainly encouraged by his attitude of "Hey, I need to do business with you guys." All the signs were promising, and we were looking forward to our discussion with him. Little did we know that we would be walking into one of the most hostile business environments that we've ever faced.

The meeting was confrontational from the get-go. At the start, Taber threw a report of our research down on the conference table and declared, "I've got seven years' worth of data that says one thing about my customer satisfaction and loyalty. And your report says something else. Either my seven years' worth of data is wrong, or you're wrong." Taber also attacked our integrity, using the words "deceptive" and "manipulative" to describe our research.

We were thrown off guard. There we were, thinking that we'd be talking about a deal with Taber, and there he was, throwing down a gauntlet. He had challenged us to disprove his results, and when we declined to play that game, he proceeded to attack our methodology and data.

Here we need to make a crucial point: Taber initially centered his assault on just one of us (Gary) and not the other (Bob). It is also important to know that Gary was basically an unknown quantity to Taber, whereas Bob had had several past dealings with him. In fact, Taber was well aware of Bob's past work, including his coauthorship of *Strategic Selling®*, the best-selling book that has trained a generation of salespeople. In addition, years ago Bob cofounded a company that Taber tried to acquire. So, throughout the years, Taber had become familiar with Bob's reputation and history in the industry.

Taber looked squarely at Gary and said, "You're the president and CEO of Miller-Williams. You explain your research to me." So Gary started talking about the methodology that we use, explaining how it leads to an accurate assessment of how customers truly feel about a vendor. Before he could get very far, though, Taber cut him short. "Basically, that's a nonanswer," he charged. "What you're telling me is that you have some sort of proprietary research method that you are either unable or unwilling to talk about."

Gary replied that we were more than willing to give details of our methodology but that we needed visual tools and a good chunk of time to fully describe the process. "Okay," Taber replied. "I'm ready. Go." But whenever Gary tried to explain something, Taber would automatically refute it. The two men butted heads on practically everything, and it was abundantly clear that Taber was going to be resistant to anything that Gary said.

Then Bob piped into the conversation. All of a sudden, Taber eased up and said he had much confidence in Bob's background and experience. He also added that over the years the one thing he had admired about Bob was his fierce personal integrity. As Taber spoke, there was a definite difference in not only his tone but also his body language. With Gary, Taber had been leaning forward, launching one question after the other. But when Bob started talking, he sat back in his chair and listened. He literally backed off.

After Bob had entered the discussion, we got to a level playing field, with Taber becoming much more receptive to hearing us out. As it turned out, there was a logical reason why our research results were different from his. In a nutshell, our survey had included end users—people who were actually using his products—whereas his studies had concentrated on the executives at the customer companies who had made the purchasing decision. Those execs had chosen Taber's company, but they weren't the ones who were in the trenches using the products. As it turns out, high-level execs can often have a very different view of a vendor than end users do—a difference that we've termed "choosers versus users."

Our cause was further aided when Gary mentioned that our firm had an in-house expert with a doctorate in statistics who had helped with the design of our research study. Gary added that we had even discussed our methodology with Tim Johnson, who works for Taber and also has a Ph.D. in statistics. "We've talked this over with Tim," Gary said, "and he told us that he had no problem with our methodology."

This threw Taber for a loop. "I need to know what Tim's looked at," he said. Quickly, one of the execs at the meeting got up and left the room, reappearing minutes later with a fax of some info that we had sent to Johnson months before. Taber studied the information closely. All of a sudden, he said, "Well, I see what you're doing here, and there's a lot of value to it. We need to be doing this." Looking directly at Gary, Taber asked, "Can you do a customer-satisfaction study for us?"

Gary replied that we could, and Taber said, "So what do you need from me?" We told him that we had to have two things: information about his competitors and his definition of the term "customer satisfaction." Moments later we knew Taber had turned a corner with us when he said, "No, no, no. I don't want you to define 'customer satisfaction' the way *I* do. I want you to define it the way *you* do."

We could hardly believe our ears. After a half hour of heated confrontation between Gary and Taber, the discussion had become conciliatory. That dramatic turnaround was due, we believe, to the fact that Gary was able to gain Taber's confidence as the result of a transfer of Bob's credibility as well as the stamp of approval from Tim Johnson, Taber's trusted expert.

HOLD YOUR GROUND, BUT
FIND THE MIDDLE GROUND

Another factor in our interchange with Taber was perhaps more important: Gary was able to withstand Taber's aggressive, intensive questioning. This point is worth further explanation. It was as if Taber was playing a game of intimidation—a common tactic of Skeptics. Had Gary capitulated, we might have easily lost the game. But Gary stood his ground without getting defensive, and that made all the difference.

Interestingly, we believe that Taber had made up his mind to work with us *before* the meeting took place. His company's sales had stagnated even though his survey results had indicated that he was doing everything right. So he knew that there was a large disconnect somewhere. Even then, he was hardly going to strike a deal with us without probing us further. The meeting, we believe, was for him to look for reasons for hiring us. Or, perhaps more accurately, because Taber is a Skeptic, he was going to see if he could find any reasons why he *shouldn't* do business with us. He was going to look for chinks in our armor, particularly Gary's.

It is important to remember that you can't change the worldview of Skeptics. Their ingrained nature tells them not to accept anything at face value, so they question everything. But there's no malice or malevolence to their attitude. They're just inherently difficult. It's the way they are, and nobody's going to alter that. So you have to adapt to and work within that framework, even when they aggressively confront and challenge you.

In such trying situations, you have to rely on your own internal mechanisms to stay grounded and centered. Always keep in mind that you know more about your area of expertise than the Skeptic does. If you're an experienced salesperson, for instance, your depth and breadth of knowledge about your company's offerings will outweigh any superficial information that the Skeptic may have. So you need to remain confident and centered in that expertise, even when the Skeptic attacks it. And you need to hold your ground, especially when the Skeptic begins to hurl numerous curveballs your way.

In addition to their suspicious nature, Skeptics tend to be rebellious. They flaunt social conventions and care little about what others think of them. When you put those two qualities together—a suspicious nature and a rebellious streak—it's no wonder that your dealings with Skeptics will often be unpredictable and off-putting. Be forewarned that things will go according to the Skeptics' pace, not yours. For our meeting with Taber, we had prepared an agenda, but as soon as he walked into the room, he assumed control of the proceedings, taking us on a journey that was far different from the one for which we had prepared.

To make matters worse, some Skeptics will skip from one subject to another, and following their train of thought can be like trying to track a kernel of corn as it pops and ricochets in the popper. They might skip from step 3 to 7, for instance, and assume that you'll be able to figure out 4, 5, and 6 for yourself. Understandably, this can easily be overwhelming. You may feel as if you're being tested, which will only heighten the tension you might be experiencing. When that happens, you need to calmly have the Skeptic retrace his steps. You could say, for example, "I'm not sure I've followed your argument. Perhaps I'm not aware of one of your assumptions, so let's go back to the base point you made about . . ." But that tactic could easily fail if you haven't already established the necessary credibility with the Skeptic.

Another unnerving habit of many Skeptics is that they will polarize an argument into black and white, leaving little room for compromise. For instance, they will take your views and exaggerate them to the point of caricature. Then they might ridicule that extreme position, which wasn't your stance at all.

A Skeptic colleague of ours frequently uses that aggravating tactic. Once, we made the point that professional baseball needs reforms because certain teams like the Yankees have huge budgets and are consequently perennial contenders in the playoffs. In contrast, we asserted, there is much more parity among NFL teams, partly because of salary caps and greater revenue sharing among the franchises. Our colleague quickly took our argument to the extreme. "Well, then," he said, "if the system is so broken, why don't we just scrap Major League Baseball altogether? And while we're at it, why don't we just make football our national pastime?" Of course, this was hardly our point.

We were merely making the case for how Major League Baseball could be improved, but our colleague had turned us into fanatics who wanted the destruction of a cherished sport.

That discussion was infuriating, to say the least, and it can be extremely difficult to maintain your composure in such situations. After all, the Skeptic has grossly misrepresented your position, and the temptation is to lash back by doing the same to him. But doing so would only leave the both of you futilely attacking straw-man arguments. The more productive alternative is to nip the problem in the bud by quickly refocusing the discussion. You might state something along the lines of "You know that's not what I was saying. I was merely making the point that . . ." In other words, you could calmly but firmly let the Skeptic know that you won't be baited.

Another effective tactic is to find the middle ground. Remember how our meeting with Darren Taber started? He essentially threw down a gauntlet and said that either he was wrong or we were. In one fell swoop, he totally polarized the discussion. For the rest of the meeting, we were careful not to denigrate his research. With Skeptics, the last thing you want to do is to impugn their reputations or egos. So we carefully explained how our and his research could both be accurate, even though the results were seemingly contradictory, because we were measuring different things. And we did not make any judgments about whose methodology was superior—we left that for Taber to decide. Finally, he was able to accept our research because he saw that it could coexist with his own data.

KEEP YOUR EMOTIONS—AND YOUR EGO—IN CHECK

Perhaps the most difficult part of our meeting with Taber was that he attacked both our integrity and the veracity of our data. But this is what Skeptics often do: They go into intimidation mode, and their social graces go out the window. They can be like attack dogs, going straight for the jugular. They will barrage you with questions and sometimes even blatantly impugn your character. Taber went so far as to imply that we had pumped up our research results just to gain publicity for our work.

It would be natural to take offense at such insinuations, and it is extremely difficult not to take them personally. But the key is to avoid that. When dealing with Skeptics, you need to depersonalize any accusations or criticisms. You should realize that such attacks have nothing to do with you or your qualifications. Skeptics are suspicious of everybody and everything. As tough as it might be, you need to remain calm as you argue your case logically, drawing on all sources of credibility that you can. Do not become defensive as you respond to the Skeptic's questions and comments, however loaded they may be. Even when the Skeptic is in full attack mode, you absolutely *must* remain unflappable.

The last thing you want to do with Skeptics is to fight fire with fire. Being confrontational with them will only increase their aggression as they fight to maintain their reputations and egos. If you try to go head-to-head with Skeptics, you risk offending them, especially if you haven't already established a solid foundation of credibility with them. On the other hand, Skeptics don't respect people who wither. If you back down, you instantly lose credibility in their eyes. In other words, you need to find the right balance. Do not match the Skeptic's aggressiveness, but be firm and confident in responding to the hardball questioning. The way you gain credibility is by having your facts right and by standing your ground.

Needless to say, it's all too easy to lose your cool when a Skeptic is trying to intimidate you. This is why we recommend that whenever possible you pair up in dealing with them. That way you can mitigate the pressure. When Taber would attack Gary, Bob would join the discussion to deflect Taber's attention and allow Gary to collect his thoughts. It was like a tag-team wrestling match. To be successful, though, both partners must have the same agenda and they must completely trust each other, so that when one person steps in, the other needn't worry that the discussion will veer off course. In our experience, we have found that two is the ideal number of partners. With three or more, it becomes increasingly difficult to ensure that everyone is on the same page. When someone's not, a meeting can quickly spiral out of control, which is the last thing you want in dealing with a Skeptic.

Of course, pairing up is not possible in many situations, such as when you're interviewing for a job. In those cases, you need to be doubly sure that you keep your emotions and your ego in check. If you don't, you could find yourself engaged in an undignified contest that you will likely lose even if you win. Consider the painful experience of Elliot Lee, a marketing professional in Boston.

Several years ago, Lee got a call from Enid Zukeran, a former colleague of his who told him about a job opening at her company, Apollo Sports, a Northeast manufacturer of sporting apparel. Apollo had been struggling recently with a dangerous slide in demographics: The average age of its customers had been slowly creeping higher as the company seemed unable to attract younger consumers. In a past job, Lee worked with Zukeran on a marketing campaign that successfully launched XtremeChill, a new sports drink targeted at teenagers and young adults. "You'd be perfect for this job," she told him. "Nobody here understands Gen X consumers like you do." She added that she had already talked to her boss, Dave Autier, about Lee. "He was very impressed with what you did with XtremeChill," she said. "He's really looking forward to meeting you."

At first, Lee was reluctant. He had just started a new job and was already working on several interesting projects there. But Zukeran told him that salaries at Apollo were substantially higher and that the position would give Lee great visibility in the industry. "You'd be a fool not to meet with Dave," she said. "At the very least, you'll get a better sense of what you're worth on the job market."

On the day of the interview, Lee was stuck in a rush-hour traffic jam. He had allowed himself a full hour to get to Autier's office—a trip that ordinarily would have taken just thirty minutes—but he was running late. Finally, he whipped into the parking lot with just a few minutes to spare and raced into the office building for his 5:00 P.M. meeting. Autier's assistant greeted him and escorted him to a conference room. Sitting there, Lee tried to compose himself. "Relax," he thought, "the ball is in Autier's court. He'll probably do most of the talking." At around 5:15, Autier strode into the conference room, introduced himself, and sat down. He then stared at Lee for several awkward seconds and finally said, "Tell me something: Why in the world should I hire somebody like you?"

Lee was beside himself. There he was, thinking that Autier would be wooing him, and all of a sudden he found himself on the defensive. Trying to collect himself, he somehow managed to mutter, "Hasn't Enid talked to you about me? We worked together for several years; she's well aware of what I can do."

Autier shot back, "I really don't care what *Enid* thinks. I want to know why *I* should hire somebody like you."

Still reeling, Lee countered, "Well, maybe a better question is why I would even want to work here in the first place."

From that point, Lee can't remember exactly what ensued. The meeting had quickly deteriorated, with both men's egos totally out of control. Everything was happening at a frightening pace, and soon Lee was attacking back, criticizing Autier for a past marketing campaign at Apollo that had flopped. Autier, on his part, said that there was a long list of far superior people for the job, including many in-house candidates. "Well, if that's the case," Lee challenged, "why did you call me in for this interview in the first place?"

Today Lee looks back at the incident and is able to laugh. "Thankfully, I didn't need the job. In fact, I didn't even particularly want it," he recalls. "And I'm sure glad I didn't get it. Working for Autier would have been a nightmare. I probably wouldn't have lasted a day, if that." But what if Lee had needed that job? What if he had been desperate for work?

Lee is a mild-mannered, agreeable person, and it's difficult to imagine him in a heated argument. He himself is at a loss to explain exactly what happened. All that he can say is this: "Somehow Autier really pushed my buttons. I mean, I really wanted to slug the guy."

Indeed, when dealing with Skeptics, it's all too easy to get swept up in the moment, particularly when you're under attack. One useful tip is to completely detach yourself from the proceedings, almost as if you're participating in a science experiment and are observing yourself from a distance. That, however, is much easier said than done. Nevertheless, when all else fails, remember this: Fighting fire with fire when dealing with a Skeptic is a losing proposition. Even if you win the battle of egos, you'll lose the war because nothing infuriates Skeptics more than when someone doesn't play their game and calls them on it, such as when Lee told Autier, in so many words, "Who do you think you're kidding? We both know that you need me more than

I need this job." Telling Skeptics that you're onto them will only win you a Pyrrhic victory, at best.

Sometimes, though, you might need to correct bad information that the Skeptic is relying on. This is a risky endeavor requiring the utmost caution. If, for instance, your Skeptic boss states incorrectly that your company's R&D costs have been spiraling out of control recently, don't respond with accusations ("You're wrong") and don't be judgmental ("You always jump to the wrong conclusion") because that will only set the Skeptic off. Instead, just present the data in a neutral, almost clinical way ("Actually, our R&D costs are just 4.8 percent of sales, which is below the industry average") and let the Skeptic come to his own conclusion. This will bolster your credibility with him while also allowing him to maintain his with you. For the Skeptic to trust you, he needs to preserve and uphold his reputation and ego, so it is crucial that you do nothing to injure his sense of self. And remember that Skeptics tend to avoid responsibility and are quick to blame others for mistakes. So be sure to place previous problems on someone else. Or, better yet, blame an uncontrollable outside factor, such as a downturn in the economy.

There is one interesting footnote to Lee's disastrous encounter with Autier. The day after the job interview, Lee called Zukeran, his former colleague, to tell her what had happened. Zukeran was perplexed. She insisted that Autier had told her that Lee was a shoo-in for the position. A few years later, when Autier was working for a different firm, one of his managers tried to hire Lee. This time, though, the meeting went much more smoothly, mainly because Lee was prepared for anything to happen. And, anyway, Autier was a completely different person, friendly and sociable, almost as if the earlier encounter had somehow earned Lee a badge of credibility. Autier offered him the job, but after some consideration Lee turned it down.

GO TO THE SOURCE OF CREDIBILITY

As mentioned earlier, you need to establish your credibility quickly with Skeptics. In some situations, this might seem like a simple task—

for example, if you have a solid reputation that is widely known throughout the industry. Even so, you should never estimate how difficult it can be to earn a Skeptic's trust. Never assume that the Skeptic will accept anything at face value. So it is crucial that whenever presenting information to back you up, you rely on the primary source of that data. With Skeptics, hearsay and other secondary or passed-along information will do little to reinforce your case. On the other hand, solid testimonial from a direct, credible source can often carry the day. Consider the experience of Rick Harris, one of our clients who is an executive at a large services-management company in the Northeast.

Harris's firm was recently bidding for some work with St. Elizabeth's Hospital, an extensive health care complex in Washington, D.C. The contract was for an array of services, including housekeeping, laundry and linen management, food and nutrition, and patient transportation (moving someone, for example, from the emergency room to surgery). St. Elizabeth's had performed most of those services in-house, but management thought that the hospital could save money by instead outsourcing those tasks. Along with Harris's company, two other firms were competing for the work.

Early on, Harris realized that winning the contract wasn't going to be easy. Like many health care organizations, St. Elizabeth's had suffered from substantial budget cutbacks, and a round of layoffs had eroded employee morale. The hospital management thought that outsourcing certain functions could lead to better services at lower costs, and a committee was formed to investigate that possibility. The committee was a cross section of St. Elizabeth's middle management, including the various department heads, such as the director of emergency medicine, the director of radiology services, the patient-care manager, and so on. Of the ten members on the committee, three were Skeptics who were far from optimistic that an outside vendor could improve things. "Their attitude was, 'Why should we think that things will be different?'" recalls Harris.

To prepare for a formal presentation to the committee, Harris and others from his company, including several technical experts, conducted an extensive on-site study at St. Elizabeth's. They interviewed department heads, including a number of the committee members, to better understand the issues involved. During some of those interviews, Harris noted that one of his people—Todd Goodman, an expert in patient transportation—seemed to impress St. Elizabeth's management with his technical knowledge and experience in the field.

After Harris and his group had finished that groundwork, Harris began to strategize how best to organize his presentation to the committee. The upcoming meeting was crucial because it would determine the committee's recommendations to the CEO and board of directors at St. Elizabeth's. "As we put our presentation together," remembers Harris, "we tried to figure out what would be the best way to get the Skeptics into our corner."

The meeting was scheduled to last for two hours, and Harris had planned a tight agenda, with himself as moderator and various people giving short presentations. At first, Harris was uncertain whether to include Goodman. "In any presentation," notes Harris, "you have just a limited number of people that you can take with you, and Todd's a typical technical guy who isn't particularly comfortable in those types of situations." In addition, Harris had planned to spend just a nominal amount of time discussing patient transportation because that particular service would be only a small portion of the overall contract. "But," says Harris, "I made the judgment to include Todd because he had established such credibility with a number of the committee members during the on-site interviews."

Harris's instincts were right. During the meeting, many of the committee's concerns focused on patient transportation, and Goodman was able to describe step by step how the new system would work, from the instant a nurse requested that a patient be moved to the time when the transport had been accomplished. One advantage of the new system, explained Goodman, would be the use of walkie-talkies instead of beepers. When a patient needs to be transferred from his room to the radiology department for a CAT scan, for example, the nursing station on that floor would call a central dispatcher, who would quickly locate the nearest available staff member for the transport. This system was much more efficient because the use of beepers ate up considerable time as people waited for others to respond to their pages.

The committee members asked a host of questions, and Goodman

was able to answer each of them thoroughly. He had a battery of information at his fingertips, including data for facilities of similar size. He
talked about the elevators for the hospital, the layout of the corridors
and patient areas, the average amount of time per patient that the
system would save, and so on. He was also able to give details of how
the new system would save money: More efficient patient transportation decreases the unnecessary idle time of expensive equipment like
MRI scanners. "I think Todd swayed many people on that committee," says Harris. "I'm glad I made the decision to include him in
the presentation. He was the ideal person to address those questions."

Interestingly, the committee spent an inordinate amount of time
on patient transportation even though the scope and size of the other
services, such as housekeeping and food and nutrition, were substantially larger. "We talked a lot about patient transportation," recalls
Harris, "but I couldn't have been happier because we had Todd, our
technical expert, there."

Goodman was particularly influential with the three Skeptics on
the committee, mainly because patient transportation had a direct
impact on their operations. And Goodman's credibility seemed to
spill over into the rest of the presentation, enabling Harris to make a
strong case for St. Elizabeth's business. "The entire tone of the
meeting changed once Todd handled all those questions," says Harris.
The upshot was that the committee did recommend Harris's company
over the other two competitors. "Of course," says Harris, "that wasn't
all due to Todd, but I'm sure that he was a major factor."

KNOWING WHAT TO DO—AND
WHEN TO DO IT

Persuading Skeptics can initially seem like a thankless task, mainly
because of their strong personalities and aggressive styles. Skeptics
make up their minds quickly, and they have definite opinions on
everything. But that doesn't mean they are completely inflexible.
When Skeptics question something, they are trying to determine why

and how they might change their minds. They can be influenced, but only when you patiently respond to all their queries and then let them make their own conclusions.

The exhibit "The Skeptic Plan" highlights what you should do before, during, and after your meetings with them. Note the amount of groundwork you'll need to do before your formal presentation in order to establish as much credibility as you can. If you're a salesperson, for example, you might arrange for the Skeptic to visit your production facility to gain his confidence in your company's ability to manufacture certain products.

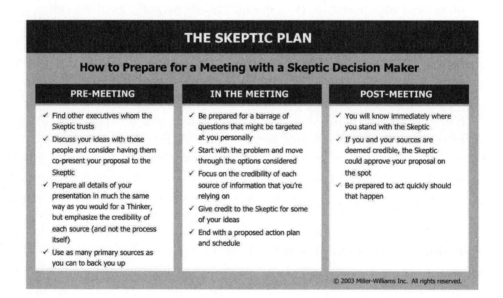

THE SKEPTIC PLAN

How to Prepare for a Meeting with a Skeptic Decision Maker

PRE-MEETING	IN THE MEETING	POST-MEETING
✓ Find other executives whom the Skeptic trusts ✓ Discuss your ideas with those people and consider having them co-present your proposal to the Skeptic ✓ Prepare all details of your presentation in much the same way as you would for a Thinker, but emphasize the credibility of each source (and not the process itself) ✓ Use as many primary sources as you can to back you up	✓ Be prepared for a barrage of questions that might be targeted at you personally ✓ Start with the problem and move through the options considered ✓ Focus on the credibility of each source of information that you're relying on ✓ Give credit to the Skeptic for some of your ideas ✓ End with a proposed action plan and schedule	✓ You will know immediately where you stand with the Skeptic ✓ If you and your sources are deemed credible, the Skeptic could approve your proposal on the spot ✓ Be prepared to act quickly should that happen

Note that an effective tactic is to credit your idea to the Skeptic. (After all, what source could be more credible than the Skeptic himself?) If, for example, you are advocating that your Skeptic colleague switch vendors to a product that has less functionality but is cheaper, you might say, "In our staff meeting last month, you mentioned that our operating costs were too high, so that got me to thinking about possible solutions." Be careful, though, that your explanation isn't contrived, and avoid helping Skeptics unless they specifically ask for it, because they prefer that you think that they know things already.

In any formal meeting, Skeptics are swayed by presentations that emphasize strength, toughness, endurance, dominance, and longevity. They respond to clear leaders in an industry and are particularly influenced by reference testimonials from people who are widely recognized and respected. Key words that will resonate with Skeptics include: *feel, grasp, grab, handle, power, commanding, action, win, suspect, trust, agreeable, demand, disrupt.*

To summarize, Skeptics can be swayed but only when you

- Remember that the name of the game is credibility. With it, you'll be able to argue your case and have them truly hear what you're saying. Without it, you might as well be talking to the wind.
- Stand firm against the Skeptic's battery of questions. If you capitulate or become visibly shaken, you'll quickly lose your credibility. But never challenge a Skeptic, even when he's wrong. Instead, find ways to reframe the disagreement so that you'll both be right.
- Avoid any knee-jerk reactions. You need to depersonalize the Skeptic's loaded questions and comments. Muster your patience and remain dispassionate and rational. The aggressive tactics of Skeptics are just par for the course. Responding with anger will weaken your case irreparably.
- Use primary sources of data to support you. Because Skeptics are innately suspicious, they are particularly distrustful of secondary information that they cannot verify for themselves.

Chapter 9

The Follower Decision Maker

Followers make decisions based on how other trusted executives have made them or on how they've made similar decisions in the past. They have a high sense of duty and can thrive in large corporations and governmental organizations. In general, Followers are

1. **Devoted to the tried and the true.** They stick with what's worked before, and they don't try to fix something that's not broken.
2. **Averse to the new.** They avoid any unexplored paths. They are not innovators, nor are they early adopters.
3. **Conscientious corporate citizens.** They are responsible decision makers who can be counted on to protect and maintain a business.
4. **Deft people handlers.** The have great diplomatic skills and are excellent listeners. They usually manage by consensus, making few political enemies.
5. **Empathetic.** They are adept at seeing the world through other people's perspectives. Their emotional intelligence tends to be high.

6. Difficult to identify. They wear many guises and can easily be confused for Charismatics, Skeptics, and Thinkers.

DEVOTED TO THE TRIED AND THE TRUE

Decades ago, mainframe computers ruled, and IBM was the king of that industry. At that time, a widespread saying in corporate America was that nobody got fired buying IBM. That aphorism exemplifies the mind-set of Followers. In short, Followers don't necessarily want the *best* solution; they want the *safest* solution. And to them, the safest solution is one that has repeatedly worked before in similar situations.

When a company is humming along, Followers are excellent at maintaining the status quo. They are adept at keeping things in steady state, and they don't often make the mistake of trying to fix something that isn't broken. Just ask Jim Parker, who succeeded Herb Kelleher as CEO of Southwest Airlines. Parker says that he knew from the outset that his job was straightforward. "My biggest challenge," he recalls, "was to maintain the direction and focus of the company."[1]

And Parker, along with President Colleen Barrett, has done just that. For instance, they have upheld Kelleher's fiscal conservatism by resisting the temptation to expand quickly to take advantage of the current woes of their competitors. Southwest has stayed true to its basic operating principles—for example, it relies on direct flights instead of using the hub-and-spoke approach—and in doing so, the company continues to be one of the most admired and profitable airlines in the world. When Parker was once asked to talk about his goals, he told the story of a Southwest flight he took right after becoming CEO of the company. He happened to be sitting next to a lawyer on that flight, and the man, after realizing who Parker was, said, "You've got a damn good airline here. Just don't [screw] it up."[2]

Even when faced with a business that needs to be fixed, Followers will rely heavily on solutions that have worked before. Consider Carly Fiorina, the CEO of Hewlett-Packard. Fiorina is a polished speaker.

She's smooth, composed, and always seems to say the right words at the right time. Nicknamed Rock Star,[3] she is photogenic and cuts a striking figure, immaculate in her Armani suits and stylishly coiffed hair. At first glance, people might easily peg Fiorina as a Charismatic. But make no mistake: When it comes to important decisions, she is much more a Follower than anything else.

When she took the helm of HP, Fiorina promised to shake things up at the sluggish Silicon Valley icon, but she was faced with the daunting task of spurring growth at a company that had mature product lines like ink-jet printers and PCs. Her solution was to rely on one of the oldest tricks in the book: Acquire another firm. First she tried to strike a $17-billion deal for the consulting business of PricewaterhouseCoopers. But that failed, and HP's stock continued to tumble. Droves of employees were laid off while morale plummeted. Fiorina's response? Launch a campaign to acquire another company, this time Compaq Computer for $19 billion. She eventually succeeded but only after a messy, expensive, and bitter proxy battle against investors led by Walter Hewlett, the son of one of HP's founders.

Wasn't Fiorina a fearless maverick for pursuing such a huge deal, particularly because high-tech mergers have such a poor track record? Yes, she took a huge risk. But, actually, Followers are not necessarily averse to risk. What Followers avoid is being the first to tread down an unexplored path. It is important to note that before her decision to acquire Compaq, Fiorina relied on McKinsey & Co., a leading consulting firm. McKinsey analyzed numerous past deals and told Fiorina that mergers tended to fail when a company had little experience in the business of the firm it was trying to acquire—which would not be the case for HP and Compaq. Fiorina must have been comforted to learn from McKinsey that in terms of an analogous situation, the HP-Compaq deal could be more like the successful megamerger of Exxon and Mobil in the petroleum industry.[4]

Of course, most executives want to be seen as innovators. So Followers might play this game: After they've moved to a new company, they will make the same decisions that they did at their previous firm and sell those changes as bold and revolutionary. When Fiorina first arrived at HP, she was troubled by the company's decentralized structure: More than eighty business groups, each focused on a separate product line like scanners, were being run as independent fiefdoms. So she reorganized the company basically into halves. The "front end" consisted of a centralized sales and marketing group that was itself essentially split in two parts, one of them targeting corporate customers and the other focusing on consumers. The "back end" was likewise split in two—printing and imaging on one hand, and computers on the other. That sweeping reorganization might have seemed like the move of a daring rebel. Fiorina, after all, was the first outsider to head HP in the company's long, fabled history. But, in actuality, what Fiorina had done was to make HP more like her old firm, Lucent Technologies, where she headed the global service-provider business after rising through the ranks at AT&T. (She helped execute AT&T's successful spin-off of Lucent in 1996.)

Transferring business practices, though, can be tricky. Consider the tale of two other executives: Steve Bennett and Bob Nardelli. Both men earned their stripes at General Electric during the golden Jack Welch era. And both have moved on to other companies, where they've tried to apply the lessons they learned at GE.

Bennett, a twenty-three-year GE veteran and former executive with GE Capital, became CEO of Intuit, the Mountain View, California, company that sells financial accounting software such as the popular Quicken and TurboTax programs. After taking the helm of Intuit in 2000, Bennett has been making all the right moves, many of them straight from GE's playbook. Intuit has cut costs and jettisoned many "noncore" businesses, such as its insurance operations. From its base in personal finance software, it has been targeting small-business customers as it moves upmarket. To do so, it has aggressively acquired several companies in an effort to provide integrated software and services offerings to customers in specific industries. Bennett and his management team describe their focused, disciplined approach to business as "strategic and operational rigor"—words that could have been spoken by Jack Welch himself. So far, so good. In 2002, Intuit's earnings surged, and the company's stock continued its ascent—all this during a terrible slump in the high-tech industry and a bear market on Wall Street.

Nardelli, who became CEO of the Home Depot in late 2000, has not fared as well. Described as a "GE man through and through,"[5] Nardelli was a rising star at GE's power systems unit but left after Jack

Welch had passed him over to tap Jeff Immelt as the next head of GE. At the Home Depot, the multibillion-dollar retailer, Nardelli has yet to shine. His critics contend that he has stumbled in trying to replicate GE's manufacturing efficiencies there. His efforts to cut down on inventory, for instance, have sometimes left stores short of stock on key products. But Nardelli has insisted that GE and the Home Depot are more alike than different: ". . . there are certain fundamentals in running a business that are pretty portable."[6] At the end of 2002, though, the Home Depot's stock had tumbled to near $20 a share, from around $40 when Nardelli first took over. All this prompted *BusinessWeek* to run an unflattering commentary with the blunt title "What Worked at GE Isn't Working at Home Depot."[7]

Of course, Bennett could run into trouble, too, especially as Intuit increasingly goes head-to-head against software giants Microsoft and Oracle. And Nardelli could yet turn the Home Depot around. But the point is this: Both executives have thus far stuck with the tried and true, implementing at their new companies what was successful at GE. Nardelli is counting on some very GE-like tactics for spurring growth at the Home Depot. He is hoping, for instance, to cultivate his in-house talent by establishing a leadership institute that is inspired by GE's fabled Crotonville facility. One of the courses that the center will teach is Six Sigma, the quality-control methodology that was one of Jack Welch's favorite hobbyhorses. Nardelli is unabashed about his efforts to replicate various GE processes at the Home Depot. "What I'm known for," he says, "is transferring best practices."[8]

AVERSE TO THE NEW

Because Followers are fearful of anything new, they will seldom be early adopters. Instead, they will make decisions based on what they know has worked before, relying heavily on their rearview mirror for guidance. The last thing they want is to be explorers, because they know that pioneers are the first to get shot with arrows. So in a business downturn, Followers will do the obvious. They will cut expenses, lay people off, divest operations, and so forth (whereas Charismatics might do just the opposite by boldly investing for an eventual upturn in the market).

Not surprisingly, Followers tend to be brand-driven. They will "buy IBM" even when a better—but untried—solution exists. What happens, though, when Followers don't have a path to follow? That question might not be hypothetical for Southwest Airlines, now that upstarts like JetBlue have entered the market, in part by mimicking Southwest's philosophy of low-cost air transportation. Jim Parker rightly realizes the dangers that confront any executive of an established leader like Southwest. "There are two traps you can fall into," he says. "One is to have an ego-driven desire to leave your mark—and to try to change things. The other is to be too passive—and fail to recognize the need for change."[9]

Another trap for Followers is to be confronted with a truly new and unique problem. In such situations, they might go into delay mode. For instance, they could become victims of "analysis paralysis," continually studying the problem but never arriving at a conclusion. Or they might say yes to a suggestion but then do nothing. And they could continue to stand on the sidelines, waiting for someone to show them a game plan that's worked before.

Walter Kiechel, the former editorial director of Harvard Business School Publishing, which puts out the *Harvard Business Review*, was faced with such a daunting situation in 2002. Suzy Wetlaufer, then the editor of the *Review*, had begun an affair with Jack Welch, the former CEO of General Electric, after interviewing him for an article. The situation raised a number of ethical and journalistic issues, putting the integrity of the *Review* under fire.

Kiechel, who was Wetlaufer's boss, was slow to act. Senior editors who were calling for Wetlaufer to resign felt that his continued inaction allowed the problem to erupt into a full-blown crisis. Instead of taking a firm stand, he had at one point sent an e-mail to the staff and signed it "Gutless Senior Management." The attempt at humor failed to ease tensions, particularly as the situation spiraled out of control. Soon it was a national scandal. The *New York Post* ran an unseemly cartoon depicting Wetlaufer sitting on a desk, her legs splayed, with a long line of men waiting to be interviewed by her. Howard Stern was taking regular potshots on his morning radio show. *Time, Newsweek, USA Today,* the *New York Times,* and a host of other publications also weighed in. Wetlaufer eventually did resign, but only after the staff had mutinied and the *Review* had suffered a severe blow to its reputation and credibility.

There is another lesson: When confronted with something that is truly new—an innovative concept or a unique problem—Followers will often say, "This is just like . . ." or "This reminds me of . . ." In other words, to understand anything foreign, Followers need to relate it to something familiar. And they will draw such connections even when they are, at best, tenuous.

During the crisis at the *Review*, Kiechel tried to downplay Wetlaufer's affair with Jack Welch by using an analogy to Norman Pearlstine, the highly respected editor in chief of Time Inc. In a meeting with his top editors, Kiechel tried to allay their concerns by telling them, "When Norm Pearlstine was trying to know Ross Perot, he babysat Perot's kids. And if you know Pearlstine, he doesn't even like children." Several editors were stunned that Kiechel would attempt such a lame comparison. "There's a difference," one senior staffer shot back, "between getting close to your sources and *f*cking* them."[10]

CONSCIENTIOUS CORPORATE CITIZENS

Such shortcomings aside, Followers can make excellent leaders and middle managers, especially at large corporations and government agencies. In fact, Followers account for more than a third of all executives, representing the largest group of the five decision-making styles. So here's the paradox: How can Followers be good leaders?

The truth is that not every organization needs bold entrepreneurs at the helm. At bureaucratic organizations like insurance companies, for instance, decisions are influenced heavily by rules and regulations—just the kind of environment in which Followers thrive. But this is not to say that Followers are uninspired automatons. Yes, they can lack the colorful managerial style of Charismatics and Skeptics, but they can also be spontaneous, making a decision on the spot when they know the solution has been proven. A Follower like Carly Fiorina might base her decisions on what others have done, but she is still a dynamic leader, able to persuade and energize others with her vision of the future.

Without a doubt, Followers can be highly effective leaders because they do not act precipitously. In their companies, they are known as responsible, reliable, stand-up people. Whereas Skeptics are the rebels of the business world, Followers are the good corporate citizens. At GE, Bob Nardelli hit all his financial targets and never made a major misstep. When he was the head of the power systems unit, profits surged by nearly sevenfold in just five years. "Jack [Welch] and I used to marvel at his ability to execute," recalls Bill Conaty, head of human resources at GE.[11]

For many Followers, the operative word is "protect": When push comes to shove, they are more interested in preserving than creating. Consider Edgar Bronfman Jr., the third-generation CEO of Seagram. His grandfather Sam Bronfman founded the firm in the Prohibition era by selling whiskey to bootleggers, and his father, Edgar Bronfman Sr., ran the company for more than two decades, diversifying and building it into a multibillion-dollar corporation.

In 2000, Edgar Jr. sold Seagram to Vivendi, the French corporation. One of his reasons for doing so was that he was reportedly haunted by a painful adage about family businesses, which goes something like this: The first generation starts a company, which the second generation grows and generates tremendous wealth. Then the third generation messes up and loses everything. In particular, Edgar Jr. was concerned that Seagram, with its Universal Studios and other entertainment assets, was going to have trouble competing against media behemoths like Disney, which had purchased ABC; Viacom, which had acquired CBS; and AOL, which had just merged with Time Warner. By selling Seagram to Vivendi, Edgar Jr. thought he would be ensuring his family's legacy. "I've talked this over with my dad," he told Jean-Marie Messier, then CEO of Vivendi. "He believes it's the best way to take care of the next generation."[12]

But the deal was disastrous. Messier made one misstep after another, ultimately leading Vivendi Universal to the brink of bankruptcy. Throughout the meltdown, the Bronfmans sustained tremendous financial losses. At one point, the value of their stake in Vivendi Universal had plummeted by more than $3 billion (in company stock and the sales of shares).[13] The debacle stirred discord within the

Bronfman clan and spurred Edgar Jr. and other Vivendi Universal board members to lead a coup that forced Messier out of office. The irony is worthy of Greek tragedy: Because of his great concerns to protect what his ancestors had built, Edgar Jr. struck a deal that steered him perilously close to what he most wanted to avoid.

Followers can be perfectly content working for a company that is number two or three in its industry. In fact, they might prefer it that way, because then they can take their cues from whatever the leader is doing. Indeed, Followers can get into trouble when they become number one, or if they're already in the top spot, they can have great difficulty staying there. A danger is that in their complacency Followers might fail to notice the warning signs of a coming storm. Case in point: General Motors.

The fall of GM has been widely recounted—it was even grist for the movie *Roger & Me*, which poked fun at the company's insular bureaucracy. The "Roger" in that documentary-like film was Roger Smith, who ran GM from 1981 to 1990. Smith was succeeded by Robert Stempel, who was himself succeeded by Jack Smith and John Smale. During the reign of those men, GM's share of the U.S. market plummeted from above 40 percent to below 30 percent.

There were numerous reasons for GM's precipitous decline, but one overarching factor might have been the way in which the company's top executives made decisions. For decades, GM's culture fostered conformity, and Followers tended to climb the corporate ladder quickest. GM's managers, for instance, attended the company's institute (instead of a university business school) to learn the GM way of doing things. All this was fine when the company was king of the hill. After all, Alfred P. Sloan, who transformed GM into the most powerful company in the world, practically wrote the book on modern corporate management.

But then things changed with the introduction of stylish, high-quality cars from Europe and Japan. Suddenly, the executives at GM didn't know how to respond because they had little guidance from their GM playbooks. While imports ate away GM's market share, the company continued to crank out uninspired gas-guzzlers, even after the crippling oil crises of the 1970s. It has taken the new CEO, Rick Wagoner, an innovative decision maker with an M.B.A. from Harvard Business School, to shake things up. He has broken with GM tradition, for instance, by tapping outsiders for crucial positions, giving them tremendous freedom and authority to do their jobs. Whether Wagoner and his executive team will be able to complete GM's massive turnaround remains to be seen, but the early signs are encouraging. The company has recently been able to stabilize its share of the U.S. market, after losing ground since the early 1980s.

One attribute that makes Followers such good corporate citizens is their tremendous sense of responsibility, a quality that they also seek in others. They encourage people to step up to the plate to solve a problem and are perfectly willing to delegate both authority and responsibility. In fact, they will sometimes outsource important decisions to trusted people. That said, Followers will not pass the buck: They will bear the ultimate responsibility for decisions that their subordinates make.

DEFT PEOPLE HANDLERS

A willingness to delegate is but one of many excellent people skills of Followers. In general, Followers are able to connect personally with their staff and colleagues, often inspiring great loyalty from them. They are diplomatic, and they can be shrewd in office politics. When there's a change in regimes, Followers usually survive. They bide their time, always being careful not to step on important toes. And they slowly but surely climb the corporate ladder, usually outlasting other talented execs who self-destruct.

Excellent people skills were among the reasons Carly Fiorina rose so high at AT&T. She was, for example, always there to reward employees who had closed big deals, showering them with flowers, balloons, and other gifts. "She won people over very quickly," remembers Bill Marx, then an executive vice president at AT&T.[14] "There were people who resented her success, but she charmed the resentment right out of them," says another person, recalling Fiorina's tenure there.[15]

Followers tend to be excellent listeners. Peter Coors, chairman of Adolph Coors Co., likes to visit distributors and bars to chat people up, and in the process he learns about his family business from customers and people on the front lines. When he's traveling, he visits local drinking establishments and buys rounds for the house. He once went into a gay bar in Boise and introduced himself, even though his company had long been at odds with gay activists. At the bar, Coors heard from two customers who criticized his firm's policy of using lie-detector tests to screen job applicants. And the bartender told him that Coors draft sometimes caused problems with his taps because the beer was packed at such high pressures. Peter Coors was genuinely interested in learning from such encounters. He would repeat the criticisms to make sure he had heard them right, and then he'd jot down the information on a cocktail napkin to make sure he wouldn't forget anything.[16]

Even when they're in the corner office, Followers are humble enough to know that they don't have all the answers. Bob Nardelli, CEO of the Home Depot, often talks with Ken Langone, a board member, first thing in the morning. Roger Penske, another board member, whom Nardelli recruited from GE's board, has been impressed with Nardelli's eagerness to hear what others have to say. "Between meetings," says Penske, "he calls and asks for advice. Typically, you don't see that."[17] And whenever Nardelli is thinking of firing someone, he usually double-checks his decision with other execs: "I say, 'Look, here's my view. Am I seeing this right?' "[18]

Followers don't ask questions just to be polite or to stroke someone's ego. They truly want good advice, even when it runs counter to their views. When that happens, Followers will fully consider the information, and if it's persuasive, they will change their course of action, even when it's painful to do so. After HP had spent a half billion dollars to acquire Bluestone Software, a company that sells "middleware"—software that enables different types of computers to talk to one another—Carly Fiorina asked someone on her staff to recommend a strategy for that business. The reply: Pull the plug on Bluestone. So just two months after Fiorina had acquired the company, HP announced that it was going to discontinue selling those products.[19]

Followers like Fiorina are often eager to be mentored by others. At Lucent, Fiorina relied on the experience and support of Henry Schacht, former chairman, and Rich McGinn, former CEO. And when she was considering taking the top job at Hewlett-Packard, she told Richard Hackborn, a well-respected HP veteran who is credited with building the company's successful printer business, that he should become chairman of the board. Ever since, Hackborn has been a staunch ally of Fiorina, particularly throughout her contentious crusade to buy Compaq.

Because they learn from the experience of others, Followers do not usually pursue half-baked ideas. They typically manage by consensus, and they make sure to obtain the proper approval before proceeding with major projects. If they're a CEO or president, for example, they get the green light from the board of directors for any important decisions. In other words, Followers will go through the proper channels. Rarely do they attempt to do an end run around people they shouldn't. And Followers like Edgar Bronfman Jr. are not prone to fits of anger or outbursts of emotion, even when things are tense. "He never seems to lose his cool, no matter what the pressure," says Edgar Bronfman Sr. "With his temperament, he could be a scratch golfer . . ."[20]

EMPATHETIC

Another important people skill of Followers is empathy: They are very good at seeing the world through other people's points of view. Followers often excel in marketing positions because they can discern what customers want. As business execs, they frequently anticipate what others will do, and their ability to read people can be uncanny. In other words, they possess more than their fair share of emotional intelligence.

Such attributes, among others, helped Carly Fiorina in her brutal proxy battle against Walter Hewlett. Fiorina was pushing hard for HP to acquire Compaq; Hewlett and others were adamantly opposed to the deal. Fiorina eventually prevailed, thanks in part to her ability to placate the concerns of key shareholders. One of those people, Vinit Bodas, a senior analyst with Brandes Investment Partners, remembers a meeting he had with her in which he wanted to ask the loaded question of whether Fiorina might divest any of HP's businesses. To diplomatically probe the subject, Bodas began by merely asking Fiorina for her general thoughts about HP printers. "Before I tell you that," Fiorina replied, "I want to tell you that we're not going to spin the printer business off."[21]

Later, after shareholders had approved the merger, Fiorina worked hard to sell the deal to employees. And she always seemed to know what to say. Meeting with a group of HP salespeople and customer-support professionals in Orlando, she was quick to tell them, "Most of you are focused on 'Do I have a job? What is my job? And who is my boss?'"[22] She then listened intently as workers told her how bad morale was and how the merger had added considerable paperwork and bureaucracy to their jobs.

As managers, Followers are good developers of talent. In fact, they often view employees as a top priority and not as a mere afterthought. In his autobiography, Edgar Bronfman Sr. talks about one of the changes that his son was implementing at Seagram. "[Edgar] is trying to do things differently," wrote the elder Bronfman. "He has determined that people are essential to the success of our enterprise and has made human resources a much higher priority than I ever did."[23]

DIFFICULT TO IDENTIFY

As discussed earlier, a casual onlooker might easily classify Carly Fiorina as a Charismatic because she certainly projects herself as a bold, innovative executive who loves big ideas. But Fiorina has consistently made huge decisions just the way a Follower would. At the *Harvard Business Review*, many staff members might have mistakenly categorized Walter Kiechel as a Thinker because he seems to process information methodically, and he often plays the part of the cerebral academic. But that is typical of most Followers: They are difficult to identify because they wear many guises. In our research, we have found that of the five decision-making styles Followers are the ones who are most often categorized incorrectly by others. (This point will be discussed in detail in the next chapter.)

Like Skeptics or Controllers, Followers might ask a battery of aggressive questions. They might engage someone in long lists of issues and repeatedly challenge that person's position. Or, like a Charismatic, they might encourage their staff to think outside the proverbial box, prodding people for innovative ideas. Or, like a Thinker, they might take considerable time as they studiously ponder all the pros and cons of a decision. In the end, though, Followers will agree to something only if they've seen it done somewhere else.

But Followers won't admit to that. They would much prefer to be perceived as bold and forward-thinking even when their decisions and actions indicate otherwise. The last thing they want is for others to view them as Followers. So they will often talk a good game about their daring plans for the future. They might say they want to aggressively grow revenues by attacking new markets. Or they might state that they are intensely searching for the next blockbuster idea. But before the rubber can hit the road, they will quickly revert to Follower mode because that's their default style of decision making.

Peter Coors once had grand plans for the company that his great-grandfather founded. He eventually did make some changes—a push into marketing and advertising, for one—but he hasn't accomplished everything that he had planned. Of course, he hasn't been completely free to push through the changes he wanted, because he lived in the shadow of his father and his uncle, who was the chairman of Coors. In contrast, though, consider how August Busch III has transformed Anheuser-Busch. Like Peter Coors, Busch III is the fourth generation of a brewing dynasty. But there the similarities end. Soon after becoming president of Anheuser-Busch, Busch III replaced a number of top execs and then usurped his father's power by convincing the company board to give him the chairmanship. From that point on, he had complete control and quickly set about to revamp Anheuser-Busch.[24] It would be safe to conclude that August Busch III is not a Follower.

WHAT FOLLOWERS SEEK—AND WHAT THEY AVOID

Followers are indeed difficult to identify, but the task can be greatly aided by looking at the various factors involved in the decision-making process. For example, how much time do people need to make important decisions? How comfortable are they with risk? Do they tend to act alone, or do they first need to talk things through with others? By investigating those and other tendencies, we were able to

APPROACH PROFILE for FOLLOWERS

When Making Decisions, Followers.....

	Average	SEEK MORE
Bargains		31
Playfulness		21
Responsibility		15
Impulsiveness		15
Fear & Uncertainty		8
Self-Absorption		8
Education		6
Intelligence & Facts	0	
Rebellion	-2	
Risk	-3	
Persistence	-5	
Competitiveness	-7	

AVOID MORE

Error ±2.9 points   © 2003 Miller-Williams Inc. (millwill.com)

Note: The data have been normalized to range from –100 (maximum aversion) to +100 (maximum desire).

determine that 36 percent of the nearly seventeen hundred business executives we surveyed were Followers. The exhibit "Approach Profile for Followers" contains a summary of the common characteristics of this category of decision maker.

A striking result from our research is that Followers lack any strong aversions. Specifically, of the twelve components we studied (risk, responsibility, impulsiveness, and so on), Followers do not actively avoid any of them in the decision-making process, and perhaps this is why they are Followers. But a common misperception is that Followers always avoid risk. Actually, they are neither risk-averse nor risk seeking. In fact, they are generally neutral when it comes to making big decisions that have some degree of uncertainty. They will avoid a certain type of risk, however: They will not try something that is unproven. Followers will go forward with a risky venture as long as that type of approach has succeeded before, but they have great trouble with something that has no prior instances of success.

Of the five styles of decision makers, Followers are the ones with the strongest desire for bargains. For them, a decrease in price can substantially offset the risks involved with trying something new and untested. In some cases, they might think that the cost of implementing something has become so low that they simply can't afford *not* to try it. Interestingly, Followers have a relatively strong desire for playfulness in the decision-making process. This is especially true when it comes to light-spirited haggling: They enjoy the give-and-take of trying to get someone to give them the best deal. Another somewhat counterintuitive finding is that Followers have a moderate desire to be impulsive. As mentioned earlier, they can be spontaneous—making a decision on the spot—but only after someone has proven to them that a proposal has worked before.

In summary, we have found that Followers

- Stick with what they know, modifying proven solutions to solve new problems.
- Seldom become pioneers because they live by the credo "the nail that sticks up gets hammered down."
- Avoid making rash decisions, instead preferring to proceed cautiously and responsibly.
- Have a personable style that others find both disarming and engaging.
- Are adroit at seeing problems and solutions through the viewpoints of others.

• Tend to lack definitive traits, making them prone to being miscategorized as Charismatics, Skeptics, or Thinkers.

The mind-set of Followers might best be encapsulated by this: They do not play to win. Instead, they play not to lose, and that's a huge difference. So, for example, when an industry is undergoing revolutionary changes, Followers can have great difficulty taking advantage of the opportunities that inevitably arise. On the other hand, when a market is mature and stable, Followers are extremely adept at defending and protecting that business. In such situations, they can be very effective leaders, because their decision making is both dependable and highly responsible.

Chapter 10

Persuading the
Follower Decision Maker

Of the five styles of decision makers, Followers are the most difficult to identify, but they can also be the simplest and most straightforward to persuade. In fact, Followers will often give you a favorable decision right on the spot, but only when you've laid the proper groundwork. Doing so requires four things.

1. **When in doubt, assume.** Followers wear many guises. When you're unsure of how to categorize someone, particularly if you're getting conflicting signals, assume that person is a Follower.
2. **Supply proof, proof, and more proof.** Provide as much evidence as possible that your proposal has been successful in a number of similar situations. All of this proof must be relevant and credible to the Follower.
3. **Keep it simple.** Don't confuse Followers with too much information. Concentrate on their problem and explain how your proposed solution has worked elsewhere in similar conditions.
4. **Link the new to the old.** Whenever you take Followers outside their comfort zone, always make sure they have a path back to what's familiar to them.

WHEN IN DOUBT, ASSUME

The toughest part about persuading Followers is identifying them in the first place. As discussed in the previous chapter, Followers are often miscategorized as Charismatics, Thinkers, or Skeptics. A major part of the problem is that Followers don't want to be known as Followers. This seems to be especially true in the United States, where mavericks and rebels have long been revered. Unfortunately, there seems to be a pejorative connotation to the word "follow," and people would rather be perceived instead as leaders. But, as everyone knows, a company with too many chiefs and too few Indians is likely headed for disaster. And the simple fact is this: Followers can be dynamic, effective business executives. Carly Fiorina is a case in point.

That said, few executives will admit to being Followers. Fiorina herself would probably deny it. But the truth is that a large fraction of executives (more than one out of three) tend to make their decisions that way. They might talk a good game—asserting, for instance, that they are bold and innovative—but in the end they will proceed only with solutions that have worked in the past.

Thus, the best way to categorize people is to look at all the decisions they've made in the past. You need to focus on what they've done and not necessarily on what they've said, because actions do indeed speak louder than words. Frequently, you might mistake Followers for Skeptics because they've aggressively challenged you. But Followers are not inherently suspicious; instead, they prefer that you help them gain a better grasp of what they don't understand. And although Followers may exhibit a take-charge style, they will usually yield when challenged, whereas Skeptics will only dig their heels in deeper. In chapter 13 ("How to Read People"), we discuss in greater detail the various distinctions between the different styles of decision making, but we have raised the issue here because Followers in particular are so difficult to identify.

Consider our experience with Julia Cliffe, a senior vice president of marketing for CaseText, a software company. (Note: To respect the confidentiality of our clients, we have used pseudonyms and have altered identifying details of the examples in this chapter.) Cliffe is a classic Follower: She will only use something that she knows has worked in the past. But, as with many Followers, she hardly fits that stereotype because of her energetic, forceful personality.

Before Cliffe arrived at CaseText, we had been working on a major project for a couple years under Cliffe's predecessor, who had hired us. After that person had left the company, we continued our work under one of his lieutenants, Doris Aratani, a vice president of marketing. Even after Cliffe had come on board, Aratani remained our point of contact, and everything was going smoothly. But then our contract came up for annual renewal, and Aratani told us that we had to speak with Cliffe to get the final approval. Because we hadn't even met Cliffe yet, we asked Aratani for some advice and coaching. Aratani told us that her new boss was a take-charge manager who made quick decisions. We were told she was open and up-front and that she was a risk taker. "She's a big-picture person," Aratani told us. From that and other information, we drew the conclusion that we would be dealing with a Charismatic.

Our first contact with Cliffe was over the phone. For that hour meeting, we had prepared by thinking of all the different ways we could sell ourselves by impressing her with innovative ideas of future research we might conduct for her. At first during the phone call, Cliffe came on very strong. She took charge of the conversation and started talking about herself: Here's who I am. Here's where I come from. And here's what I've done. We learned, for instance, of the work she had done when she was at a major consulting firm before she joined CaseText.

After she had finished introducing herself in that fashion, we started talking about our background. Cliffe seemed particularly impressed with the fact that one of us had coauthored the best-seller *Strategic Selling*®. "I have your book right here on my bookshelf," she said. From that point, she appeared to be especially receptive and collegial. In fact, she confided in us, "Here are all my problems," and essentially did a huge data dump of the various issues she was facing. As we absorbed that information, she said, "So tell me how you can help me."

Throughout the discussion, Cliffe kept on saying that she wanted big ideas and innovative solutions. Indeed, she almost seemed to be challenging us to come up with creative, out-of-the-box approaches, which is exactly what a Charismatic would do. But whenever we proposed something, she would reject it right off. Instead of saying, "That's interesting. Tell me more," she would quickly express her disapproval, saying, "No, no, no. That won't work," without even attempting to explore the possibilities. Her lack of any natural curiosity about what we were proposing was frustrating. And whenever she did ask any questions, they were always along the lines of "Where have you done that before?" and "Is this something any of your other clients are using?"

Another big surprise was that Cliffe seemed completely uninterested in our extensive survey on how executives make decisions—research that is the basis for this book. We were excited about the study because we had just finished analyzing the data and had gotten what we thought were a number of valuable insights. To our knowledge, nobody had done a survey like this, and we were eager to apply our results. We told Cliffe, for example, that the findings from our study could help CaseText become more successful at closing big deals. But she didn't even probe us for more details. Why wasn't she interested in learning about the differences between Charismatics, Thinkers, Skeptics, Followers, and Controllers? we wondered.

Moreover, we told Cliffe that traditional research on customer satisfaction has become insufficient because it isn't forward-looking. It just gives you a rearview-mirror perspective of how your customers *used* to feel. Instead, we told her that we thought a better approach was to track customers' expectations by asking them what their ideal solution or experience would be. But Cliffe rejected that idea before we even finished explaining it. We're not sure she even understood what we were trying to tell her, and this was puzzling because a Charismatic would surely have been interested in hearing more.

We were confused. Even though Cliffe had been asking for ideas, she wasn't receptive to them. Such mixed signals were our first big tip-off that our initial categorization of her was wrong. Even when Charismatics aren't impressed with certain ideas, they will at least try to keep the discussion going to brainstorm for other possibilities. With Cliffe, all we got was negative feedback and discouraging responses. There was none of the give-and-take that Charismatics enjoy.

Another interesting thing was that Cliffe kept on relating our discussion to things she had done in the past. She would repeatedly say

things like, "When I was at my previous company, we did some work that . . ." and "I remember working on a similar project in which . . ." At first, we weren't sure if she was trying to impress us with her experience, but later we realized it was an important clue to something else.

Lastly, during our conversation, Cliffe told us about one of Case-Text's board members who had criticized some of the work we had been doing for the company. He had objections to our research methodology and had questioned Cliffe intensively about them. Cliffe told us about the criticisms, and then she said, "What would you have me say to him?" In essence, she was asking for us to tell her how to defend work that had been done for her department.

After our phone meeting, Aratani told us how surprised she was at Cliffe's lack of interest in our suggestions. But in retrospect, everything seemed to add up when we figured out that Cliffe was a Follower. That was why she wasn't really interested in new ideas and was always asking whether we had implemented our suggestions elsewhere. That was also why she often tried to relate our discussion to her past experience. And that was probably why she wanted our guidance for dealing with that board member.

After we had identified Cliffe correctly, our job became simple. We sent her about ten case studies of similar projects that we had done for a variety of clients. We then told her that we could supply a detailed report of any of those examples if she was willing to sign a nondisclosure agreement for protecting the proprietary information of our clients. But she said, "No, no, that's not necessary. I've seen enough," and she renewed our contract. At that point, we hadn't even met her in person yet. Because she's a Follower, we believe that two factors were sufficient to give us the green light: our association with *Strategic Selling*® and the case studies that we had sent.

Often, to identify Followers, you need to use the process of elimination. Cliffe, for example, wasn't receptive to new ideas, so we ruled out her being a Charismatic. She didn't appear to be process-oriented or data-driven, so we were doubtful that she was a Thinker. She wasn't inherently suspicious toward anything we were telling her (she was just uninterested), so we didn't think she was a Skeptic. And she didn't have the mind-set of "everything has to funnel through me," so we discounted the possibility of her being a Controller. After ruling out those four categories, we were left with the conclusion that she was a Follower, and then her behavior all seemed to make sense.

Our experience with Cliffe brings up the following useful rule of thumb: Assume someone is a Follower unless proven otherwise. In general, the other four types of decision makers tend to show their characteristics more definitively. So when you're having a tough time classifying someone, that's a good indication that you might be dealing with a Follower. And when you're getting mixed signals (as we were with Cliffe), that's another sign that the person is a Follower. Furthermore, remember that Followers are the largest of the five groups of decision makers, accounting for more than a third of all executives. So if you have to make a guess, statistically speaking, the wisest strategy would be to assume that someone is a Follower unless there's evidence to the contrary. Lastly, and perhaps most important, you'll never get burned by trying to persuade someone as if he's a Follower (even if he's not), because supplying proof that your solution has worked in the past will be an effective argument with any type of executive.

From our research, we have two additional rules of thumb. As mentioned earlier, Followers rarely identify themselves as Followers. Most often they describe themselves as Charismatics because the word "follow" has a negative connotation, particularly in the business world. In general, people would much rather perceive themselves as leading (which tends to be associated with strength) rather than following (which tends to be associated with weakness). On a related note, we have found that people who categorize themselves as Followers are usually not. We can vividly remember arguing with an executive who is a classic Thinker. When we asked him why he insisted that he was a Follower, he said that he never made a decision when he didn't have a good handle on all the risks involved. But then we told him that that's a characteristic of Thinkers: They don't make a move until they have quantified all risks by using a methodical process.

SUPPLY PROOF, PROOF, AND MORE PROOF

Although Followers are difficult to identify, persuading them is straightforward. They can be the easiest of all decision makers to influence, but you still need to know which buttons to push—and which to avoid. To obtain buy-in from Followers, you must be careful that you don't take them outside their comfort zone. Anything unfamiliar raises red flags, and the only way Followers can justify making a change is when they are certain that others have succeeded in that path. Not surprisingly, Followers are influenced heavily by references and testimonials, particularly from trusted sources.

When dealing with Followers, sell yourself *only* if you have a strong track record of success and have the evidence to support you. Working for an established leader can be a huge advantage—the "nobody lost his job buying IBM" syndrome that was discussed in the previous chapter. So if you're a salesperson selling BMW cars, you'll have an easy time with Follower customers. To them, an established brand with a good reputation sells itself, and the best thing you can do is make sure you don't get in the way of the purchase.

But if you or your company lacks the necessary track record, you need to look for past decisions by the Follower that support your views. Or you could find similar decisions by other executives whom the Follower trusts. Without such proof, Followers won't proceed, although they won't admit to this. They might even give the appearance of "yes" but then stall when it comes to making the decision. On the other hand, Followers can be impulsive and make a decision on the spot when they have the information they need—that something is a well-known brand with a solid reputation or that it's succeeded in many similar situations before.

Key words to use with a Follower include: *previous, just like before, similar to, what works, old way.* Ideally, Followers want solutions that are proven (yet appear to be innovative), trusted (but seem to be new), and safe (yet are perceived as leading-edge). At the end of the day, what they need to know most is that they won't lose their shirts or their jobs. This is why they rarely make bold, out-of-the-box decisions. Given the choice, they would much rather err on the side of caution and simply pass on taking high-risk/high-payoff gambles. More often than not, they will make their decisions based on the way it's always been, or based on the same way that someone they trust has decided. Consequently, with Followers, you can almost never have too much proof that something has worked before.

That lesson was key to us in our recent dealings with a major client, a multibillion-dollar corporation with various operating divisions. We had done extensive research for one of those divisions, which had then used our data to implement new programs for growing its business in certain areas. The division was able to achieve impressive results, catching the eye of the company's president, who then recommended that Al Lundquist, who heads another of the company's divisions, meet with us. Lundquist's group had recently been struggling, losing several key accounts.

A big clue that Lundquist was a Follower was in how he viewed our upcoming meeting. He had just had a bad year, with several defections among his major accounts, and he desperately wanted to get back on course. This is typical of Followers. When a business is changing quickly, they're not particularly agile at anticipating problems. Their corrections tend to be after the fact, when they're already in trouble. And their corrections tend to be mainly to get things back to where they were. In contrast, other types of decision makers (Charismatics, for instance) might view a problem as an opportunity not only to get back on track but also to make some improvements so that they'll actually come out ahead in the long run.

After we had determined that Lundquist was a Follower, we knew that proof was going to be crucial. So we got permission from the other division head—the executive for whom we had done earlier research—to use his data to show what we had done for his business group. We compiled several other case studies from other clients as well.

Our first meeting with Lundquist was in his president's conference room on the top floor of the headquarters building, but the president wasn't present. This was probably for the best, because we knew that even though we had the president's tacit approval, we were going to have to sell ourselves to Lundquist. Our plan was to show him all the similar projects we had done and to describe the impact of each. Then we would explain exactly what we could do for his division.

We started with a thorough description of our work for the sister division of Lundquist's unit. After we had given all those details, we talked about a project for another client in the same industry. Then we discussed similar projects in other industries. In other words, we began with our strongest suit and then went in descending order of importance and relevance. Our strategy was to start with our best proof to get Lundquist's attention, and then each subsequent example would continue to reinforce our main points. This approach tends to work best not only for Followers but for all executives, who tend to be extremely busy people. When delivering such a presentation, citing numerous examples in descending order, you know you've proven your case when the Follower says, "Okay, I've got it. You don't need to show me more." At that point, the Follower is convinced that your proposal will work. But if at the end of your presentation the Follower says, "Is that it?" then you know you're in trouble. Fortunately, all of the examples we cited were pertinent, credible, and sufficient for Lundquist, and he asked us to come back to do a presentation for his senior executive team. Two weeks later we did that, and we got the contract.

But what happens when you don't have enough proof to sway a Follower? Remember that Followers tend to be bargain hunters, as we noted in the previous chapter. In fact, of the twelve components we studied (risk, responsibility, impulsiveness, and so on), the strongest desire for Followers is for bargains. So if you're a salesperson and have trouble convincing a Follower to buy something based on a product's past history, then consider lowering the price. This will help decrease the risk for him to try something new. In a sense, you will be sharing the risk with him. Also remember that playfulness and impulsiveness are two other desires for Followers. So haggling in a lighthearted way and offering Followers a time-sensitive price can often tilt the balance your way.

With Lundquist, even though we had sold him on our past record, that wasn't quite enough for him to give us the go-ahead because at the time he was having a budget crunch in his division. When we suggested that his president might be willing to subsidize a portion of the project from the company's corporate overhead, Lundquist jumped at the opportunity, and we closed the deal shortly thereafter.

KEEP IT SIMPLE

Followers don't like to admit that they are Followers. They want others to think they're innovative, so sometimes you might want to play to that desire. But be careful not to take Followers too far outside of their comfort zone. Being innovative with a Follower can easily backfire. One of the biggest mistakes that people make in trying to sell a Follower is they complicate the task unnecessarily. Yes, Followers need to have abundant proof that something is proven, but they don't really need much else. This is why, of the five types of decision makers, Followers are the easiest to persuade. Often, though, the process can seem too easy, and it's tempting to do more than you should. In our research, we found that although 36 percent of all executives are Followers, only 6 percent of sales presentations are targeted that way. Of all executives, Followers are the ones whom people waste the most time trying to persuade, when little effort is actually necessary.

We ourselves almost made the mistake a couple years ago when we were contacted by two potential clients: the director and VP of marketing for a large division of a corporation that sells software and consulting services. The executives were in charge of marketing sophisticated products that enable companies to simulate various "what if" scenarios. Using such programs, a retail chain could determine, for example, how much the sales volume would increase if it decreased prices by 4 percent. Alternatively, it could estimate how much the volume would fall if it increased prices by the same amount. By running a slew of such simulations, the retail chain could figure out the optimum pricing structure for maximizing profits.

The capability to run such "what if" scenarios would be valuable to any business, but the two executives from that corporation were interested in obtaining a way to quantify that value. They were looking for a methodology to help them determine, for example, that a customer had increased its operating profits by $2.2 million through the use of their software. They contacted us because they had heard about similar work that we had done for another client.

In our first conversation over the phone with them, it was clear from the beginning that they were sold on us. So we began to talk about how we could do research that was even better and more insightful than we had done for our previous client. We were taking them down all these different paths, giving them interesting ideas for them to consider. Their responses to all those suggestions were uniformly enthusiastic, so we were looking forward to commencing the work.

Then a month or two went by and nothing happened. The project had stalled.

We then realized that we had made the mistake of trying to sell too much too quickly. The only thing that those two executives wanted to know was that we could do a project for them that was similar to the research we had done for our past client. That's all they wanted to know. They didn't need anything else from us, and, actually, they didn't *want* anything else. Unwittingly, we had complicated matters by discussing additional work that in retrospect must have made them somewhat wary because it was too innovative and unproven.

To correct our mistake, we had one of our research associates contact the two executives to deliver a straightforward presentation that would simply state exactly what we had done for our previous client and how that work could be adapted, with slight modifications, for their project. With that, we got the contract for the research. They sent us a check for $30,000 to commence the work—and we hadn't even met them in person yet!

The lesson was clear: Those two executives were Followers, and, as such, all they needed to see was how our research methodology had been proven in a similar project. In essence, we won their business based solely on the work we had done for our previous client. It was as cut-and-dried as that, and we didn't need to complicate matters. Followers need only a certain amount of information—mainly proof that something works—and that's that.

Later, as we worked on that project and were getting results for them, we were able to bring up some of the other ideas that we had floated in that first phone meeting. But now, because we had already proven ourselves on this new project, the two executives were much more receptive. In fact, the project has doubled in size, and we anticipate its growing further. As the scope expands, though, we have been careful to grow it incrementally and to always make sure that any novel concepts are tied back to the original project. For example, when we increased the number of their customers that we surveyed, we told them, "We'll be using exactly the same methodology. But because we'll have a larger sampling size, statistically we'll be able to tell you a lot of other things about your customers that we couldn't before. We'll have additional insights like . . ."

Furthermore, whenever we've proposed to do additional work, we've always commenced that conversation with the results from our latest research for them. We'd say, "Here are the most recent insights and here's what they mean." We start by supplying additional proof that our methodology is working and then suggest new ideas for future directions that the project could take.

LINK THE NEW TO THE OLD

Our experience with those two executives brings home the importance of linking the new to the familiar. Followers need to work with solutions that are proven. Whenever you try to sell anything that is novel to them, you need to show how it is similar to something that's worked in the past. And you should reassure them by emphasizing those similarities. When talking to them, you might say something along the lines of "This is the way that you've always done it. The only difference is . . ." If you fail to make that type of connection, Followers are likely to reject your proposal, however terrific it might be.

What if you're trying to sell a Follower on something that is truly new and unique? In such cases, you still must find a way to relate the novel system to something that is familiar. Remember that Followers always try to understand things by relating to their past experiences: "This is just like . . ." or "This reminds me of . . ." You should encourage them to make such connections. The last thing you want is to throw something new at them without providing the proper frame of reference.

Consider a client of ours that manufactures major household appliances, such as refrigerators, gas and electric ranges, washers, and dryers. Several years ago, the company wanted to implement a new system for its vast network of dealers. In the past, it had been sending a heavy box of material twice a month to each of its hundreds of dealers around the country. The box contained marketing brochures for the company's numerous brands, along with pricing data, information on rebates and special programs, and so on. But not every dealer needed all that material, and the inefficiency was costing millions of dollars every year. So the company implemented a "pull" system: All that information would be posted on a Web site, and the dealers could select only what they needed (for example, the latest details on rebates) and print just that on high-resolution color printers supplied by our client. The new system sounded terrific in theory, but it was a flop in the field. Dealers weren't using it, and our client was becoming frustrated by their resistance.

We were hired to get to the root of the problem, and to do that, we conducted an extensive survey of the dealers. One of the first things we learned was that most of them were very conservative business-people who did not particularly like change. Many of them had run operations pretty much the same way for decades. Their advertising in the local papers, for instance, was pretty much the same kind of ads that they had always used. Of course, running such an operation is not rocket science, but these dealers rarely deviated from their past business practices. We didn't actually conduct a study of their decision-making styles, but we would be surprised if most of them weren't Followers.

The next thing we discovered was that our client had been trying to encourage the dealers to use the Web system by emphasizing how new and improved it was, proclaiming that it was "leading-edge," "better," "new," "innovative," and so forth. But this type of language only made the dealers anxious. They specifically did not want some newfangled system with a lot of bells and whistles. What they wanted was to know that they could find the important data that they needed. The common complaint was this: "I want to know that I can quickly get the information that I need to run my business."

With that in mind, we recommended to our client that they stop trying to sell the new system by touting how innovative it was. We advised that they emphasize how similar the new system was to the old way of doing things. So a typical memo to announce a new feature might read something like this: "In the past, to determine the rebates for a particular model and brand, you had to look at two different documents—the Listing of Product Serial Numbers and the Rebate Update Newsletter. Now, in the new system, that information is all in one place: the Rebate Summary, which you can access easily through the following Web page…"

That insight was a big "aha" to our client, and managers there began to rethink all their correspondence. The general theme switched from "Look at how terrific the new system is" to "The new system is just like the old way you've been doing things, but it's better and easier to use." That change made a big difference. The dealers now were comforted because they were assured that something they depended on was still going to be there. To them, the old system was proven, and they absolutely did not want to give it up, but they would trade it in for an improved version. When our client began to position the Web system as a modified, improved version of the familiar way of doing things, resistance from the dealers dropped substantially, and the feedback was much more positive.

Of course, to some degree everyone dislikes change, and people are all comforted by familiar things. Human beings are, after all, creatures of habit. But this is particularly true for Followers. They are almost compulsive about wanting to continue to use what's worked before, whereas other types of executives are much more open to being pioneers. Charismatics, for instance, might be attracted to a novel solution just because it *is* new. They might be intrigued and attracted to all the gee-whiz features and options. Thinkers might also be swayed if you could methodically prove how the new system is better. In contrast, sometimes the only way to convince Followers of a truly innovative solution is to get someone else to succeed with it first—their need for reassurance is that great.

KNOWING WHAT TO DO—AND WHEN TO DO IT

As discussed earlier, the most important—and difficult—thing is to identify Followers properly in the first place. Any mistake there could be fatal. If, for example, you misidentify a Follower as a Charismatic and then you try to impress him with your bold, innovative ideas, the Follower will likely tune you out. Also with Charismatics, you want to discuss the risks of your proposal and delineate how you're going to minimize them, but any discussion of risks with Followers will only heighten their anxieties. With Followers, you need to show that your proposal has minimal risk, based on the number of times it's been implemented successfully in the past.

An important thing to remember with Followers is that they tend to play defense rather than offense. In other words, they are usually reactive rather than proactive. In most cases, their trigger event occurs when something upsets the status quo—for example, when a competitor instigates a price war. When that happens, the primary goal for Followers is to get things back on course. You might be able to prepare them for something that's on the horizon, but they will not act until a problem has already become manifest. This type of rearview-mirror approach to management is typical of many Followers, such as Al Lundquist, who was spurred to action only after the defection of some of his key customers.

The exhibit "The Follower Plan" gives an overview of what you should do before, during, and after your meetings with Followers. Note that your primary tool will be case examples, including any ref-

THE FOLLOWER PLAN

How to Prepare for a Meeting with a Follower Decision Maker

PRE-MEETING	IN THE MEETING	POST-MEETING
✓ Build numerous case studies for your solution	✓ Present information in the same order as for Thinkers and Skeptics; the key difference is the depth of your case studies	✓ The default mode of Followers is the status quo, so they may not make a move until their problem becomes pressing
✓ Include examples outside the industry so the Follower can feel innovative	✓ Connect your proposal to whatever is familiar to the Follower	✓ Consider ways to lower the cost of your solution to lessen the risk of buying
✓ Omit instances of when your solution has failed (but be prepared to discuss them)	✓ Show how your strategy has succeeded elsewhere while other options have failed	✓ Continually reinforce how your option has succeeded in past situations that were similar to the Follower's current circumstances
✓ Include costs and show that your proposal is the cheapest, on a risk-adjusted basis, because it is a solution that has been proven	✓ Compare the costs of each option under consideration	

erences and testimonials that you can gather. Essentially, you must show in detail how your proposal has succeeded in many other places under conditions that are similar to the Follower's. Remember that Followers are good at putting themselves in the shoes of others, so case studies will be particularly effective. You should be prepared to discuss the risks of your proposal—as well as your measures to minimize those risks—but don't bring that subject up unless the Follower does. If, however, the Follower is considering other options, you might want to talk about the risks of those alternatives, including instances in which they failed in the past.

In summary, persuading Followers is fairly straightforward, providing that you

- Remember that people will rarely admit that they are Followers. Instead, they will pretend, for example, to be Charismatics by portraying themselves as "big ideas" people. When in doubt, assume that the person you're dealing with is a Follower, until proven otherwise.
- Provide as much proof as possible that your proposal has worked in similar situations in the past. Followers absolutely need to feel comfortable that something is proven before they proceed with it. When you don't have the necessary track record, consider appealing to the Follower's desire for bargains.
- Don't overplay your hand. Followers basically want to know just two things: how your solution has worked before and how it will help them solve their problem. Providing them with other information can unnecessarily complicate and obstruct their decision-making processes.
- Before proposing anything new, be sure to lay the proper foundation. Discuss the familiar way of doing something and then link that to the novel solution. For Followers, any tethers to the past will minimize their anxieties as they venture outside their comfort zone.

Chapter 11

The Controller Decision Maker

Controllers can be frustrating to work with because of their desire to be in charge of all aspects of the decision-making process. But they can be very effective leaders, especially in situations that require a strong, take-charge presence. Among their defining qualities, Controllers are

1. **Driven by fear.** They are constantly on the lookout for whatever might adversely affect them or their organizations. In other words, they never allow themselves to become complacent.
2. **Proactive.** They do not sit on their hands, waiting for others to act. They step up to the plate and do what needs to be done.
3. **Fiercely self-reliant.** They do things their way, and they can make big decisions without advice or input from others.
4. **Absolute and resolute.** They tend to see the world in black and white, and they are unshakable in their beliefs.
5. **Meticulous.** They have an impressive faculty for detail. They can handle a staggering amount of information and minutiae.

6. Unyielding perfectionists. They constantly push themselves—as well as those around them. Their view is that any
job can always be done faster, cheaper, and with higher
quality.

DRIVEN BY FEAR

Fear is the primary emotion that drives Controllers. They are chronic
worriers, and they tend to become particularly anxious whenever
faced with the unknown. If a new competitor enters the market, they
prepare for the worst. When there's a restructuring in their organization, they assume the changes will affect them negatively. If they are
the leaders in their industry, they view every development, such as a
new technology or governmental regulation, as a threat to their position.

That ever-vigilant mind-set can be a potent ally in business. In fact,
fear can enable an organization to anticipate problems while they are
still manageable. Andy Grove, former CEO and cofounder of Intel
whose motto is "Only the paranoid survive," credits fear for much of
his company's success. "The most important role of managers is to
create an environment in which people are passionately dedicated to
winning in the marketplace," says Grove. "Fear plays a major role in
creating and maintaining such passion. Fear of competition, fear of
bankruptcy, fear of being wrong, and fear of losing can all be powerful
motivators."[1] For one thing, asserts Grove, a culture of fear has helped
Intel overcome complacency.

It is difficult to argue with Grove, who, besides being the chairman
of Intel, also teaches at the Stanford Graduate School of Business. In
the fast-changing high-tech industry, in which today's leaders quickly
become tomorrow's has-beens, Intel has managed to stay at the fore-
front of the chip business for decades. Of course, the company has
had its ups and downs, but throughout them it has consistently main-
tained its dominant position as the organization that sets the agenda
for others to follow.

Controllers can be phenomenally successful in business. Take Martha Stewart. Although her accomplishments have been overshadowed by the criminal charges stemming from her stock trading, the fact is that Stewart is among the savviest entrepreneurs around. She has taken a simple idea—that tasteful, graceful living is available to everyone—and turned it into a formidable empire, establishing one of the best-known brands in the world. Her company, Martha Stewart Living Omnimedia, is a multimedia juggernaut, with revenues from magazines, books, TV, radio, and merchandising royalties. In the dog-eat-dog world of business, Stewart never allowed others to get the upper hand. "She gave everybody the shiv before they gave it to her," notes the media critic Michael Wolff.[2]

Ross Perot, too, has been one of the great success stories of U.S. capitalism. Back in the 1960s, he left IBM, where he had earned himself the reputation as a master salesman, to found Electronic Data Systems (EDS), which he grew into a multibillion-dollar corporation. After selling that company to General Motors for a tidy sum, he went on to start another firm, Perot Systems. Perot's shrewd and tough approach to business is amply captured by one of his favorite sayings from Thornton Wilder: "Every good and excellent thing in the world stands moment by moment on the razor-edge of danger and must be fought for."

Although a healthy dose of fear gives Controllers their competitive edge, often enabling them to accomplish the impossible, an excessive amount of that emotion is hardly productive. It can make them freeze in their tracks, for instance. Or they might interpret situations in the most negative ways, seeing enemies and fights where none exist. They might also fixate on worst-case scenarios, even though those circumstances are extremely unlikely to occur. And excessive fear can constrain the decision-making processes of Controllers, making them unduly self-absorbed and inordinately focused on details. In short, fear can be either a strength or a weakness, and successful Controllers learn to manage and channel that emotion in productive and advantageous ways.

PROACTIVE

When an omelet is needed, Controllers won't hesitate to crack the eggs themselves. They will take charge instead of waiting for others to act. And to get results, they won't hesitate to dismantle the old way of doing things and replace it with their own solution, even if that means stepping on numerous toes. This focused and no-nonsense approach to business can lead to spectacular results.

When Jose Ignacio Lopez de Arriortua arrived at the headquarters of General Motors in the spring of 1992, the company had its back against the wall. It was bleeding red ink, having lost $4.5 billion the year before, stirring the board to oust Robert Stempel, CEO and chairman, just a couple years into his tenure. Lopez was tapped by the incoming CEO, Jack Smith, to become head of worldwide purchasing. Lopez's marching orders were simple: Cut the costs of manufacturing GM vehicles.

With that directive, Lopez quickly took action. He made GM suppliers, even those that were subsidiaries of the company, go through rounds and rounds of bidding. Those that survived were then asked to lower their prices even further. For suppliers that claimed they were already running at their absolute leanest, he would sometimes send efficiency experts to their plants to show them exactly how they could trim additional costs from their operations.[3] He reportedly tore up existing contracts and instructed the vendors to resubmit their bids, but this time with greater price reductions.[4]

Many might argue with Lopez's "my way or the highway" methods, and his controversial career (he left GM for Volkswagen, sparking a nasty, expensive legal brawl between the two companies) has become a case study for business-school students. That said, Lopez's results were breathtaking. In just a year since arriving in Detroit, he helped save GM billions of dollars. As a testament to his effectiveness, on the day that a newspaper announced that he was leaving GM, the company's stock fell 3.4 percent.[5]

Controllers do not hesitate to take action when something is not to their liking, even if the problem might better be addressed by those with direct authority and responsibility. The classic case here is

George Steinbrenner, the owner of the New York Yankees baseball franchise. Known as the Boss, Steinbrenner has become notorious for publicly dressing down his players to the media. In one of his most infamous remarks, he called Hideki Irabu, then a Yankees pitcher, a "fat, pussy toad." More recently, before the 2003 season, Steinbrenner stirred things up when he told a newspaper reporter that Derek Jeter, the Yankees' star shortstop, wasn't focused enough on baseball. Later Steinbrenner would say, "I am the way I am. I got my message through. If I'm paying a guy $16 million, I want him to listen."[6] Although other owners might have handled the situation differently — letting their managers or coaches have one-on-ones with the players in question — the Yankees' record of success speaks for itself. The team is a perennial contender in the postseason, and the franchise is one of the most lucrative in any sport.

Especially when the going gets rough, Controllers feel the urgency to take action, and this can be wise or not. In the late 1970s, when two EDS employees were being held hostage in Iran, Ross Perot didn't wait for the United States government to resolve the crisis. He enlisted the help of Green Beret Colonel Arthur "Bull" Simons, who led a commando team into Tehran to bust the two men out of jail, escaping safely into Turkey. The daring adventure was the stuff of fiction, and in fact the best-selling author Ken Follett would later write about the jailbreak in his thriller *On Wings of Eagles*.

On the other hand, during the Ford Explorer crisis, which led to a massive recall of the SUV's Firestone tires, Jacques Nasser, then CEO of Ford, took it upon himself to go on national TV to reassure the public. In the commercials, he came across as wooden and rehearsed. Chairman Bill Ford Jr., the personable great-grandson of the company founder, would have been a more effective spokesman, assert some critics. Moreover, Nasser had the filming done at Ford's headquarters. A better approach, say PR experts, would have been to tape Nasser in the field, comforting customers and talking with Ford dealers.

FIERCELY SELF-RELIANT

Controllers are extremely independent. They do it their way, and they succeed or fail based on their own abilities. Unlike Followers, Controllers do not need pioneers to blaze a trail for them. They have their own internal compass that tells them what to do, always pointing them to their own true north. Whatever they achieve, Controllers do so on their own—and in their own way. They are supremely self-reliant, and their intense drive can be impressive. At times, it seems as if they will single-handedly accomplish tasks through sheer willpower alone that others would find far too daunting to even attempt.

When it comes to big decisions, Controllers need to be in control of the overall process. All information must go through them, and they will make the decision when they want to and not necessarily when others need them to. Furthermore, they don't particularly require the advice of their staff and colleagues. In fact, the only input that Controllers really want is their own, because that's the only source that they can truly trust. Again, much of this is related to the important role that fear plays in their outlook. For instance, Controllers might summarily dismiss a person's opinions because they assume that individual has an agenda that conflicts with theirs.

Not surprisingly, Controllers tend to be organizational loners, and they can be very self-absorbed, a trait that leads to their making decisions based solely on their own input. Although a Controller might talk to others about a decision, he will seldom genuinely listen to them or truly consider their advice. Consensus management is not a strength. Controllers might even ignore everyone else and make their decision by going purely with their gut feelings. They won't hesitate to make unilateral decisions, even when an organization's culture and customs dictate a more inclusive process.

Meetings with Controllers can be unpredictable affairs. They might be confrontational, assuming that others are trying to take advantage of them. Or they might be completely silent, reflecting their tendency toward self-absorption. Or they might become impatient, wondering why someone is unable to see things their way. Whereas Followers are good at putting themselves in the shoes of others, Controllers can see things only through their own perspective. "My reality problem," admits Rosie O'Donnell, "is that I think everyone thinks the way I think."[7]

Another reality problem with Controllers is that they are used to having their own way, and they will often insist on getting it. Because they are driven by fear, Controllers need to have control, which gives them a greater sense of security. Before Martha Stewart launched her own business as caterer and domestic diva, she was a stockbroker at Monness, Williams & Sidel. She didn't take to that career, however, because of one thing. "What bothered Martha about the stock market was that there was an aspect she couldn't control, and that was stock prices," says her former boss, Andrew Monness.[8]

A loss of control is perhaps what Controllers fear most, and this can be either a strength or a weakness, depending on the circumstances. Perhaps nowhere is that dichotomy better exemplified than with Stewart. Her need to control her editorial content—and ultimately her own destiny—led her to buy back her flagship magazine, *Martha Stewart Living,* from Time Warner, which was one of the wisest business decisions she ever made. On the other hand, her micromanaging a transaction of her ImClone shares while en route from the United States to Mexico might well be one of her biggest mistakes, triggering investigations by the Justice Department, the SEC, and Congress.

The desire to micromanage has led more than a few Controllers astray. When Nasser was running Ford, he had sixteen executives reporting directly to him, whereas GM's CEO had just nine. And when Nasser was promoted to CEO from his position as head of worldwide automotive operations, he didn't fill his former position. He also didn't appoint a COO, so that in effect there was no clear number two person. All this led *BusinessWeek* to publish an editorial with the headline "Ford: Jacques Nasser Can't Do It All." The commentary criticized Nasser for reportedly trying to do too much too quickly, implementing a host of sweeping initiatives, including a major shift in strategy to move Ford into service-related businesses, such as auto repair and insurance, that might have stretched the company too thin. As Ford's troubles deepened in 2001—the company's market share had eroded, morale was low, and manufacturing quality had slipped—the response from Nasser, whose career was on the line, was to grip the company reins even tighter. "I'm going to spend a great deal of my time in the product arena," he proclaimed. "I'll be all over every single brand and every single product in this company as of yesterday."[9] By the end of the year, however, Nasser had been shown the door.

ABSOLUTE AND RESOLUTE

Controllers tend to be clear, precise, and straightforward. They have immutable rules that define what is acceptable and what is not. To them, there is the right way (usually their way) and the wrong way, with no middle ground. In other words, everything is either black or white; grays are prohibited. It's that simple.

The upside of this view of the world is that Controllers are often able to distill complex, messy problems into stark terms that are easy to comprehend. They make it abundantly clear what they want and when they want it. They are rarely ambiguous, leaving everyone knowing exactly what's expected of them. The downside, though, is that Controllers can sometimes be unnecessarily rigid, issuing decrees that leave little room for negotiation. When Ross Perot was head of EDS, he made his views clear on the kind of workers he wanted. He once told a reporter, "If we have a married employee who has a girlfriend, we terminate him. He's got a lifetime contract with his wife, and if she can't trust him, how can I?"[10]

That cut-and-dried attitude can be very effective in business, as evidenced by Perot's spectacular success with EDS. At the same time, though, it can also cause Controllers to miss big opportunities. When Arthur Blank and Bernie Marcus were cofounding the Home Depot in 1978, Perot was interested in investing $2 million in the venture. But the deal fell through when Perot commented on Marcus's four-year-old Cadillac: "My people don't drive Cadillacs. My guys at EDS drive Chevrolets." Perot then repeated that remark twice. "And when he said it the third time," recalls Marcus, "I realized this was never going to work . . . If this guy is going to be bothered by what kind of car I am driving, how much aggravation are we going to have when we have to make really big decisions?"[11] Marcus and Blank then looked elsewhere for their seed money, and the big loser was Perot. More than twenty years later, as the Home Depot became a national chain, his proposed investment would have been worth about $60 billion.

Another downside is that Controllers can fixate on something and then impose illogical and even counterproductive rules to constantly remind everyone of its importance. For example, to impress upon everyone the importance of being punctual, a Controller might decree that the entrance to the employee parking lot be locked at 8:00 every morning, forcing tardy workers (even those with good excuses) to park their cars blocks away, making them that much later in getting to their jobs. The rules can even become eccentricities that others view as trite, inane, or even ludicrous. When Jose Ignacio Lopez was at GM, for instance, he insisted that his people switch wearing their watches from their left wrists to their right (or vice versa) so that they would be constantly aware of their deadlines for meeting certain goals.

Controllers can be counted on to speak their minds, and that's why they often don't excel at large corporations. "If I'd stayed at IBM," says Perot, "I'd be somewhere in middle management getting in trouble and being asked to take early retirement." The reason is simple. "When I got up to the bite-your-tongue level," he says, "that's when I would have gotten in trouble."[12]

Controllers are not particularly adaptive to change. Once they've explained what they want, that's it. Their ideas and orders become gospel, and they assume that others will follow them accordingly. Furthermore, Controllers rarely capitulate. They stand on their principles and focus on what needs to be done. And they accomplish that, whatever the obstacles. When Jacques Nasser was at Ford, he was known for rarely taking no for an answer. "He's like Chinese water torture," says someone who knew him there. "If he doesn't get the answer he wants, he just keeps coming back."[13]

It must be noted, however, that Nasser's uncompromising attitude was among the very qualities that propelled him so quickly up the corporate ladder. Well known as a turnaround specialist, he helped restore order to several of Ford's international units throughout his long, varied career there. When he eventually became head of Ford's worldwide automotive operations, he trimmed costs by several billion dollars in just two years, enabling the company to become the world's most profitable auto manufacturer in the late 1990s.

That said, the tough mind-set of Controllers can also lead to ugly battles. They are not especially skilled at working out their differences with others, and when things don't go their way, they often take their marbles and head home. Consider the recent brawl between Rosie O'Donnell, the comedian and former talk-show host, and Gruner + Jahr, the publishing company that put out *Rosie*, the now-defunct magazine. That partnership has dissolved into a flurry of bitter accusations, nasty threats, and expensive lawsuits. What infuriated O'Donnell is that others allegedly usurped her control over the editorial operations of *Rosie*, her namesake publication. "They took control of my magazine from me," she charges, "and told my staff not to take directives from me, or to listen to me, that *he* now controlled the brand *and* the name, and if I didn't like it I can sue him . . ."[14]

The "he" in those remarks is Dan Brewster, the CEO of G + J's operations in the United States. After O'Donnell had announced that she would quit *Rosie*, G + J pulled the plug on the magazine, and Brewster had this to say: "Not liking the terms of a signed contract is not an excuse to simply walk away, leaving a wake of destruction. But I guess that's obvious to a sane person."[15] Although the official court verdict awarded damages to neither party, it is evident that both sides will have ultimately lost, sustaining considerable damage to their reputations and finances.

And therein lies the problem. Sometimes Controllers can be so fixated on being right that they lose the big picture. In contrast, other executives will realize that being right is sometimes not as important as being effective. That type of pragmatism eludes many Controllers who are overly rigid, stubbornly holding their positions even as the evidence mounts against them. To make matters worse, few Controllers have excelled in the fine art of compromise. Not surprisingly, some of the most bitter disputes have involved Controllers: Rosie O'Donnell's public slugfest against G + J and its CEO, Daniel Brewster; Ross Perot's intense clashes with GM's top management and board; Jose Ignacio Lopez's defection to Volkswagen, which sparked an expensive and lengthy legal battle against GM; and George Steinbrenner's repeated firings and rehirings of manager Billy Martin.

METICULOUS

Fear makes Controllers abhor uncertainty and ambiguity, which is why they will often focus on the pure facts and analytics of an argument. They will review information in a logical, clinical fashion. They are sticklers for accuracy and will often be inordinately concerned with minutiae. Their attention to detail is exacting, thorough, and even excruciating.

Martha Stewart's meticulousness has become the stuff of legend. It has, in fact, been the basis of her multimedia empire. She doesn't just wrap her bushes in burlap for the winter; the fabric is custom-fitted to the exact shapes of the individual plants.[16] "She out-detailed everybody in a detail game,"[17] says Michael Wolff, the media critic. As Stewart became embroiled in the ImClone scandal, the image of her as perfect hostess provided much fodder for biting satire. "A subpoena should be served with a nice appetizer," quipped Conan O'Brien, the late-night comic.

Ross Perot has a similar exactitude. After Ken Follett had written *On Wings of Eagles,* the account of the jailbreak that freed two EDS employees, Follett sent a fourth draft of the manuscript to Perot. "[Follett] bet me a Rolls-Royce that I couldn't find any errors," recalls Perot. "I found two. I said, 'It's Admiral Mountbatten, not General. And you spelled McDonald's wrong.'" (Follett later sent Perot a miniature Rolls-Royce on a key chain. "I didn't say what size you'd get," he told Perot.)[18]

Perot's fondness for details and charts was on ample display for the U.S. public when he twice ran for president. In 1996, during his second campaign, he devoted an entire infomercial to describe details of the seven-step process he uses to solve problems. Jacques Nasser, too, has a fondness for charts. When he held the number two job at Ford, he had weekly meetings with employees to teach them about shareholder value, price-to-earnings ratio, return on investment, and other business basics. Using flip chart after flip chart, he would spend hours with groups of workers in lecture halls, manufacturing plants, and other company facilities.[19]

That kind of thorough precision takes great effort. Luckily for

Stewart, she can get by on just three or four hours of sleep a night, leaving her with more than her fair share of the day to run her company. At Ford, workers had to get used to Nasser's long hours as well as his eagle eyes. "Designers just weren't used to working late and having the president walk up behind them, look over their shoulder, and say, 'What about moving that bumper down a bit?'" recalls one Ford employee.[20]

Such attention to detail is a double-edged sword. On the plus side, Controllers won't likely miss something tiny that might nonetheless have important ramifications, such as a footnote in a contract that substantially alters a deal. And Controllers leave little to chance. Stewart, for instance, travels with two laptop computers, in case one should break. So, with a competent Controller in charge, a crucial presentation to a major customer will go off exactly as planned, and a major product will be launched without the usual glitches and snafus.

On the minus side, however, sometimes the focus on detail is motivated by overwhelming fear. When Controllers are afraid of making a mistake, they will concern themselves unduly with the details of a proposal. They worry that if they overlook something, it will surely come back and bite them. And they don't want to lose control, so they need every piece of data. This is why they will constantly have people chasing down one piece of information after another — the latest quarterly results, recent market research, an article in a trade magazine, a press release from a competitor, and so on, ad infinitum. In addition to being a delay tactic, the requests can be part of a larger issue of control. To put it bluntly, some Controllers almost seem to enjoy making people jump through hoops. Few things are more frustrating than when a final decision rests with a Controller who is afraid of making a move.

Ultimately, Controllers will make up their own minds on their own time. And although they seek accuracy and facts, that does not necessarily mean their decisions will be intelligent and rational. In fact, they might not even look at the information they've requested. Sometimes their egos or fears get the best of them, and they jump to illogical conclusions. Another problem is that Controllers can focus too much on the trees and not see the forest. That kind of myopia can be devastating. Take Martha Stewart. By selling her ImClone stock when she did, she saved a tiny fraction of her total net worth. But by her own estimate, the resulting fallout from that transaction has cost her about $400 million, from the subsequent decline in value of her holdings in her own company as well as from legal fees and lost business opportunities.[21]

UNYIELDING PERFECTIONISTS

Controllers tend to be perfectionists, both particular and picky. They want initiatives to be implemented without a hitch, which is why they often have trouble delegating to others. Contrast that with Charismatics, who are not afraid of getting something wrong because they know that mistakes are par for the course. (What Charismatics can't stand is when people repeat their errors.)

Controllers often have strong personalities and can even be overbearing. In their minds, they are the best salespeople, the best marketing experts, the best business strategists, and so on. They can also be volatile, making snap remarks that alienate others. They might misinterpret things and fly off the handle. Their demeanor can turn on the dime, often earning them the reputation as the Dr. Jekyll and Mr. Hyde of their organizations.

As bosses, Controllers are tough and demanding. Their hard-driving style can be off-putting, and they often come across as brusque and insensitive. Furthermore, their perfectionism can make them difficult taskmasters. Before hiring Joe Torre, George Steinbrenner went through twenty-one managers in twenty-four years. And while most teams would be elated to have the Yankees' remarkable record—winning four World Series in five years from 1996 to 2000—that has hardly made Steinbrenner a complacent man. At their best, Controllers motivate and push people to achievements beyond their highest expectations. At their worst, Controllers use their positions of authority to instill fear, resorting to intimidation and bullying. The behavior of some Controllers has even bordered on the abusive, as they rely primarily on "the fear factor" to rule.

Part of the problem is that Controllers are often not able to see how others view them. They can have a major blind spot to how they are coming across. When Martha Stewart was being investigated for her sale of ImClone stock, she understandably granted few interviews. But in one that she did, she seemed unaware of how her comments might exacerbate the public's antipathy toward her. When the reporter admired her silver chopsticks, she told him, "In China they say, 'The thinner the chopsticks, the higher the social status.' Of course, I got the thinnest I could find."[22]

Controllers hate when anything goes wrong, and when something does, they will usually avoid being held accountable. Instead, they assume others are at fault. They might even take the following attitude: "No one can really approach my level of understanding and competence, because if they could, they wouldn't make so many errors." Again, contrast that with the attitude of Charismatics, who are very willing to take responsibility for their decisions. Controllers will distance themselves from a mistake, and they can be blamers. In organizations run by Controllers, when something goes wrong, people run for cover, afraid that they'll get tagged with the fault. Vendors, too, have it rough. After a Controller has decided on a particular supplier, when something goes wrong, he will cancel the contract and quickly move on to the next vendor. Sometimes the salespeople of the first supplier don't even realize what's happened until they've already lost the Controller as a customer. Moreover, when problems surface, many Controllers have the bad habit of shooting the messenger.

For all their faults, though, Controllers can be highly effective executives, particularly in situations that require someone to be firmly at the helm. Consider what happened to EDS after Ross Perot had sold the firm to General Motors, which subsequently divested it. EDS has recently hit turbulent waters. The company has been losing ground to IBM, and it has clashed with A. T. Kearney, the consulting firm it acquired. Moreover, its accounting practices have come under scrutiny. In the fall of 2002, the SEC initiated a probe of the company's finances, an inquiry that has escalated into a formal investigation. Amid this, CEO Richard Brown was replaced in 2003, all while many top consultants at A. T. Kearney had reportedly hired lawyers to help them negotiate their resignations from the firm.[23] As the situation threatened to spiral out of control, longtime EDS staffers have wondered whether things would have gotten so bad had Perot still been in the corner office. Similarly, onlookers might question whether companies like Arthur Andersen and Enron would have suffered such complete meltdowns had someone at the helm ensured that all employees, including top execs, were abiding by ethical and business codes of conduct.

WHAT CONTROLLERS SEEK—AND WHAT THEY AVOID

Although Controllers tend to be micromanagers, not all micromanagers have a Controller style of decision making. As mentioned in chapter 7 ("The Skeptic Decision Maker"), Tom Siebel, the cofounder and CEO of Siebel Systems, is something of a control freak, intimately involved with the operational details of his company. But when it comes to making important decisions, Siebel is much more a Skeptic than Controller.

APPROACH PROFILE for CONTROLLERS

When Making Decisions, Controllers.....

	Average	SEEK MORE
Self-Absorption		79
Fear & Uncertainty		58
Rebellion		37
Impulsiveness		29
Bargains	-2	
Playfulness	-5	
Competitiveness	-14	
Risk	-45	
Persistence	-49	
Education	-52	
Intelligence & Facts	-52	
Responsibility	-54	

AVOID MORE

Error ±2.9 points   © 2003 Miller-Williams Inc. (millwill.com)

Note: The data have been normalized to range from –100 (maximum aversion) to +100 (maximum desire).

To avoid mistaking people's personalities for their decision-making styles, our survey of nearly seventeen hundred executives looked specifically at people's behaviors when making important decisions—for example, their willingness (or even desire) to take risks and assume the responsibility for them. By studying an array of such tendencies, we found that almost one out of ten executives is a Controller.

The most striking thing about people in this category of decision making is that they have a number of extreme likes and dislikes, as shown in the exhibit "Approach Profile for Controllers." In particular, note how strong their tendency toward self-absorption is. In fact, that quantity was nearly off our scale. Controllers also have a strong tendency to make decisions based on fear and uncertainty, and they very much desire to be both rebellious and impulsive.

Controllers also have several extreme aversions. They strongly avoid education and intelligence and facts, which relates back to their tendency toward self-absorption. Specifically, even though Controllers might ask for a lot of information, they won't actually use it to make their decision. All they really need is their own input and gut feelings. Also note how strongly Controllers will avoid both risk and responsibility: They are terrified of making a wrong move (a fear that is sometimes paralyzing), and when things go wrong, they can be blamers. Lastly, we should point out the extent to which Controllers dislike people who are persistent. Again, as mentioned earlier, Controllers make decisions based on their own timetable, and they hate being pressured by others to move any faster than that.

Key results from our study are that Controllers

- Use fear as their ally, which helps them to avoid the dangers of complacency.
- Take charge to restore order, especially in chaotic situations.
- Make decisions, even major ones, mainly relying on their own input, steadfastly resisting organizational and political pressures to sway them.
- Are unequivocal and unwavering in knowing exactly what they want and when they want it.

- Tirelessly leave nothing to chance, as they concern themselves with the details and minutiae of any proposal.
- Relentlessly push to do everything faster, more cheaply, and with better quality.

Not surprisingly, Controllers tend to evoke strong emotions in others. They are either loved or loathed. On the one hand, they can instill fervent loyalty among their employees because of their straight-talking styles and their steadfast commitment to principles. On the other hand, they can be demanding and frustrating to work with. That said, in certain situations—particularly when a company is under-going tremendous disruptions to its business—Controllers can be unparalleled in their effectiveness to get the job done, both within budget and on schedule.

Chapter 12

Persuading the
Controller Decision Maker

Controllers are the most difficult executives to work with. In actuality, they can't really be persuaded; they must persuade themselves. Even so, there are two factors that can help tip things your way: time and fear. You need considerable amounts of time because Controllers do things according to their own schedule, not yours. And you must manage and minimize their fear in order for them to act. In essence, you need to

1. **Enable action but don't force it.** Provide Controllers with all the information they need. Then back off and wait patiently until something compels them to act.
2. **Fly below the radar.** Often the best way to handle Controllers is to keep your contact to a minimum and instead work through their lieutenants.
3. **Build alliances.** Partner with people who are adept at improvising to get things done within the Controllers' various systems, rules, and regulations.
4. **Draw your line and hold to it.** With Controllers, you often reach an impasse. When that happens, it's imperative that you know exactly what is negotiable—and what isn't.

ENABLE ACTION BUT DON'T FORCE IT

The most important thing to remember about Controllers is that they operate out of fear, which can make them misconstrue even your best intentions. For instance, they might mistakenly assume that you have ulterior motives when you don't. They could become combative, questioning you aggressively and relentlessly. All this can be aggravating, but the best response is to remain composed and patient. You have to avoid becoming defensive and resist the natural inclination to take things personally.

That, of course, is much easier said than done. But it can be very empowering to realize that Controllers are, at their core, operating out of fear. In some cases, they might actually be secretly terrified of making a decision, especially when numerous unknowns are involved. When that happens, Controllers can be particularly difficult, but the worst thing you can do is to return any of their aggression with some of your own. That only adds fuel to the fire, heightening their fears. Instead, handle them almost as you would a snarling animal—by being calm, unemotional, and reassuring.

The secret to working with Controllers is that you need to overcome their internal fears, which they will pretend they don't have. They might cover them up by paying an inordinate amount of attention to the intricate details of processes and methods, continually requesting additional information from you. Dealing with Controllers can often be a frustrating game of cat and mouse, with you always chasing down some problem or information at their request.

Controllers might not even look at the materials they've asked for, but it's important that you jump through the hoops anyway. Becoming frustrated or angry with Controllers only exacerbates their fears. Instead, calm them by being patiently responsive to their requests. The trick is to enable Controllers to overcome their fears without calling attention to them. One of the worst things you can do is to say something along the lines of "What are you so afraid of?" That just spooks Controllers even more, which is the last thing you want to do.

In meetings, Controllers can be very self-absorbed, so be prepared for long silences during your interactions. And remember that even though Controllers seek accuracy and facts, that does not necessarily translate into their making rational decisions, as they sometimes jump to illogical conclusions. To persuade Controllers, your argument needs to be highly structured and linear. They want details, but only if presented through an expert. Controllers are influenced most by proposals that display a sense of strength, discipline, authority, command, and rigidity—all supported by data analysis. They are particularly drawn to take-charge approaches that present themselves as being unstoppable and unbeatable. To evoke that feeling, use the following key words: *power, handle, physical, grab, keep them honest, make them pay, just do it, details, facts, reason, logic.*

Ultimately, though, you can't really sell Controllers on anything. They make up their own minds on their own schedules. They tend to make decisions in a vacuum, using just their own input. Controllers can't really be persuaded, because they need to always be in control. You have to let them make their decisions based on *their* analysis, not yours. In practice, the only way to sell an idea to Controllers is not to sell, but instead to give them the opportunity to buy. Your best bet is simply to supply them with the information they need and hope that they convince themselves.

That tactic is often successful because it allows Controllers to think an idea is theirs. Controllers are much more prone to act when they feel some ownership of a proposal, so you should encourage any such connections. For example, you might refer to a public utterance or stance of the Controller: "You've always emphasized that our customers are our number one priority. The proposed restructuring will better align our business units to those customers." Or you might find a parallel from the Controller's past: "When you were at Johnson & Johnson, you did a similar restructuring within your business unit." If you can't find a way to link your solution to the Controller, then at least try to credit her with helping to identify the problem: "At our executive retreat, you mentioned that our overhead costs have gotten way out of control. That got me to thinking about how we could streamline the organization by restructuring to centralize key functions."

Even then, Controllers can take an inordinate amount of time to make a decision, and until they're ready to act, they might keep asking you for one piece of information after another. That frustrating process could continue until there's a compelling trigger event—disastrous quarterly results, for instance—that simply forces their hand. Before that happens, bide your time and gently wear the Controller down so that when the trigger event does occur, she'll move quickly. It's a tricky process. You want to highlight significant information so that the Controller eventually forces herself to make a move—as opposed to your forcing her to take action. A common mistake is to be too aggressive in pushing your proposal. When that happens, Controllers are likely to see you as part of the problem and not the solution. Be forewarned that Controllers tend to be blamers, and they won't hesitate to shoot the messenger.

One tactic that sometimes works is to give Controllers a deadline that is dictated by an external factor (and not by you): "Our window of opportunity will close in six months because that's when our competitor will be opening a dozen branches in this region." Or if you're a salesperson dealing with a Controller, you could gently remind him of an upcoming event that is beyond your control: "As you know, the U.S. government will be imposing new tariffs on our products starting this fall."

Even when Controllers know they need to act, they can still slow things by being too involved, usually by overexerting their authority. Or they might try to change the rules in the middle of a game. In such situations, the best response is to be patient but firm. Consider our experience with Tim Wainwright, a senior executive at a high-tech company in Southern California. (Note: To respect the confidentiality of our clients, we have used pseudonyms and have altered identifying details of the examples in this chapter.) Wainwright is a textbook Controller, always insisting that everything funnel through him. We actually weren't hired by Wainwright but by Charles Morrison, the CEO of the company, who wanted us to do a research study to help them understand how to serve their customers better in a changing market.

The project proceeded according to schedule, and when it came time for us to renew our contract, we got a quick approval from Morrison. But then Wainwright told us, "Wait a minute. I have a few questions before we move forward." He then bombarded us with numerous pointed queries: "What is this particular line item?" and "Why are you charging us for that?" and "Shouldn't this have been included in the previous contract?" and so on.

We were caught off guard, to say the least, because Morrison, Wainwright's boss, had already approved everything. But we answered each of the questions patiently, remembering that Controllers operate out of fear, so they often have trouble letting go of something. They want a lower price; otherwise, they think they'll be perceived as weak negotiators. Or they've got to get a project done ahead of schedule; otherwise, they'll be seen as pushovers for not driving people harder.

In actuality, the only thing we needed from Wainwright was for him to choose one of three options that we had already worked out with Morrison. It should have been a straightforward decision, but it wasn't because Wainwright kept on trying to combine the options. "That's not what we agreed on with Morrison," we told him, "but if you want to expand the scope of the project, we could do that for an additional cost." We then referred him to a document that Morrison had approved that clearly confirmed what we were saying. Wainwright then replied, "Okay, I'll go with just option two."

FLY BELOW THE RADAR

With Wainwright, we were thankful that we had the support of his boss to help us. Even so, we never forced his hand; we merely guided it. But what if we didn't have that kind of leverage? In such cases, sometimes the best approach is to keep your contact with Controllers to a minimum and instead work directly with their lieutenants. That's the strategy we used in our dealings with Kevin Dillon, who is the head of a large division of a Fortune 500 corporation.

Several years ago, we did research for another division of that company, which helped it to expand its market. That success caught the eye of the company's president, who suggested that we meet with Dillon. But when we tried to do so, we got the distinct impression that he was avoiding us because he always seemed to be unavailable when we were in town. When we finally did get to meet with him, he wasn't all that interested in what we had to say. His first words were, "I only have fifteen minutes for you," and then he proceeded to do almost all of the talking for the better part of an hour. Before he left the meeting, he told us to work with his vice president of sales, Tony Rusting, and his head of marketing, Dana Jacobs. "Those guys will make the final recommendations to me," Dillon said.

Right off the bat, we knew that Dillon wasn't a Follower, because he wasn't swayed favorably by the results we had gotten for his sister division. He was going to make up his *own* mind and wasn't going to be influenced by what we had done. In fact, not only did our success with the other group fail to impress him, it was almost a *negative*, as far as he was concerned. Furthermore, he made it abundantly clear how indignant he was that his boss, the president of the company, had suggested we could help him. That rebelliousness made us think that Dillon was either a Skeptic or a Controller, and we would later learn that he was the latter.

Actually, Dillon's turning us over to Rusting and Jacobs was a blessing in disguise. Both men have been very responsive to us, and the research project has proceeded smoothly. Thanks to them, we have kept our dealings with Dillon to a minimum, which has been fine by us. In fact, we don't have any contact with him unless he initiates it himself. That unspoken arrangement has worked well because, through Rusting and Jacobs, we know exactly what we need to do and we've been productive in executing that scope of work. The project has stayed on course, even though Dillon has yet to officially endorse it.

At first glance, Dillon's behavior might be puzzling. After all, wouldn't a Controller *want* to be involved? Remember, though, that Controllers often avoid taking responsibility, and they tend to be blamers. By keeping his distance, Dillon has an escape route. If the project fails, Rusting and Jacobs will probably take the heat, as Dillon can blame them for faulty implementation. Moreover, he can claim that he gave the project his tacit approval only because the president of the company was pushing for it.

Such organizational politics are not the topic of this book; the important point is that when dealing with Controllers, you're often better off working directly with their lieutenants. In this case, it was actually Dillon who made that suggestion, but if he hadn't, we might have proposed it ourselves. The arrangement has certainly worked to our benefit.

There is another lesson here. As we've gotten to know Rusting and Jacobs through our work with them, we've come to appreciate how demanding a boss Dillon can be. One of Rusting and Jacobs's tactics is to avoid one-on-one meetings with him. When they need to talk to him about something, particularly a problem they're having, they see him together. This confirms what we have found from our own experiences. Some of the worst battles with Controllers come in one-on-one situations. As discussed in the previous chapter, Controllers can be very difficult to work with because they operate out of fear and they tend to be relentless perfectionists. In one-on-one meetings, Controllers might feel empowered to do whatever they please. They might chew someone out, their behavior even bordering on the abusive. Having another person present at a meeting helps to keep a lid on that—almost as if the presence of a witness keeps the Controller in check. The last thing you want is to be dealing with an out-of-control Controller.

Be careful, though, that you don't give Controllers even the slightest impression that you're ganging up on them. To avoid that, you need to frame the meeting as a discussion and then let the Controller take charge. You might even openly invite him to do so. You and your colleague could say, "We were talking about something and wanted your input." Such diplomacy helps to prevent Controllers from feeling like they're cornered, and it also lessens their fear that something is happening behind their backs.

Although we advise our clients to fly below the radar when dealing with Controllers, doing so can be tricky. This is especially true when Controllers are in charge of the money, the resources, and the people. In such situations, they control the game, and the only way you can win is by finding inventive ways to work within that system—all while being careful not to bring undue attention to yourself.

Years ago, we worked with ClarityBase, an up-and-coming software company. We were enthusiastic about the project because the firm had an exciting new product, and it needed us to study exactly how that software package was enabling its customers to gain an advantage over their competitors. The big problem, though, was that the chief operating officer of the company was a total Controller.

The stories about Paul Bradshaw, the COO, are legion, but perhaps the following anecdote provides an ample illustration. At a company kickoff with eight hundred salespeople present, Bradshaw delivered these words: "Here is the new sales presentation that I want every single one of you to learn so that you can give it in your sleep. I don't want you to change one single thing. This is the way it's to be done. And you are to use it with all customers, *exactly* this way." Then, for the next hour and a half, he went through a PowerPoint presentation that was absolutely dreadful. There were more than a hundred slides about ClarityBase's products, and every one contained arcane insider language and indecipherable acronyms. At the end of his talk, Bradshaw warned the audience, "You're going to be tested on this presentation. Every single one of you is going to learn it, backwards and forwards." During the coffee break, people were mumbling to each other, shaking their heads. "Can you believe this latest from the Great Committee of One?" someone sighed. "Boy, is he out of touch."

Needless to say, we stayed out of Bradshaw's line of sight as much as possible. Here again, we were fortunate to be working primarily with his lieutenants, in this case, Karl Edmondson, the vice president of marketing, and Patricia Holt, the senior VP of customer service. For months, everything went smoothly, but then we hit a snag. Our work had ramped up to about $260,000 on an annual basis, and Bradshaw had just decreed that any expense over $50,000 would have to be signed by him. When Edmondson and Holt asked him to approve the $260,000, he balked, saying it was too much money.

We sat down with Edmondson to discuss different options for narrowing the scope of our project. But the problem was that for every piece that we suggested we could eliminate, Edmondson insisted that it was essential. After much discussion, he realized that there was no way we could bring the cost down to a figure that Bradshaw would find acceptable. Finally, Edmondson recommended that we break the project into large chunks, each of which would be less than $50,000. That way, he explained, he could sign the invoices himself.

Obviously, we would be running the risk that Bradshaw might eventually discover what Edmondson was doing. Controllers tend to be very detail-oriented, so it was quite possible that Bradshaw would one day discover the separate line items in ClarityBase's overall budget that were associated with our project. And if he did, he would probably be furious. He might have even fired us right then and there, leaving us holding the bag for work we had done but hadn't been paid for. As it turned out, though, Bradshaw himself was fired two months later, and we were able to complete the project without incident.

What if things hadn't worked out that neatly? On our part, we weren't unduly concerned because we wouldn't be issuing a final report of the study until the project was near its completion. That report was essential for ClarityBase because it would pull together all of the data we were collecting, including a detailed analysis of that information. Without that document, all our research would be incomprehensible to ClarityBase. So, for us, the final report was a bargaining chip. We believe that Edmondson's plan, should he run into trouble with Bradshaw, was to say, "We've invested so much in the research already. We need to finish the project or everything will be wasted."

Backing anyone into a corner, especially a Controller, is extremely risky. When you're outside the organization (as we were with Clarity-Base), the safest approach is to have insiders (like Edmondson) be the ones to box the Controller in. But when you're inside the organization, the better approach is to use an external factor. For instance, you might cite deep price cuts by a competitor: "If we don't do something in response, we're likely to suffer defections among a dozen of our major accounts." Even then, Controllers usually take a wait-and-see attitude. But when the event does start to occur (for example, a key customer takes its business elsewhere), they will at least be sensitized to the news and will then move quickly.

BUILD ALLIANCES

Working with Controllers is never simple or straightforward. Because they are driven by fear, they are likely to misconstrue even the most benign situations, seeing enemies and problems where none exist. Consequently, we strongly advise our clients that when dealing with Controllers, they absolutely must have good coaching from colleagues and others who want them to succeed. With Kevin Dillon, we received excellent guidance from Tony Rusting and Dana Jacobs. For Paul Bradshaw, we benefited tremendously from Karl Edmondson's help.

Our finding those allies wasn't a matter of dumb luck. In any organization or group run by a Controller, there will usually be people who have to routinely come up with creative solutions to get their jobs done. If the Controller has implemented systems that are unnecessarily rigid, they probably know where all the loopholes are. These people can be tremendous allies, helping you to accomplish what you need to do without running afoul of the Controller. You must tap into their knowledge and follow their lead. As an example of what we mean, consider our experience with Reinartz-Katzen, a European company that manufactures industrial materials. The cofounder and owner of that firm is Gerhard Reinartz, a brilliant man who also happens to be a classic Controller.

Years ago, we received a call from John Marcus, the president of Reinartz-Katzen North America, who said that Reinartz wanted us to present a seminar at the company's annual conference in Lausanne, Switzerland. Before that, though, Marcus said that Reinartz wanted to meet us in person. Marcus then told us exactly how to play that meeting. "Let Reinartz be in charge," he said. "Let him tell you what he wants. All he's really doing is checking you out. Just don't raise any red flags with him and you'll be fine." As it turned out, that advice was excellent, and our meeting with Reinartz went without a hitch.

The seminar itself, though, was a different story. Reinartz had brought together all of his top managers and salespeople from around the world, a group of about three hundred. We had barely been introduced before Reinartz began to take over. Every time we tried to explain a concept, he would jump in, expanding on the point we wanted to make. To make matters worse, he was also twisting what we were saying to suit his own agenda. If nothing else, the situation was ironic: Reinartz had gone to considerable expense to set the seminar up, and there he was, unwittingly sabotaging it.

Finally, the group recessed for a coffee break. Marcus, our supporter and ally, came over to us, and we asked him, "What are we supposed to do here?" From his response, we knew that he had handled numerous situations like this. "Leave it to me," he reassured us. He then took Reinartz aside and diplomatically told him, "I think we could make better use of our time and resources if we let our speakers present their material, and then during the workshop you could roam around the room and personally coach people." And that's exactly what Reinartz did. It wasn't the ideal solution, but at least it was workable.

Throughout that day, we noticed how Marcus and other country presidents worked together to ensure that their respective staffs would get the most out of our presentation. For instance, when it came time for people to break into small workshop groups, they made sure that certain people (mainly those who weren't genuinely interested in learning) were isolated in one group—conveniently located for Reinartz to coach. At every step of the way, it seemed that Marcus and his colleagues knew exactly what to do. Without their help, the seminar might well have been a disaster.

With Controllers, that's often the case—you need the help of allies to get work done. We know many Controllers who regularly have knee-jerk reactions to isolated incidents. When just one employee abuses a vacation policy, for example, they respond by issuing a draconian decree that does more harm than good: "Absolutely no one, under any circumstances, is allowed to carry over a single day of vacation time from one year to the next." At those types of organizations, employees regularly help each other to deal with policies that are often illogical and unnecessarily rigid. Those people can be a valuable source of useful advice and helpful tips. In any business situation, coaching from people in the know is always important, but when you're dealing with Controllers, it is absolutely essential.

Recently, we've been working with two executives from a business unit of a large corporation. The group is in trouble: Its core market has stagnated; sales are declining; competitors have been gaining ground. The two executives—Ram Ghoshal, the chief information officer, and Lynne Sheehan, head of sales and marketing—want to explore the possibilities of entering new, related markets. For that project, we could easily conduct customer research to help them determine what their best options might be. The problem, though, is that the head of their business unit is Roger Bryant, a die-hard Controller.

Two years ago, at the annual strategy meeting of senior execs, Bryant did the bulk of the talking, and everybody pretty much sat there and listened. To get people more involved at last year's meeting, Bryant didn't attend. But at that brainstorming session, every time somebody proposed anything, another person would say, "No, Bryant won't go for that." So even though Bryant wasn't physically there, his presence was still felt by everyone, and the meeting didn't go any better than it had the previous year.

Now the business unit desperately needs fresh ideas for generating new revenues, and we have proposed to Ghoshal and Sheehan that

we could do two different surveys of their current and potential customers to determine what new markets have the greatest untapped potential value. Our meetings with them have been going well, but they can't get Bryant to budge in giving us the go-ahead. But they've come up with an interesting solution.

We have already commenced a different research project for another business unit at the same company. Ghoshal and Sheehan have worked out a deal with that group. The plan is for us to begin the research for Ghoshal and Sheehan but to piggyback it on the work for the other group. Ghoshal and Sheehan would then transfer a partial payment of $20,000 to that business unit as compensation for the pilot research. Next, they will use the resulting data to make a stronger case to Bryant for going after certain new markets. If all goes well, Bryant will review that preliminary information, which will make him understand how his market has been shifting, and he will give his approval to conduct a full-blown research project to get detailed results.

Whether everything will go according to this plan is anybody's guess. Controllers operate out of fear, so the big question is which will produce less anxiety in Bryant: the fear of doing nothing and having revenues continue to decline, or the fear of entering a new market. Two factors could tip things in Ghoshal and Sheehan's favor. First, Controllers are analytical and they are drawn to data, so the information from the pilot research will have an inherent appeal to Bryant. Second, Ghoshal and Sheehan will be careful to structure their argument in just the right way. Even though Bryant's strategy of continuing on course hasn't been effective for a couple years, Ghoshal and Sheehan won't talk about that. Instead, they will say that their core market has been undergoing a fundamental transformation that is opening up new opportunities. That way they won't appear to be criticizing Bryant's leadership, thus allowing him to save face while also encouraging him to move forward.

At first glance, Ghoshal and Sheehan's tactics might appear to be manipulative. In one sense, they are because they do help skillfully manage a difficult situation. But in a different sense, they are not manipulative in that they are neither unscrupulous nor unfair. On our part, we would greatly prefer working on this project in a more straightforward fashion. But, at the same time, we agree with the pragmatism of Ghoshal and Sheehan. Of course, people would prefer going from

A to B on a straight path, but that's not always possible when dealing with Controllers. Often you'll need to take a circuitous route that in the end will get you there faster and with fewer headaches.

DRAW YOUR LINE AND HOLD TO IT

Occasionally, even circuitous routes won't work. The Controller might be intractable, and you could lack the necessary time to work through his lieutenants. When that happens, you need to know exactly where your bottom line is, and you must steadfastly hold to it. Controllers often try to push things whenever they can. In doing so, they can be very persistent and forceful in eroding your position. To avoid that, you must always have a clear idea of exactly what is nego-tiable—and what isn't.

Remember Tim Wainwright, the senior executive that we had so much trouble with? Actually, that project almost never happened. Ini-tially, we had declined to submit a bid for the work because we had already been having so much difficulty with Wainwright. He was always questioning us: our methodology, our expertise, our motives. That attitude was going to make the project impossible, so we decided against applying for the work. To inform the company, we wrote to Charles Morrison, the CEO, who had originally requested that we be involved. Our letter was very diplomatic, essentially saying, "This is an interesting project, but we don't think that we're a good fit, so we're withdrawing our bid."

Soon after receiving our letter, Morrison called. "What's going on here?" he asked. "You're a perfect fit. You're just what we need." We tried to dance around the issue, but Morrison was insistent on knowing exactly what had happened. Finally, we admitted that Wain-wright was a factor. In so many words, we told Morrison that although the research sounded very interesting, it probably would do none of us any good if we took on the project unless people there were going to be on board with us.

"Don't worry about Wainwright," Morrison told us. "I'll take care of things." And that's what must have happened, because the project proceeded smoothly, with Wainwright being very agreeable and responsive to working with us. But then, when we were negotiating a new contract to continue the project, we ran into trouble, with Wainwright aggressively questioning everything about our proposal even though it had already been approved by Morrison. Eventually, we were able to resolve things with Wainwright, but had we reached an impasse, we might have considered withdrawing from the project again. In our minds, we knew exactly what our agreement with Morrison was—in fact, we had a written document to support us—and we weren't going to let Wainwright change things in midstream.

That experience brings up a crucial lesson. When dealing with Controllers, get anything important in writing. We were fortunate that we had a document, approved by Wainwright's boss, that spelled everything out. That way we could be firm with him when he tried to alter the rules of the game. Be forewarned that Controllers can complicate even simple decisions. To prevent that, a paper trail of memos, letters, contracts, and other documents can help tremendously. Without such support, concluding your negotiations with Controllers might be frustratingly elusive, like trying to grab a slippery bar of soap.

Another important lesson is that although we had the support of Wainwright's boss, we never pushed that fact. Because Controllers rarely capitulate unless they are completely boxed in, the temptation is to get to them by using their bosses as leverage. But we strongly advise against pulling rank on anyone, especially Controllers. Besides being a questionable business practice, that tactic will likely backfire. The Controller will never ever forget what you did. Even twenty years later, at a different company in a different industry, it could come back to haunt you. Nobody likes having someone do an end run to the boss, and this is especially true for Controllers. As discussed in the previous chapter, Controllers operate primarily out of fear and they tend to be rebellious, so using anyone who has authority over them will always be, at best, dicey. Sometimes even the slightest perception of this happening will set the Controller off. We learned that lesson the hard way with Kevin Dillon, the divisional head whom we talked about previously.

In our early dealings with him, when we were first discussing the kind of research we could do for him, we mentioned that Brian Tucker, his boss, had told us that the company might be able to fund some of our work with $175,000 from the corporate overhead budget. That was a mistake. Dillon flew off the handle, becoming both defensive and defiant. In no uncertain terms, he told us, "Brian Tucker doesn't really have anything to do with what we do in this division. This is my decision, not his." At that point, our conversation with Dillon was effectively over, and we were fortunate that Tony Rusting and Dana Jacobs, his two lieutenants, were there to keep the ball from dropping.

Later we would learn from them that Dillon had thought we were out of line for supposedly threatening to go over his head. We were stunned. We had used Tucker's name merely to make a suggestion that we thought might be helpful, but Dillon didn't take it that way. This, unfortunately, is typical of the behavior of many Controllers. Because they operate out of fear, they often misconstrue things in the worst way. They misread a neutral or even friendly situation and respond as if it were hostile. With Controllers, you can almost never be too careful. *Assume they will take things out of context,* so be sure to minimize the ways in which they might misinterpret anything that you say or do. The sad thing is that their misinterpretation often becomes a self-fulfilling prophecy, turning potential allies into enemies.

In a real sense, Dillon was behaving like a snarling, cornered animal. In such situations, the last thing you should do is become emotional, which will only make matters worse. Instead, you have to maintain your calm as you reassure the Controller of your intentions. With Dillon, we didn't return his aggression, which would have only escalated his fears. We simply let the matter drop, thinking we would later let someone else, perhaps Rusting or Jacobs, explain to him what we were trying to suggest.

KNOWING WHAT TO DO—AND WHEN TO DO IT

By their very nature, Controllers are extremely difficult to influence. In fact, you can't really persuade them; you can only enable them to persuade themselves. They need to make decisions in their own way—often through much self-absorption—and they need to do so on their own schedules, regardless of your or others' deadlines. Any attempt to rush them will usually be counterproductive, so your best strategy is to be patient until the Controller is ready to act.

In actuality, Controllers make their moves only when there's a strong trigger event, such as the defection of key customers. Otherwise, they are bound to keep asking for one more piece of data after another. In such situations, you should respond to the requests without getting frustrated. Your goal is simply to make the Controller aware of the trigger event so that when it does occur, he will move swiftly to respond.

The exhibit "The Controller Plan" provides a summary of what you should do before, during, and after your meetings with Controllers. Note that dealing with Controllers is often a counterintuitive process. For instance, often the best meeting is no meeting at all. The better approach is to have others, particularly those whom the Controller trusts, work behind the scenes to build your case for you. If that succeeds, the Controller will eventually call the meeting himself to

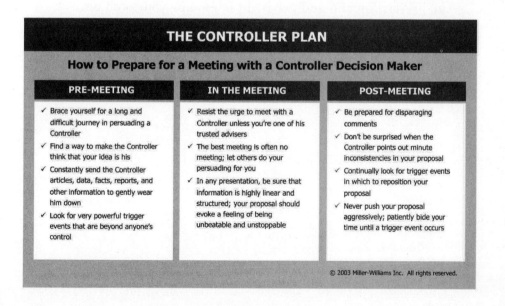

THE CONTROLLER PLAN

How to Prepare for a Meeting with a Controller Decision Maker

PRE-MEETING	IN THE MEETING	POST-MEETING
✓ Brace yourself for a long and difficult journey in persuading a Controller	✓ Resist the urge to meet with a Controller unless you're one of his trusted advisers	✓ Be prepared for disparaging comments
✓ Find a way to make the Controller think that your idea is his	✓ The best meeting is often no meeting; let others do your persuading for you	✓ Don't be surprised when the Controller points out minute inconsistencies in your proposal
✓ Constantly send the Controller articles, data, facts, reports, and other information to gently wear him down	✓ In any presentation, be sure that information is highly linear and structured; your proposal should evoke a feeling of being unbeatable and unstoppable	✓ Continually look for trigger events in which to reposition your proposal
✓ Look for very powerful trigger events that are beyond anyone's control		✓ Never push your proposal aggressively; patiently bide your time until a trigger event occurs

discuss your proposal. Remember that Controllers often need to be in charge of all aspects of the decision-making process.

To summarize, although you can't really persuade Controllers, you can greatly increase your chances of success with them if you

- Let it happen; don't try to *make* it happen. You need to provide Controllers with all the information they need to make their decision, and then you have to back off, allowing them to come to their own conclusions, using their own analyses and in their own time.
- Avoid run-ins with Controllers by working mainly through their lieutenants. Such arrangements allow Controllers to feel less compelled to exert their authority over your proposal.
- Get coaching from people who are adept at getting their jobs done within the Controller's system. These people are invaluable sources of useful advice and helpful tips. Without them, you could easily fail.
- Always have a clear idea of exactly what you need as well as what you can compromise. Stand firm in holding that line; Controllers can be very forceful and persistent in eroding your position.

PART 3

THE PRAGMATICS
OF PERSUASION

PART 3

THE PRAGMATICS
OF PERSUASION

Chapter 13

How to Read People

Before you begin to influence others, you need to categorize them accurately. Otherwise, the best persuasive skills in the world could easily backfire, particularly if you misidentify a Charismatic as a Controller, or a Skeptic as a Follower. To avoid such costly mistakes, you need to

1. **Heed actions.** Pay particular attention to how people handle complex decisions with serious consequences. For instance, how much input do they need from others?
2. **Use the process of elimination.** For anyone who is difficult to identify, narrow the choices by first eliminating any categories that obviously don't apply. Then continue to observe that person's behavior to rule out additional possibilities.
3. **Focus on *risk* and *responsibility*.** The surest way to classify people is by looking at how they handle both risk and responsibility when making important decisions. Those two quantities are diagrammed in the *behavioral dial*, a simple but powerful tool for categorizing others.

HEED ACTIONS

To classify people's decision styles, you need to look at how they make *big* decisions. By that we mean important choices with serious consequences. Executives are busy people, and they regularly make dozens of decisions on a daily basis. Most of those, though, are relatively minor ones, and many might even be considered to be slam dunks. Just because an executive makes those types of decisions on the fly does not necessarily mean that she's a Charismatic or Skeptic who loves risk. When categorizing people, you need to look at how they make big decisions, particularly complicated, messy ones that have no easy answers. Examples include the acquisition of a company, the hiring or promoting of someone to a key position, the closing of a division, a reorganization, the substantial investment in a new technology. How people handle those types of actions provides valuable insight into their decision-making styles.

In the previous chapter, we talked about Kevin Dillon, who heads a major division of a Fortune 500 corporation. Dillon has a dynamic, energetic personality. Several years ago, when he was promoted to his current position, we met him along with several of his senior execs. At the time, he seemed enthusiastic and enthralled with new ideas, especially when we talked about a research methodology that we had just developed for profiling customers more accurately. Back then, we hadn't yet conducted our extensive survey of executives—research that is the basis of this book—but had we known about the five categories of decision makers, we most likely would have classified Dillon as a Charismatic.

But our talks with him didn't go anywhere, and we ended up working instead with another division of that company. This was an early sign that Dillon wasn't a Charismatic; if he had been, he would have wanted to be first to use our new methodology. (As it turned out, the head of the other division *is* a classic Charismatic decision maker, who is always pushing us for our latest ideas.) We couldn't be sure about Dillon, though, for several reasons. His marketing vice president seemed to resist our methodology, perhaps because of a "not invented here" reluctance to try anything from the outside, and we thought that maybe that person had stalled the project. In addition,

Dillon's division had acquired several other companies and gone through a major reorganization, so we thought he might not have wanted to take on another project just yet. Lastly, because we ourselves had become very busy with other clients, we never aggressively followed up with Dillon to give him a detailed proposal of the research we could do for him. As we now know, Charismatics need such an implementation document before they proceed with any major project.

So there were various plausible reasons why Dillon didn't pursue any work with us even though his early enthusiasm had indicated otherwise. Only later did we discover the true reason: He's not a Charismatic, but a Controller. That's why, several years later, when we were having serious discussions about finally proceeding with the research, he balked. When he had to put some money where his mouth was, he wouldn't proceed. Controllers greatly avoid risk, and he wasn't going to fund anything that he couldn't control and that he wasn't absolutely sure was going to work. By paying close attention to Dillon's actions over a period of time, we were eventually able to classify his decision style accurately.

We should note that by advising you to look closely at people's actions, we are not talking about their body language. A widespread notion in pop psychology is that people's body language is a gateway to their thinking. Some of that research has merit—when someone is jutting his jaw and puffing his chest, he is likely reacting aggressively to you—but much of it is dubious. We are not convinced, for example, that just because a person has folded his arms across his chest and crossed his legs that he is highly doubtful of what he's hearing.

Another important point of our story about Dillon is that categorizing someone's decision-making style is a complicated process. You might have a working hypothesis, and even when there's evidence to contradict it, you sometimes won't be sure exactly whether that information is directly related. So you hold on to a faulty assumption. But that's par for the course. The important thing is that you constantly test your assumptions, and you have to be ready to revise them when you do have solid proof that they're wrong.

Incidentally, classifying Dillon was made more difficult because we weren't getting a clear read from two executives who reported directly to him. One of them thought he was a Charismatic (which confirmed our earlier mistaken assumption), and the other thought he was a Follower. But when we highlighted the various characteristics of Controllers at a seminar we gave for the company, both executives immediately had an "aha" moment, and during a break they told us they finally figured out that Dillon is a Controller. This, by the way, often happens. You might struggle trying to categorize someone, but when you finally figure it out, all the pieces fall into place. At that point, everything will seem so obvious that you'll wonder why you took so long to put it all together.

As we discussed in chapter 2 ("How Does Persuasion Work?"), everyone has elements of each of the five styles, and often people can have two (or more) prevailing styles. For example, someone might be roughly 60 percent Thinker and 40 percent Charismatic. In such situations, you want to focus on the dominant style because it tends to drive the decision-making process. That's the person's default mode, which he will use particularly in high-pressure situations in which he needs to make crucial decisions. Once in a while, a client of ours insists that someone is split down the middle, 50 percent Follower and 50 percent Controller, say. But our research shows that everyone has a dominant default style, and when push comes to shove, they use it. Incidentally, a common reason for someone appearing to have two styles is that his decision making differs from his personality (for example, he's a Follower who micromanages others, making him appear to be a Controller). In such cases, you obviously have to focus on the person's decision style and not his personality.

That's not to say that people always use their default style. Indeed, much of decision making is situational: People sometimes use a different decision-making style in a different environment. For example, at work a person could be a Follower, but at home she could be more of a Thinker, mainly to balance her husband, who is a Charismatic. In other words, people can adapt their styles to complement that of their bosses, colleagues, spouses, and friends. We have noticed ourselves often doing that. One of us (Bob) is a Charismatic, and the other (Gary) is a Thinker. We believe we generally make good decisions together and that our business partnership works because we balance each other's natural style.

When one of us isn't around and the other has to make a quick, important decision, he tries to emulate the other's style to ensure that nothing is overlooked. For example, when Gary isn't around, Bob forces himself to go through the whole Thinker methodology, looking at all the pros and cons of a decision. He can double-check to ensure that he's asked the opinions of everyone involved to obtain as balanced a view as possible. And then he can make a decision. If people were to observe Bob in such situations, they might easily categorize him as a Thinker. The lesson here is that when you're classifying someone, you need to look at how that person makes decisions in the environment you're interested in. Otherwise, you might easily make mistakes.

If people can adapt their decision-making styles, can they also change their default mode? We have not done specific research to address that question, but our belief is that the answer is yes. We believe, however, that the process would be slow and evolutionary. As we mentioned in chapter 2, people develop their default style over years, and if they're successful, they stick with it. If, on the other hand, they've repeatedly made bad decisions that have hurt their careers, those mistakes could lead to their making subtle changes in their thinking processes to avoid further setbacks, and over the years their default mode could evolve from one style to another.

USE THE PROCESS OF ELIMINATION

Often you'll meet a person who is obviously and undoubtedly one of the five categories. The executives we've talked about in the previous chapters are examples of such people. Fed chairman Alan Greenspan, for instance, is undeniably a Thinker. There is simply no question about that. He makes decisions in a methodical, balanced way, and he fits all of the characteristics of a Thinker.

Generally speaking, with the exception of Followers, the other categories tend to show themselves definitively. Skeptics, for instance, often even announce themselves that way. When you're dealing with them, you frequently know it because they will tell you so. They'll say things like, "You're really going to have to convince me on this" or "I'm really doubtful about your proposal" or "I'm going to play devil's advocate here."

In many cases, though, things aren't so cut-and-dried. For such situations, we recommend a process of elimination, and the following acid tests can help you to narrow the possibilities quickly:

1. Is he always looking for the next big idea, and does he want information in headlines and bulleted items? If the answer is no, he's not a Charismatic.
2. Is she process-oriented and balanced, always weighing the pros and cons of a decision? If the answer is no, she's not a Thinker.
3. Is he suspicious of every piece of data, and does he sometimes make snap judgments? If the answer is no, he's not a Skeptic.
4. Does he need to be in charge of the decision-making process, with everything funneling through him (which often makes him the bottleneck), and does he tend to blame others for his mistakes? If the answer is no, he's not a Controller.
5. Does she move forward *only* with solutions that have worked before, in some variation or another? If the answer is no, she's not a Follower.

Note that the acid test for Followers is saved for last. This was done on purpose. Generally speaking, if you can rule out the other categories, the person you are dealing with is a Follower. As discussed in chapter 10 ("Persuading the Follower Decision Maker"), assuming someone is a Follower unless proven otherwise is an effective strategy for several reasons. First, Followers are the largest group (accounting for more than one out of three executives), so if you had to guess, your best odds would be to assume that a person is a Follower. Second, the other four styles tend to show themselves more definitively, whereas Followers tend to be chameleon-like. Especially if you're getting mixed signals from someone, assume he's a Follower. Third, you can't really go wrong by persuading someone as if he's a Follower because all executives (including Charismatics, Thinkers, Skeptics, and Controllers) are swayed positively by proof that something has worked successfully before.

In addition to the acid tests, the following criteria can be helpful in ruling out certain categories:

- If he truly needs other people's opinions before making a move, he's not a Controller.
- If she has trouble understanding the perspectives of others, she's not a Follower.
- If she is prone to "analysis paralysis," she's probably not a Charismatic or Skeptic.
- If he can make an important, complex decision on the spot, he's likely not a Thinker or Controller.
- If his knee-jerk reaction is to say no to everything until convinced otherwise, he's not a Charismatic and probably not a Thinker.
- If he doesn't have strong opinions, he's likely not a Skeptic or Controller.
- If she's far more concerned with costs than with features and benefits, she's not a Charismatic.
- If you can *never* get him to change his mind, he's probably a Controller.

FOCUS ON RISK AND RESPONSIBILITY

After using the process of elimination, you might find that you're down to two possibilities. Our clients frequently make comments along the lines of "He's either a Controller or a Skeptic" or "I think she's a Thinker, but she might be a Follower" or "He's a Charismatic, but he's also got strong elements of being a Thinker." Even after much additional deliberation, they find that they can't make the final determination between their two categories. In such cases, the *behavioral dial* can be a very effective tool.

The dial consists of two concentric circles, with the outer circle divided into quadrants (see the exhibit "The Behavioral Dial"). Thinkers are represented by the inner circle because they are the most balanced of the decision-making styles. Of the twelve components discussed in chapter 2, the strongest for Thinkers are that they

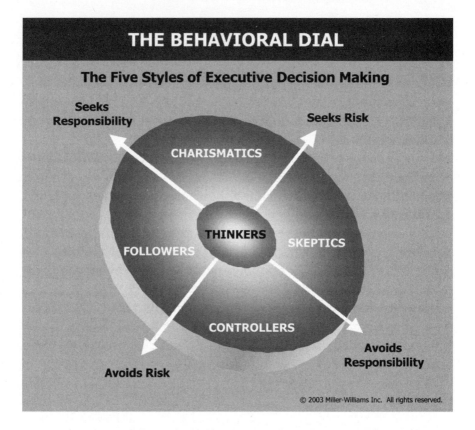

seek competitiveness and bargains and they avoid risk. These preferences, however, are relatively mild when compared to the likes and
dislikes of the other four categories of decision makers.

Charismatics and Controllers are in opposite quadrants because
they do not share any of their strongest desires. In fact, many of their
preferences are contrary. Charismatics seek responsibility, persistence
in others, risk, education, competitiveness, and intelligence and facts,
which are all things that Controllers avoid. On the other hand, Controllers operate out of fear, self-absorption, and impulsiveness, which
Charismatics shun. Followers and Skeptics are in opposite quadrants
for a similar reason: Those two groups have no strong desires in
common.

Of the twelve components, the two that elicit the strongest reactions among all four non-Thinker styles are the desire for (or avoidance of) risk and the desire for (or avoidance of) responsibility.
Specifically, Charismatics and Skeptics seek risk; Controllers and Fol-

lowers avoid it. Furthermore, Charismatics and Followers desire
responsibility; Skeptics and Controllers shun it. Thus, the behavioral
dial has two axes, one for risk and the other for responsibility, that
divide the outer circle into quadrants.

The dial can be a useful tool for categorizing someone, particularly
if that person has any strong reactions to either risk or responsibility.
(If the person doesn't, he might well be a Thinker.) To aid you in
using the dial, several subtle distinctions are in order. Both Charismatics and Followers seek responsibility, but they do so in different
ways, and the difference is related to how they view risk. Charismatics
seek the risk of trying out big new ideas, and in doing so they want
both the authority for making those decisions and the accountability
for making them. That is, they step up to the plate and are willing to
take full responsibility for their decisions, even when the fault lies
elsewhere.

Followers, on the other hand, are somewhat neutral to risk in general, but they are very averse to trying out anything that hasn't been
successful in the past. This is why they always gravitate toward proven
solutions. When something goes wrong, Followers don't necessarily
blame others, but they might use the excuse of "Well, the solution
worked before, so my decision was justifiable." In other words, Followers want the authority to make big decisions and they do want to
be held accountable for them, but they are not necessarily quick to
accept the fault for mistakes. This is why they usually take the safe
route of doing only what has succeeded in the past. In contrast, Skeptics and Controllers are completely averse to responsibility, and that's
why they are quick to point the finger at others when something goes
wrong.

Both Followers and Controllers are averse to risk, but here again
there's a difference. Followers avoid the risk of anything unproven,
whereas Controllers have a more general aversion. They fear any
decision with factors that are outside their control. Moreover, they are
very afraid of being wrong, and sometimes that fear can paralyze
them. On the other hand, Charismatics and Skeptics both seek risk,
but again they do so for different reasons. Charismatics seek the risk
of trying out big new ideas, whereas Skeptics like to live on the edge
by bucking the conventional wisdom, which relates back to their
desire to be rebellious. Furthermore, Skeptics like making big deci-

sions because they want the payoff if they're right but they do not want the responsibility for their actions (contrast that with Charismatics). In fact, very rarely will Skeptics admit when they are wrong.

The behavioral dial is a simple but powerful tool that can help you reduce the complex process of decision making into two main components: risk and responsibility. Those two quantities are perhaps the two most important characteristics of decision making. In fact, they are in many ways related to the other ten attributes that we described in chapter 2, such as a person's desire for (or avoidance of) self-absorption, rebellion, bargains, competitiveness, and so on. For example, Skeptics tend to be rebellious when making big decisions because they seek risk. Followers, on the other hand, have no desire for rebellion because they don't want to assume the risk of moving beyond the status quo.

As mentioned earlier, the behavioral dial can be particularly useful in resolving situations in which you've narrowed someone down to two categories. In the previous chapter, we talked about how Kevin Dillon took offense with us when we merely mentioned to him that his boss, the company's president, might be able to help him by giving him funds from the corporate overhead budget. "This is my decision, not his," Dillon brusquely told us, making it abundantly clear that he wasn't going to let anyone, even his boss, tell him what to do. That extreme reaction—Dillon was perfectly willing to cut off his nose to spite his face—made us think that he was either a Skeptic or a Controller, because those two types of executives tend to be rebellious in making important decisions. But then we thought about how risk-averse Dillon was. Throughout his career, he was never a "big ideas" guy, and he had always found ways to avoid both the risks and the responsibilities of major decisions. That was how he had climbed the corporate ladder. His aversion to taking risks made us realize that Dillon was a Controller and not a Skeptic, because although Skeptics avoid the responsibility of big decisions, they thrive on the risk.

We recently had another instance in which the behavioral dial helped us to resolve someone's decision style. We've been working with a large services corporation headquartered on the West Coast. Our main contact for the project is Jill Maccoby, a marketing manager for the company. We hadn't been sure about Maccoby's decision-making style because she exhibits traits of Followers and Controllers, both of whom are averse to risk, something that she definitely is. Throughout the project, we've been issuing regular reports to update people on our research results. The documents, which have included Maccoby's name, have been going to key executives at the company. Even though the results have thus far been impressive, Maccoby has told us that she either wants her name removed from the reports or wants us to include other people's names. When we told her that we included her name because she has been spearheading the study, guiding us at various points along the way, she nevertheless adamantly insisted that we not attribute anything to her unless we also cite others who are more tangentially involved. "If this project doesn't work out," she told us, "I'm not getting fired over it." That strong avoidance of responsibility—her not wanting to leave her fingerprints on anything that could be used against her—made us decide that she's a Controller and not a Follower, because the latter would be much more willing to be held accountable.

The behavioral dial can also help you to understand certain interpersonal dynamics. In our experience, we have known many Charismatics who have butted heads with Controllers, and the behavioral dial explains why. Those two groups mix like oil and water because they have little in common. The same can be said of Followers and Skeptics, who also tend to rub each other the wrong way.

Not surprisingly, Charismatics are rarely miscategorized as Controllers (and vice versa). And neither are Followers often misidentified as Skeptics (and vice versa). When you've used the process of elimination to categorize someone, you won't usually be left with the two possibilities being Charismatic versus Controller, or Follower versus Skeptic. Instead, the more common confusion comes between categories that are adjacent to each other on the behavioral dial, such as between Controllers and Skeptics (as was the case with Dillon) or Followers and Controllers (as was the case with Maccoby).

Lastly, the behavioral dial can alert you to when you need to be extra careful in persuading someone. Unless you're a Thinker, you need to be particularly aware when you're trying to influence a person who is opposite you on the behavioral dial. For instance, Skeptics must be wary when working with Followers. In such situations, you have to be especially vigilant to shed yourself of your own perspective and tailor your presentation to the other person because any argu-

ments that you might find persuasive could easily have the opposite
effect on that individual.

Categorizing people's decision-making styles takes considerable
effort and time. For months, you might have thought that someone
was a Thinker, and then something happens and you realize you're
wrong. So you change the categorization and watch for evidence that
either confirms or disproves your revised assumption. Eventually, by
continually testing your assumptions and revising them when necessary, you can identify people accurately. The important point is that
you need to keep an open mind; otherwise, you're bound to make
mistakes. We initially thought Kevin Dillon was a Charismatic, and
only years later, when we were actually working with him, did we
identify him as a Controller.

At the time, when we were still trying to figure him out, we continually discussed his behavior with each other. We can't emphasize
enough the importance of comparing notes. Particularly when we
have a disagreement about a particular person (whether she's a
Thinker or Controller, for example), we talk with each other and go
through our reasoning. Often, through that discussion, we reach an
"aha" moment when the person's behavior and actions all seem to
make sense. Frequently, one of us convinces the other, or we both go
through the process of elimination as we figure that person out. For
fun, we've even analyzed fictional characters. One of our favorite
movies is A *Few Good Men*, starring Tom Cruise and Jack Nicholson,
and we've had lively arguments about Cruise's character in that film.
(The character played by Nicholson is obviously a Controller. In the
climactic courtroom scene, the only way that Cruise's character can
get Nicholson's character to capitulate is to completely back him into
a corner, forcing him to contradict himself.) Such discussions can be
instructive, helping you to hone your skills. As the saying goes, practice makes perfect.

Our categorizations of the 1,684 executives in our study were based
on a test that initially had 240 questions for probing people's decision-
making processes. Through a careful analysis, we were able to reduce
the survey to fifteen key questions for capturing the essential behaviors of people, such as their tendency to be impulsive when making

important decisions and their propensity to be self-absorbed. More recently, we've distilled our test to six questions for quicker categorizations. To arrive at those questions, we conducted an extensive statistical analysis, and although this short test isn't as accurate as our more detailed survey, it does provide a simple but powerful way to classify others.

The test, available through our Web site at the URL www.mill-will.com/persuade.html, assesses people's behavior in making important decisions with respect to their being

1. Playful or serious
2. Calm or worrying
3. Suspicious or trusting
4. Self-disciplined or weak-willed
5. Straightforward or imaginative
6. Disorganized or organized

We invite you to test our Web site for yourself, perhaps by trying to classify the decision-making styles of your boss or colleagues. For each of the six characteristics, you rate someone on a seven-point scale. For the first question, for instance, a person can be rated as extremely playful, moderately playful, somewhat playful, neither playful nor serious, somewhat serious, moderately serious, or extremely serious. The answers are then mapped onto the twelve components (for example, a person's tendency to seek or avoid risk) that we discussed in chapter 2. In fact, all of those twelve attributes are blends of the answers from two to four of the six questions. To determine the twelve components for a particular individual, algorithms perform the calculations by assigning various weights to the different answers, depending on what those values are.

Although the computations are complicated and beyond the scope of this book, our Web site can perform the necessary number analysis. All you need to do is enter data for a particular person—your boss or even your spouse, for instance—and our Web server does the number crunching for categorizing that individual. We should note, however, that our Web site provides initial assessments. It does not give any easy, definitive answers. Instead, the preliminary categorizations provide good working hypotheses that you can then test.

• • •

In summary, classifying people requires the hard work of observing them over a significant amount of time. To avoid mistakes, you should remember to:

• Note people's actions, especially when they make important, complicated decisions with serious consequences. How people handle such situations provides valuable insight into their decision styles.
• Rule out the obvious. Often it's easier to determine what people are not, rather than what they are. Use the process of elimination to narrow the possibilities.
• Focus on risk and responsibility. The behavioral dial, which categorizes people by the amount of risk and responsibility they're willing to assume when making big decisions, can help you make the final determination, especially in cases in which you've narrowed someone down to two categories.

Chapter 14

Common Mistakes

Classifying someone's decision-making style is a complicated undertaking that takes considerable time and effort. Be forewarned that the process is fraught with potential pitfalls. Specifically, we have found that people often confuse

1. **Words versus actions.** When it comes to decision making, actions do indeed speak louder than words. Don't be seduced by what someone says. Instead, pay attention to that person's actions.
2. **Personality versus decision-making style.** People's personalities can be dramatically different than the way they make decisions. Don't confuse the two.
3. **A specific instance versus general behavior.** Never base your classification of someone's decision style on just one case, especially if that example is currently playing itself out.
4. **Skeptics versus Controllers.** Skeptics and Controllers share many characteristics, but they make decisions in very different ways.
5. **Thinkers versus Controllers.** Although Thinkers and Controllers both need copious data from market analyses, reports, and other materials, they do not use such information in the same way.

6. Followers versus everybody else. Followers often appear to be something else, mainly because that's the way they tend to project themselves.

WORDS VERSUS ACTIONS

David Faber, financial reporter for CNBC, is a well-respected, tough journalist. He has little patience with CEOs and other corporate execs who don't deliver results, and he doesn't sugarcoat his views. He simply calls things like he sees them, and he can be brutally honest and unsparing. Even so, he is the first to concede that he's occasionally been duped by smooth-talking execs.

He admits, for instance, that he was taken for a ride by Rich McGinn, then CEO of Lucent Technologies. At the time, Lucent had just missed its quarterly earnings estimate, and there were rumblings that the company might be headed for trouble. But McGinn talked a good game. "He took personal responsibility for Lucent's revenue shortfall, identified the division that had caused it, and promised to hold accountable managers whose targets hadn't been met," recalls Faber. "But McGinn faked me—and a couple of million investors—out . . . McGinn and the rest of his management team . . . had flooded the product channel, cutting prices and piling orders on customers . . . That mind-set led to aggressive accounting and questionable sales."[1] Later, as Lucent's troubles became public, the company's market value plummeted by more than $200 billion.

The lesson, according to Faber, is that CEOs and other top execs are so well coached, smooth, and polished nowadays that you can't really trust what they're saying. Instead, asserts Faber, you have to look at their actions. Do they, for instance, put their money where their mouths are, retaining significant stock ownership, well beyond the standard options? Or are they selling off their holdings, even as they tout a rosy future for the company?

Similarly, we believe that the best way to classify executives is to focus not necessarily on what they say or the amount of time they spend talking about something. Instead, look at their actions. Look at how and when they commit their resources (dollars, time, and people). This helps you to read their decision-making style. As the sayings go, talk is cheap, and actions do indeed speak louder than words. It's all too easy, though, to be seduced into believing what someone says, especially when that person is a forceful, dynamic speaker. As discussed in chapter 9 ("The Follower Decision Maker"), many people have been fooled into thinking that Carly Fiorina, the CEO of Hewlett-Packard, is a bold risk taker who loves big, new ideas. In actuality, her decision making consistently indicates that she is much more of a Follower than a Charismatic.

PERSONALITY VERSUS DECISION-MAKING STYLE

The example of Carly Fiorina raises another important point. In addition to confusing words and actions, people often make the mistake of mixing up personality with decision-making style. The confusion is understandable because there is a correlation between the two, but it's not absolute, and, more important, it does not run in both directions. That is, for example, Skeptics do tend to have a suspicious nature, but not every doubting Thomas is a Skeptic decision maker.

In our experience, we have found that the most common errors occur with Charismatics and Controllers. Charismatics do tend to have charismatic personalities. Richard Branson, for instance, is a Charismatic decision maker who also happens to have a very dynamic, charming personality. But people with charisma are not necessarily Charismatic decision makers. Case in point: Larry Ellison, who has an energetic, engaging, and magnetic personality. But when it comes to making decisions, he is most definitely a Skeptic. Similarly, many Controller decision makers might easily be labeled as micromanagers. Martha Stewart, for instance, is well known for her eagle-eyed attention to detail. But not all micromanagers are Controller decision makers. Tom Siebel, the CEO of the software giant Siebel Systems, for example, might have intimate knowledge of all the operational details of his company, but he makes his important decisions like a Skeptic and not a Controller.

We ourselves have learned never to underestimate the power of someone's personality to overshadow that individual's decision style. A former colleague of ours, whom we've known for years, has always loved new ideas. But he doesn't want to think much beyond the big concept, and his usual mode of operation is to throw out numerous suggestions and then head on to something else, a process that has been described as swooping down from a helicopter, dropping a bunch of eggs, most of which get smashed, and then flying off. This former colleague also has a vibrant, energetic, charming personality, which only seemed to confirm that he's a Charismatic decision maker.

Recently, though, we've come to realize that he can't be a Charismatic because he's a blamer. Nothing is ever his fault, and this extreme avoidance of responsibility has made us realize he's either a Controller or a Skeptic. Going back to the behavioral dial that we discussed in the previous chapter, we have thus figured out that he must be a Skeptic because he does indeed take risks. Moreover, others can get him to change his mind, albeit with considerable effort. (Controllers tend to adamantly hold on to their views, even when they're wrong.) Our former colleague's personality probably helped to fool us into thinking that he's a Charismatic even though there was evidence to the contrary. If his personality had been different, we probably would have been able to figure him out much sooner. The lesson is this: Not everyone's personality is going to match their decision-making style. By assuming that it will, you could easily misclassify someone and, worse, you could continue to hold on to that mistake even after there's conclusive proof to the contrary.

A SPECIFIC INSTANCE VERSUS GENERAL BEHAVIOR

As discussed in the previous chapter, classifying someone's decision style is a complicated, iterative process. Many people, however, make the mistake of trying to identify someone based on just one case. Making any generalization based on only one data point is never a great idea, and that's particularly so when trying to assess how someone makes decisions.

Myriad extenuating circumstances can easily affect people's behavior. Maybe a particular decision wasn't that important, so they made it quickly without going through their usual process. Or they might have been forced into quick action by some factor that is unknown to you. Or maybe their boss made the decision for them and they just implemented it. Or they might have adapted their style to a particular situation that demanded them to—for example, their business partner was on vacation, so they assumed his decision style to ensure that they didn't overlook anything. The list of possibilities goes on.

Because of such factors, you need to look at a number of important decisions that the person has made. By doing so, you can find *patterns* of behavior, similar to a police detective determining a suspect's MO, or mode of operation. You might not always have the number of data points that you'd like. The absolute bare minimum is two, because then at least you'll be alerted to any apparent inconsistencies, which would signal that you need additional information. Even after you think you've classified someone's decision style accurately, you should observe that person's future decision making to continually check that you haven't made a mistake.

All this takes considerable time and effort, but you can cover a lot of ground by asking others for advice. Especially if you're outside the organization, you need to get good coaching from people who work with the person whose decision style you're trying to classify. Ideally, you want to get various perspectives, including those of the person's boss, colleagues, and staff. Asking those people certain questions can help you to get the additional data points you need. Does she usually need a lot of time, or can she make an important decision on the spot? Does she seek out the opinions of others? Does she need to understand for herself every step in a proposal? The answers to such questions will greatly illuminate that person's behavior and tendencies.

One of the worst things you can do is to classify someone's decision style based on a single data point, *especially* if that instance is a situation that is currently unfolding. A person's behavior for a decision that has not yet been made can be dangerously misleading because you are bound to misinterpret certain clues and tendencies. We have seen too many people make costly mistakes when they've tried to take the shortcut of classifying someone's decision style on the fly. From those experiences, we have come to believe that you can't really understand how someone has made a decision until after he's made it. Only then can you conduct a postmortem that will provide useful insight into that person's decision style. It's analogous to what many financial experts say about the stock market: You can never identify a market bubble when it's happening. You can tell only after the fact.

What is particularly difficult about identifying a person's decision style is that all of the five categories share various characteristics with each other. In our experience, we have found that there are three big sources of confusion: distinguishing between Skeptics and Controllers; Thinkers and Controllers; and Followers and everyone else.

SKEPTICS VERSUS CONTROLLERS

Skeptics and Controllers are easily mistaken for each other, and it's no wonder why. Both tend to have strong personalities. Both are opinionated, headstrong, and occasionally even arrogant. And both avoid responsibility, quickly blaming others when things go wrong. From outward appearances, Skeptics and Controllers look very much alike. Beneath the surface, though, they differ in fundamental ways.

The primary distinction between Skeptics and Controllers is this: The motivations that drive their behavior are totally opposite. Skeptics are fearless decision makers. They are supremely confident that they always make the right choices. In sharp contrast, Controllers are driven by fear. They constantly worry that the decision they are about to make could be wrong. This is why, as shown on the behavioral dial discussed in the previous chapter, Skeptics are risk seekers, whereas Controllers are not, and that difference plays out in a number of ways.

Skeptics sometimes make important decisions right on the spot. Once they understand the issues involved, they can be very quick to pull the trigger. You might not like their decision, especially when it runs counter to what you've recommended, but at least you'll quickly know where you stand. And Skeptics won't hesitate to tell you exactly why they've rejected something that you've proposed.

Controllers, on the other hand, must have considerable time to make a decision. Often they make a decision only when they absolutely have to. In fact, their fear can be so overwhelming that they might do anything to avoid having to make a decision. But they would never admit that. Instead, they delay the process by repeatedly saying things like, "Tell me a little more about your proposal" or "Just get me this piece of information and I'll decide" or "Let me think about it." Then, weeks or even months later, they might say, "Well, I'd really like to see more data about . . ." With Controllers, you might never know exactly where your proposal stands.

Another key difference is that Skeptics do eventually want to select the best option. They truly do want to make the right decision, even if it means they'll have to change their minds. But they can be fiercely resistant to doing so, and their strong egos might make them very disagreeable during that process. They could even become insufferable, but they usually have some flexibility and will change before they are forced to. Of course, they might blame someone else for their earlier mistake, but at least they are willing to reverse a bad decision.

Controllers, by contrast, don't necessarily want to get to the right answer. They want to drive to *their* answer. Controllers often have the attitude of "I'm always right, so don't confuse me with the facts." This is why Controllers tend to want yes-people around them. (In contrast, Skeptics respect those who do stand up to them and argue an airtight case.) Moreover, Controllers are loath to backpedal on anything, especially if they'll have to admit that they were wrong. In other words, Controllers change their minds only when they are absolutely forced to. For that to happen, they need to be painted into a corner.

Lastly, both Skeptics and Controllers seek rebellion in making big decisions, but here again there's a crucial difference. Skeptics have an open, almost prideful, rebelliousness. Simply put, they don't care what others think, and they won't hesitate to take on the establishment. They buck the conventional wisdom because, to them, rules are made to be broken. In short, Skeptics are *fearless* rebels.

Controllers are completely different. They are *fearful* rebels. That is, their rebellion is driven by fear. They might be so afraid of making a move, for instance, that they resist demands from their boss to do so. In other words, their fear of making a mistake can make them think nothing of going up against authority figures. Interestingly, Controllers are taken aback when they learn that others perceive them as being difficult. In fact, they sometimes take great umbrage at that, because they do care what others think of them, and they can genuinely be unaware of how they are coming across. (In contrast, Skeptics are quick to admit that they can be exasperating to work with, and they might even brag about that.)

THINKERS VERSUS CONTROLLERS

Thinkers and Controllers are also often confused for each other because of certain shared traits. Both are logical, analytical, thorough, data-intensive, meticulous, and detail-oriented. And Controllers can appear to be just as methodical and process-oriented as Thinkers, both using highly structured and linear approaches to business. But again, although Thinkers and Controllers share many traits, the motivations underlying those traits differ greatly.

Thinkers are motivated primarily by their need for balance. They discipline themselves to be thorough in their analyses to ensure that they haven't missed anything important. They want diverse perspectives so that they can consider every single pro and con. This is why they painstakingly process all relevant data, and it's also why they are methodical and process-oriented—to make sure that they've covered all the bases.

For Controllers, the motivation is fear, which makes them excessively afraid of making a mistake or of getting the short end of the stick. That's why Controllers don't allow themselves to overlook anything: They fear that it will surely come back and bite them. They're so fearful something will go wrong that they often overreact by insisting that they have every single piece of data that could possibly be relevant. When Controllers are terrified of making a move, they can keep on asking for information, partly as a stalling tactic but also as a means of exerting some control over the decision-making process. Like Thinkers, Controllers are generally interested in the minutiae, but they don't necessarily use that information. In fact, although Controllers seek accuracy and facts, that does not mean their decisions are always intelligent and rational. Sometimes their egos or fears get in the way and they jump to illogical conclusions.

To add to the confusion, many Thinkers can be just as aggressive and intimidating as Controllers. As we noted earlier, Roberto Goizueta, former CEO of Coca-Cola, would grill his subordinates so relentlessly that the grueling sessions became known throughout the company as the Spanish Inquisition. With Thinkers, though, you can gain their respect by having all your ducks in a row. When you've logically thought things through and you've double- and triple-checked all your data as well as every step in your methodology, you have a good shot at persuading them because Thinkers actually do process all relevant information. In sharp contrast, Controllers might not even look at the material they've requested because they might have already made up their minds. So having all your ducks in a row won't necessarily gain you anything with Controllers. And therein lies the bottom line: Thinkers can be persuaded, but Controllers can't.

That crucial difference is reflected in the types of organizations they run. When a Thinker is the head of a business unit or division, everybody understands that their proposals might have to withstand some intensive probing and grueling questions, but eventually the best ideas usually prevail. When a Controller is at the helm, people are likely to walk around on eggshells, wondering whether their views can coexist within the Controller's "my way or the highway" system. Because Controllers rule with a "committee of one" mentality, employees know they need to conform to that, even if it's illogical and counterproductive to do so.

FOLLOWERS VERSUS EVERYBODY ELSE

The last common confusion is with Followers, who are difficult to identify because they are such chameleons. As discussed in chapter 9

("The Follower Decision Maker"), many Followers purposely present themselves as something else—for example, as risk-taking Charismatics or methodical Thinkers. But when push comes to shove, they move forward *only* with solutions that have worked successfully in the past.

Because Followers wear many guises, we advise our clients that especially when they're getting mixed signals from someone, they should assume the person is a Follower until proven otherwise. As discussed in chapter 10 ("Persuading the Follower Decision Maker"), that rule of thumb is effective because the other four styles—Charismatics, Thinkers, Skeptics, and Controllers—tend to show themselves more definitively. Also, Followers are the largest of the five categories, accounting for more than one-third of all executives. Big corporations, in particular, tend to be filled with Followers in middle management as well as in the executive suites because those types of organizations tend to reward this style of decision making. Furthermore, assuming that someone is a Follower won't damage your case if that person turns out to be something else.

In our seminars, we are frequently asked, "Is there any strategy that will work in persuading all five styles of decision makers?" The answer is no, there is no silver bullet. As we've discussed throughout this book, each style of decision maker requires a specific strategy. That said, everybody tends to respond favorably to proof that something has been successful elsewhere. That's why so many sales presentations contain one PowerPoint slide that lists the vendor's previous customers, especially if they include blue-chip companies like Merrill Lynch, IBM, General Motors, Johnson & Johnson, and so on. Note that this is the exact strategy that you would use in persuading a Follower; that is, you would provide proof that your proposal has worked successfully before. In other words, assuming that people are Followers and persuading them that way won't do any harm even if they turn out to be Charismatics, Thinkers, Skeptics, or Controllers, because all five styles are swayed favorably by proof.

Another rule of thumb is that when asked, Followers usually claim to be something else. Many executives who are familiar with our work often identify themselves to us as Charismatics or Thinkers when we know for a fact that they are Followers. In our experience, people are

notoriously inaccurate when classifying their own decision styles. We can cite countless examples of executives claiming to be one thing when their actions have totally contradicted that. The most common instances are Followers who adamantly insist that they are something else.

People who do identify themselves as Followers tend not to be. Often they turn out to be Thinkers. What they're looking at—when they incorrectly identify themselves—is how uncomfortable they are with risk. They might remember instances when they didn't understand the risks involved, which made them back away from action—something that a Follower would do. But that is precisely what Thinkers do, too. Until they are confident that they've thoroughly understood and assessed the risks of moving forward with a proposal, they avoid taking action. This is classic Thinker behavior.

A major reason why Followers are so often misidentified is that they have no defining aversions (see exhibit "Approach Profile for Followers" in chapter 9). They are even comfortable with risk, although they do avoid one type of risk, that of trying something that hasn't been done successfully before. Followers have no overwhelming desires either. Of the twelve components we studied, their greatest desire is for bargains, but the strength of that preference is just moderate. In this respect, Followers can appear to be like Thinkers, who also have a moderate desire for bargains as well as no overwhelming likes or dislikes. Moreover, Followers and Thinkers are both cautious decision makers, which can add to the confusion between the two.

Although both Followers and Thinkers seek bargains, they do so for different reasons. For Followers, bargains help to lessen the risk of trying anything unproven. This is why we advise our clients who are salespeople that when they're trying to sell any new product or service to a Follower, they might have to lower its price until it becomes too tempting not to try ("It's such a good deal that I can't afford to pass it up"). For Followers, a bargain is a *substitute* for a lack of proof that something has worked before. By lowering the price of something, you're implicitly telling the Follower that you are willing to share the risk with him, and that helps to gain his trust. In that sense, Followers are very bargain-*driven*.

Thinkers, on the other hand, are bargain-*oriented*. They always know and accept that with any decision, there's a certain amount of risk. And Thinkers don't necessarily need proof that something has worked before. In fact, they are perfectly willing to try novel things. But Thinkers still need to go through their methodical process to determine that something truly is the best option. If the uncertainty in that process is substantial, bargains can help to lessen it to an acceptable level. In other words, price is just one of many factors that Thinkers consider when making their decisions.

Once in a while, when you're classifying someone's decision style, you'll have no trouble because that person is obviously and undeniably a Charismatic, for instance, immediately swept up by new ideas and never asking about risks and costs. More often than not, though, you'll struggle. Because everyone contains elements of all five styles, accurately determining someone's default mode of decision making is usually a complex process, requiring much observation over a long period of time. You need to watch that person in action making a number of important decisions, and you should be wary of the following common traps:

- Don't be fooled by what executives say. Instead, pay attention to their actions—constantly question whether they're actually putting their money where their mouths are—and look for *patterns* of behavior.
- Someone's personality is merely a hint of how that individual makes decisions. Avoid confusing personalities with decision-making styles. The two are only partially correlated and only in a limited way.
- One instance of someone making a decision is far too little information to draw any conclusions, particularly if that example is currently unfolding.
- Skeptics and Controllers share many defining characteristics, but they differ in one crucial way: Skeptics are risk seekers, and Controllers are not.
- Both Thinkers and Controllers are data-intensive and process-oriented, but they do not analyze information in the same way.

Thinkers process all relevant data to arrive at their conclusions; Controllers have a far less balanced approach.

- Followers are frequently mistaken for something else, mainly because that's how they tend to present themselves. When in doubt, assume the person you're dealing with is a Follower until you have strong evidence otherwise.

Chapter 15

Putting Persuasion to the Test

Knowledge of the five styles of decision making can help you to understand why certain persuasion tactics work while others don't. Indeed, the ways in which Charismatics, Thinkers, Skeptics, Followers, and Controllers make decisions should make you reconsider how you've been handling certain situations. By testing your assumptions and long-held beliefs, you can fine-tune and sharpen your persuasion skills. In particular, you should note that

1. **Persuasion can be custom-tailored to a large audience.** When giving a speech to a large group, you can maximize your impact by structuring your presentation with the five styles in mind.
2. **Small groups require specific tactics.** Targeting Skeptics and Controllers is generally not the most efficient use of resources. You'll typically get the most bang for the buck by focusing on Charismatics, Thinkers, and Followers.
3. **Decision styles affect teams.** To assemble the best team for a particular goal, consider each member's style of decision making.
4. **It's not about you.** Always focus on the other person and don't fall into the trap of trying to persuade people as you yourself would like to be persuaded.

5. There is no perfect elevator pitch. Forget trying to hone the perfect pitch. Persuasion is a dialogue, not a monologue.

PERSUASION CAN BE CUSTOM-TAILORED TO A LARGE AUDIENCE

Throughout this book, we've mainly talked about one-on-one interactions between you and the decision maker. But what if you're not dealing with just one individual? What if you're trying to persuade a large audience? Say you're giving a speech at a conference of hundreds of business executives. How should you structure and deliver that presentation? Knowledge of the five decision styles provides valuable clues.

First off, provide people with a quick road map of how your speech will unfold. As long as that overview makes sense, you will hook the Thinkers because they'll identify with the logical sequence of your talk. From that point on, Thinkers are the least of your worries because they will spend the time to work through your arguments, searching for the nuggets of information that they're looking for. In other words, Thinkers stick with you as long as your presentation is logical and they know they'll eventually get the information they need. You also really don't need to worry about Controllers because they are on their own and beyond your ability to sway in a group setting anyway.

The three types of people you need to focus on are the Charismatics, Skeptics, and Followers. Your basic game plan is to first establish your credibility and provide proof that you know what you're talking about. This will put the Skeptics and Followers at ease. The thing you have to hang your hat on with Skeptics and Followers is your personal integrity and your track record. After establishing that, you need to launch into your ideas quickly before losing the attention of the Charismatics.

A typical presentation might unfold like this: Give a brief overview of what you're going to say. Then establish your credibility (this is who I am) and support that with proof (here's what I've done). Note that, to some extent, credibility and proof go hand in hand, and you can usually establish both simultaneously. Next, provide an overview of your talk with bulleted items, which will hook the Charismatics. Later, when you drill down to discuss those items, you'll consolidate that support, and if you present those details in a logical, methodical fashion, you'll eventually get the Thinkers fully behind you. Moreover, if you've done everything right and people are getting on board, you might even hook some of the Controllers.

If you're a salesperson using PowerPoint as a visual aid and have limited yourself to ten slides, you might structure your discussion by starting off with a quick outline of your talk and then present the following:

Slide 1. Who I am: Describe what your company does and why it's important.

Slide 2. What I've done: Give list of well-known customers.

Slide 3. In a nutshell, what I do and how that differs from competitors: Provide overview with bulleted items and one-line descriptions of the competitive advantages of your company.

Slides 4 through 9. Details of what I do: Give information to support slide 3.

Slide 10. Summary of what I just told you: Highlight the main points of your presentation.

Note that this presentation pretty much follows the old advice of tell them what you're going to tell them; tell them; and then tell them what you've just told them. In other words, give an overview, flesh that overview out, and then summarize everything. There's a reason why that formula works. You'll hook Charismatics because of your big idea. You'll get Thinkers because of the way you've approached things logically. And you'll get the majority of the Followers. The only people you'll have trouble reaching are Controllers and die-hard Skeptics who happen to be averse to your ideas. Fortunately, Controllers account for less than 10 percent of all executives. The population of Skeptics is twice that size, but many of them are persuadable *when* you establish enough credibility.

Incidentally, *Paths to Persuasion* is organized with exactly those principles in mind. Chapter 1 presents the main idea, introducing the five styles of decision makers with quick one-line descriptions (for readers who are Charismatics). Chapter 2 talks about our past work and gives details of our research study to provide proof and establish our credibility (for readers who are Followers and Skeptics). And chapters 3 through this one provide all the details (for readers who are Thinkers). Also note that each chapter (except for the introduction and conclusion) has been written by using the same principles: quick overview, details presented logically, and brief summary.

The point is that with large audiences it's impossible to custom-tailor your presentation to each individual person. But, at the same time, you shouldn't treat the audience as a homogeneous entity. Every large group contains its fair share of Charismatics, Thinkers, Skeptics, Followers, and Controllers, and by remembering the relative sizes of those categories and noting how each is likely to be swayed, you can deliver the presentation that will best reach the greatest number of people.

SMALL GROUPS REQUIRE
SPECIFIC TACTICS

Our advice on how to structure a presentation sounds simple and logical. It might even seem so obvious that it's not worth mentioning. But it is, because people frequently make the same basic mistakes over and over. From our research, for example, we have found that 78 percent of sales presentations focus on Skeptics and Controllers even though those two groups represent just 28 percent of all executives. Salespeople tend to anticipate push-back from Skeptics and Controllers, so they structure their arguments that way. In doing so, they often shoot themselves in the feet by overcompensating, concentrating on issues that others find unimportant. In contrast, only 6 percent of sales presentations are geared toward Followers, yet that group accounts for 36 percent of executives. To make matters worse, Skeptics and Controllers can be much tougher to persuade than Followers, Charismatics, and Thinkers.

Of course, in any meeting, the best strategy is to gear your presentation to the decision style of the person who has the ultimate authority. But sometimes that's not possible. For instance, you might be meeting with a committee in which each person has an equal vote. In such situations, be careful not to let the Skeptics and Controllers dominate the discussion.

Unfortunately, that's much easier said than done. Remember that Skeptics and Controllers tend to have strong personalities and rebellious natures. Because of that, they are frequently disruptive during a meeting, and the common response—and mistake—is to spend too much time catering to them. As the saying goes, the squeaky wheel gets the grease. The underlying assumption is that once you've persuaded the rebels, everyone else will fall into step. But the smarter strategy is to concentrate on the others—Followers, for example—and hope that their support will eventually sway the Skeptics and Controllers.

One of the best examples of this is the classic film *12 Angry Men*. In the dramatic movie, Henry Fonda plays a juror who is eventually able to convince his fellow jurors that they should vote not guilty even though each of them initially thinks the defendant committed a murder. Fonda's character is a classic Thinker, always insisting that everyone go through a methodical process to assess each piece of evidence, including all the testimony from witnesses. Thanks to his incessant and logical probing, he's soon able to sway the Followers in the group. Then, through more rational questioning of the evidence, everyone else slowly comes around, one by one.

The point is that Fonda's character doesn't waste his time trying to argue with the extreme Skeptics and Controllers. One of them is a racial bigot who, referring to the Hispanic defendant, argues that "all those people are like that." Fonda's character doesn't get sidetracked into responding to such irrational statements. Instead, he continues his logical analysis, slowly picking apart the prosecutor's case. At the end, the one holdout Controller is forced to capitulate, after everyone else has already declared there's no way they could proclaim the defendant guilty beyond a reasonable doubt.

In business, one tactic to help you avoid having Skeptics or Controllers hijack your discussion is to preview your proposal individually with their lieutenants to get advice and coaching from them before the big meeting. That way you can ferret out and handle their concerns ahead of time and then fine-tune your proposal. But, as discussed earlier, be careful not to overcompensate by spending too much time on issues that concern only Skeptics and Controllers and nobody else.

Another valuable lesson of *12 Angry Men* is that Fonda's character is able to sway the group mainly by attacking the credibility of the witnesses and the other evidence presented. Earlier we talked about how, with any group, you need to quickly establish your credibility and proof before presenting your arguments. In the case of Fonda's character, he had to get people to change their minds, so he did the reverse: He chipped away at the credibility of the witnesses and exposed how shaky their testimony and other evidence were. By doing so, he was able to slowly but surely unravel the prosecutor's case. Once credibility and proof suffer damage, *everything* becomes suspect.

DECISION STYLES AFFECT TEAMS

Whereas *12 Angry Men* is a work of fiction, the way in which decision styles affect the interpersonal dynamics of a group is not. The subject is important in business because companies routinely rely on teams to get work done. When setting one up, though, many managers fail to fully think about the proper composition of the group. They might select people simply by looking at each individual's skill set. Smarter managers will also take into account the personalities of the team members to ensure that the chemistry is right. Another factor in this equation should be each person's decision-making style.

In our experience, we have found that the best teams consist of a variety of styles because in that way diverse viewpoints are represented. A group with mainly Charismatics and Followers is bound to overlook things that a more balanced team (one that also includes Thinkers, Skeptics, and Controllers) will not. To that end, we know of organizations that build executive teams by consciously and actively considering people's decision styles. They might tap a person who's a Skeptic, say, from a pool of equally qualified candidates if that type of decision maker isn't already represented.

Not only can you change the decision-making behavior of teams by judiciously selecting the mix of the individuals involved, you can also design a particular group to accomplish certain goals. For example, if you're putting together a team that will implement processes that are proven and well defined—that is, the group doesn't need to do anything innovative; it just needs to get the wash out, day after day—then you might do well to include a fair share of Followers and Controllers. On the other hand, if your company is going through a tough time, losing customers and market share, and you're assembling a brainstorming team to correct things, then you better include Charismatics and Thinkers, because the former are likely to find the best ideas (and they aren't afraid of taking chances with them) and the latter will help investigate those proposals thoroughly to avoid precipitous action.

Company leadership is also greatly affected by decision styles. Specifically, we have noticed how certain combinations can result in winning partnerships. Consider Coca-Cola during the 1980s through the mid-1990s, when the company recaptured its former glory by transforming itself into an unstoppable multibillion-dollar diversified giant. During those halcyon days, Coca-Cola was led by Roberto Goizueta (a Thinker), then chairman and CEO, and Don Keough (a Charismatic), then president. The potent combination was perhaps the most effective pairing of executives of that generation. A more recent example is Microsoft founder Bill Gates (a Thinker) and CEO Steve Ballmer (a Charismatic). Charismatics and Thinkers aren't the only decision styles that play well off each other. Oracle, for instance, thrived under the leadership of cofounder Larry Ellison (a Skeptic) and Ray Lane (a Thinker), former president and COO.

On the other hand, certain combinations mix like oil and water. Specifically, Charismatics and Controllers as well as Skeptics and Followers tend to make bad pairings. As discussed in chapter 13 ("How to Read People"), the behavioral dial helps to explain why. Those two pairings—Charismatics and Controllers, and Skeptics and Followers—represent decision styles that share none of their strongest desires or aversions in making decisions. (Thinkers can be fine with anyone, especially other Thinkers, because they have no strong likes or dislikes—that's why they're positioned in the center of the behavioral dial.) Charismatics, for instance, are definite risk seekers, while Controllers are most certainly not. Furthermore, pairings of the same decision styles tend not to be as effective, mainly because there's nothing to counterbalance the weaknesses of the individuals. A Controller teamed with another Controller, for instance, could easily spell disaster, as both persons insist on doing things their way. A recent example of a failed partnership of two people with the same decision styles is former AOL Time Warner execs Steve Case and Ted Turner, both classic Skeptics.

IT'S NOT ABOUT YOU

One reason certain combinations tend to be combustible is that the people involved are either unable or unwilling to understand and appreciate the other's views and style of decision making. And that is not a healthy environment for persuasion to take place. You are much more likely to sway someone when you can forget your own perspective and replace it with that of the other person.

Simply put, it's not about you. It's not really about your proposal, no matter how terrific it might be. And it's not about your company, even if it is the market leader. Moreover, it is most definitely not about what you want or need. Instead, it's all about the other person. It's about her needs, her concerns, her issues. By addressing them, you greatly increase your chances of persuading her.

All this might sound painfully obvious. But the truth is that many businesspeople, especially those in sales, have been brainwashed into thinking that persuasion is all about showing, telling, explaining, and instructing. So they give canned, regurgitated presentations that come off as studied and phony. They might spend hours practicing a beautifully constructed pitch that when delivered impresses only themselves and not the intended recipient. And that is absolutely not the goal. You do not want to be forcing your message onto someone, hoping that it will stick. Instead, you want to establish a joint effort in which the both of you work together to solve a common problem.

On a related note, Charlotte Beers, the well-respected advertising and PR expert who was U.S. undersecretary for public diplomacy and public affairs, has this advice: First, think of the *reaction* you want. If, for instance, you need to have a difficult conversation with someone and are unsure of what to say, you should first determine how you want that individual to react to your talk. Once you've figured that out, you'll be much better able to structure exactly what you need to say. You'll also know the appropriate tone to use. In other words, even if you're furious about something, it's still not about your blowing some steam off; it's about how you want the other person to respond to you.

Actually, as far as persuasion goes, there's only one time when it *is* about you, and that's with respect to the other person's decision style. You need to be aware of your own decision-making style in relation to that of the person you're trying to persuade. As discussed in chapter 13 ("How to Read People"), you should be particularly careful when you're trying to influence someone who's on the opposite side of the behavioral dial. If you're a Follower who's trying to persuade a Skeptic, for instance, be forewarned that you might be skating on thin ice. In such situations, be especially aware that things you find persuasive could easily have the opposite effect on the other person. To avoid mistakes, you might do well to have someone else partner with you. If you're a Charismatic who has to argue your case to a Controller, for example, you could greatly improve your chances by having a Thinker with you to provide all the necessary data in a methodical way to suit the Controller.

THERE IS NO PERFECT ELEVATOR PITCH

In numerous ways, people often perpetuate the misconception that persuasion is more about them and not the person they're trying to sway. A good example of that is the myth of the perfect elevator pitch. Here's the scenario: You're riding in an elevator that stops on a floor. The executive you've been trying unsuccessfully for months to schedule a meeting with steps in, presenting you with the perfect opportunity. But you have just thirty seconds to make your case. What do you say?

A while ago, we ourselves taught clients to have a short speech ready for those situations in which they're introduced to someone and need to quickly give the person a handle on who they are. Although it's called an elevator speech, it actually has widespread applicability not only in business (networking with other execs at a conference or convention, for instance) but also in myriad social situations such as cocktail parties, because people are inherently curious about the work that others do.

Incidentally, in more than forty years in business, only once have we actually witnessed someone literally trying to give a pitch in an elevator. This happened years ago, and, coincidentally, it occurred right after we had given a seminar in which we had talked about delivering a thirty-second pitch. The presentation, given at a hotel in Atlanta, had just concluded, and we were in an elevator with several of the attendees, who were all wearing badges with their company names. A stranger got on the elevator, noticed the name badge of one of the people, and asked him what his company did. Our seminar participant then spouted his elevator speech, which he had probably just honed during our workshop. After he had finished, the other guy's response was, "Oh, okay," followed by an awkward silence. The fellow looked like he was sorry he had asked the question in the first place, and he quickly exited the elevator when it reached his floor—hardly the reaction that our seminar attendee was hoping for.

Since then, we have radically changed our thinking on the topic. To wit: The perfect elevator pitch does not exist. It's a business myth. In other words, there is no such thing as a short speech that is going to work for everybody. As we've discussed in this book, Charismatics, Thinkers, Skeptics, Followers, and Controllers are all swayed by different things, and something that is persuasive to a Charismatic might have just the opposite effect on a Controller. Moreover, there can also be variation within a single decision style: One Controller might be substantially different from another.

For those reasons, we now advise our clients that their elevator speech should become a dialogue. They should open with a brief statement followed by a question that solicits further communication, something along the lines of "I'm the CFO for Centra. Have you heard of us?" The goal is to immediately hook the other person into a conversation:

"Sorry, I don't know your company. What does it do?"

"We're in the teleconferencing business. Are you familiar with that?"

"Oh, so you sell those expensive pieces of teleconferencing equipment."

"Actually, those companies are our competitors. Centra develops software that enables people to use the Web for conducting their group-oriented business activities in real time."

"That sounds interesting. How does that work?"

From that point on, you're well into a dialogue. For people who work for a widely known company, the conversation would still begin with a brief statement and a query to establish a dialogue: "I'm a regional sales manager for Hewlett-Packard. We've had quite a year since the merger with Compaq. Have you followed that at all?" Again, the goal is to encourage dialogue:

"Only the little that I've read in the press. So how are things there?"

"Well, it's been about a year now, and we're actually ahead of schedule in terms of our cost savings."

"That's interesting. How did you accomplish that?"

"It's what we euphemistically call consolidation, which means selecting between two perfectly qualified people for the same job."

"That must be tough."

"Yeah, no matter how you do it, it still causes a lot of trauma."

The goal of establishing a dialogue is twofold. First, it gives you a good indication of the interests of the other person, whether they include your company's stock market performance, recent restructuring, change in leadership, acquisition of another firm, or something else. Second, the longer the other person talks, the more hints you'll get regarding his decision style. For instance, is he intrigued by the new technologies and products from your company? Or is he more interested in details of recent layoffs and other cost-cutting measures?

In essence, persuasion is much more about questioning and listening than having the exact right thing to say. Specifically, persuasion is much more likely to occur when you are able to educate the other person through an open dialogue. Remember that push-back often comes from preconceived notions that are inaccurate. By questioning and listening to the other person, you'll be able to identify where those knowledge gaps are, which will help you to focus your discussion to address them. That's why the best mechanism for persuasion is dialogue, not monologue. In other words, you have to establish a conversation because that's when you're most likely to sway the other person. Persuasion is most effective when it involves interaction: asking, probing, listening, discussing, solving—all jointly taking place among two or more people.

By understanding the five styles of decision makers, you can greatly sharpen your persuasive skills for handling one-on-one interactions. Furthermore, we have found that knowledge of how Charismatics, Thinkers, Skeptics, Followers, and Controllers make decisions provides valuable insight into numerous other situations. It has also made us revisit certain widely held business assumptions. Specifically, we now know that

- Large audiences can be swayed most effectively by structuring your presentation in a specific order that quickly puts Thinkers at ease and then hooks Followers, Skeptics, and Charismatics.
- When trying to persuade a small group, resist the natural temptation to cater to those who are disruptive (usually the die-hard Skeptics and Controllers). Instead, focus on the Charismatics, Thinkers, and Followers.
- Teams are more effective when they contain a mix of decision styles.
- Persuasion is about the other person, not you. You are much more likely to sway someone if you can forget your own perspective and replace it with that of the other person.
- The perfect elevator pitch is a myth. Instead of delivering a monologue, concentrate on establishing a dialogue with the other individual.

Chapter 16

Conclusion

At a conference not long ago of about four hundred people, including CIOs and procurement executives, we gave a speech in which we described the five styles of decision making. We talked about the differences between Charismatics, Thinkers, Skeptics, Followers, and Controllers and then described the various tactics for influencing each. During the question-and-answer session, a woman stood up and said, "For eight months, I've had a $14-million proposal sitting in the executive suite of my company. And now I know why it's been stuck." Many in the audience nodded their heads, as if to indicate that they, too, had just figured out why a deal of theirs had recently been stalled.

That type of realization is a common reaction when people learn about the five decision styles. Remember Jason Wheeler, the entrepreneur we talked about in chapters 1 and 4? He and his business partner lost a $100,000 investment to help launch the career of a new urban recording artist. After Wheeler had attended our seminar and learned about the five styles of decision making, he had a similar "aha" moment. He then realized the crucial mistake he had made in failing to secure the $100,000 by not providing the potential investor (a Charismatic) with a detailed business plan of the proposed venture. As we discussed in chapter 2, the decision making of executives appears mysterious and inexplicable only when you're not aware of the underlying principles governing that behavior.

As you've read through this book, we hope that you've had your own similar moments of revelation. Perhaps now you understand a little more clearly the time when your boss denied you a promotion, even though you were the most qualified for it. Or maybe you can now make sense of those occasions when potential customers suddenly changed their minds and signed on with your competitor. The power of our framework is that it helps decode behavior that might on the surface seem puzzling.

After reading chapters 3 through 12, you might look at certain prominent executives in a different way. Specifically, you might now understand why Carly Fiorina, the CEO of Hewlett-Packard, pushed through the merger with Compaq, even against tremendous shareholder resistance. Or you might have additional insight into how Fed chairman Alan Greenspan determines whether or not to raise interest rates—a huge decision with countless ramifications for the economy. Perhaps you've even begun to rethink how certain executives in your own company tend to make decisions. If, for instance, you've had to work with a classic Controller in your organization, you might now be better equipped to deal with that person's behavior.

For those times when you've had difficulty reading someone, chapter 13 might have provided you with valuable insights, and perhaps you are already using the behavioral dial, with its focus on risk and responsibility, to identify people's decision-making styles. If you've made bad mistakes in the past (thinking, for instance, that someone was a bold innovator when in fact she was extremely risk-averse), chapter 14 might have helped you understand those errors. From chapter 15, you might have picked up other useful tips—for example, ways to improve your public speaking, to large audiences as well as small groups. From that chapter, you might have also gained insight into why certain teams of people tend to perform better than others. Moreover, the next time the classic movie *12 Angry Men* airs on TV, you might watch it from a whole new perspective.

We have found that people who learn about the five styles of decision making inevitably begin to wonder about deploying our framework to numerous other situations. One issue that our clients often raise is whether the five styles are applicable to different cultures and countries. Although our study was conducted predominantly in the United States, every time we have presented our results to executives with experience working internationally, they confirmed that our five decision styles are indeed universal. They do add, however, that the relative percentages of the styles might change across different cultures.

Our own hypothesis, which we have not yet investigated quantitatively, is that different countries do have different percentages of decision styles. We believe, for instance, that the relative percentage of Charismatic executives in the United States is probably higher than that for the rest of the world. Similarly, Follower executives might be more prominent in Japan. We should emphasize, however, that our belief is not based on any presumption that, for example, more Charismatics are born in the United States than anywhere else. Instead, we assert that various cultures and organizations tend to reward certain styles of decision making, so the relative percentages of the five styles as represented by business execs are likely to vary from country to country.

On a related note, people usually wonder whether certain decision styles are better suited for particular job functions, leading to differences in the relative representations of those styles. For example, is the percentage of Controllers higher for COOs and comptrollers than for executives in general? Do Charismatics tend to fill certain roles, such as VP of strategy and new business development? Are Thinkers more likely to be found in purchasing and procurement functions, because of the emphasis there on using logical, comparative analyses? In the future, we plan to investigate those and other issues as we continue our research in executive decision styles.

For us, we have been continually surprised by the various ways in which people have begun to apply our framework. A question that we are often asked is whether our tools would be effective for untangling domestic issues. After learning about the behavioral dial, a participant in our seminar remarked, "Now I see why my wife and I have so much trouble making big decisions together: She's a Follower and I'm a Skeptic." Our comment to him was that we hadn't really thought about applying our tools that way (and we have absolutely no intention of getting into the field of marriage counseling), but maybe one day someone will.

Perhaps one of the most intriguing applications of our framework came from a colleague of ours whose theory is that many fictional works build dramatic tension through characters who have different styles of decision making. That way the characters can better play off one another. In particular, TV sitcoms seem to work well with such a formula. The classic *I Love Lucy*, for instance, had a Charismatic (Lucy), a Skeptic (Ricky), a Follower (Ethel), and a Controller (Fred). *Seinfeld* had a Skeptic (Jerry), a Follower (Elaine), a Controller (George), and a Charismatic (Kramer).

On a more serious note, we believe that knowledge of the five styles not only improves your ability to sway others, it also helps you with your own decision-making skills, particularly in business. For instance, if you're a Follower who's heading a division that's struggling to find new growth markets, you might do well to surround yourself with Charismatics and Thinkers to help you spot emerging opportunities. If, on the other hand, you're a Skeptic and you need help to implement a merger between your organization and another, you might consider tapping the services of competent Followers who have undergone similar mergers.

To be sure, our biggest hope is that you continue to apply our framework in different ways. But now here's our challenge. We don't just want you to use what you've learned to conduct postmortems, dissecting decisions that have turned against you to understand why that happened. Although playing Monday-morning quarterback does provide valuable insights, we also want you to apply the persuasion tools more proactively. Beginning with the next major decision that you're involved in, use the behavioral dial to help you identify the type of person you're dealing with. If you think he's a Skeptic, for example, turn to chapters 7, 13, and 14 to confirm your hypothesis. Then use the information in chapter 8 to develop the best strategy for convincing him to see things your way. You might even develop your own new tactics for influencing that type of decision style. In short, we don't want you to follow just the paths to persuasion that we've paved for you. We want you to explore some untrodden ground for yourself.

Throughout this book, we ourselves have been trying to persuade someone—namely, you—to use our framework, but in the previous chapter we emphasized how persuasion should always be a two-way communication. Unfortunately, the format of books only allows information to be transmitted and not received. But in the spirit of our basic message that persuasion requires a dialogue, we invite you to visit our Web site and take our persuasion test (the URL is www.mill-will.com/persuade.html). You can also use the contact information there to correspond with us. In particular, we'd be interested in learning about the different paths to persuasion that you've been discovering for yourself.

Appendix I

About the Research

Our initial study investigating the decision-making processes of executives was conducted from January 1999 to June 2001. For the project, we interviewed 1,684 executives through e-mail, fax, phone, and in person. The participants were from diverse industries, including automotive; consulting; consumer durables, apparel, and retail; services; software; technology; and telecommunications. We asked those executives specifically about their purchasing decisions, but we contend that the results have broad applicability to decision making in general.

More than 97 percent of the participants were from the United States, with the remainder from Australia and Canada. When we present our results at various seminars, executives from multinational companies often question how applicable our research is to them. But after we explain the five different styles in detail, they invariably confirm that based on their experiences the framework does indeed apply internationally, though they sometimes say that the relative percentages of the five categories might be different. A frequent comment we've heard is that in Japan the percentage of Followers might be higher than the 36 percent from our study.

At this point, we have not investigated such issues quantitatively; all we have is anecdotal evidence of possible differences between cultures. That said, we should emphasize that we are not asserting that any country differences (should they indeed exist) are a result of genetic factors. In other words, we don't believe that Japan could have more Follower executives because a greater number of Followers are born there. Instead, we contend that if there is indeed such a difference between Japan and the United States, it is because Japanese corporations might tend to reward and promote a Follower style of decision making more so than U.S. companies, which may be more likely to reward the innovative risk-taking behavior of Charismatics. At any rate, we contend that human nature is human nature. That is, we strongly believe that the decision styles of Charismatics, Thinkers, Followers, Skeptics, and Controllers are universal because they describe fundamental human behavior. So we would expect the five styles to be present in any culture or region of the world, although their relative percentages might differ.

In terms of age, about 46 percent of the study participants were under thirty-five years old; another 46 percent were between thirty-five and fifty-four years old; the remaining 8 percent were fifty-five and older. The split between men and women was roughly fifty-fifty. Here we should note that the purpose of our survey was to study a wide sampling of executives to capture the behavior of the key decision makers in corporate America. We defined "executives" as directors and professional managers who typically held titles from the VP level up. They were the heads of business units who had their own P&L responsibilities (or they were on the senior team that had P&L responsibilities). In short, our sampling is representative of the people driving business decisions today.

If we had looked at the upper echelon of corporate America—just CEOs, COOs, CFOs, and other "C" titles—the average age of the participants would have been higher, and the breakdown would have been more skewed toward men. But we recognize that, especially in matrix organizations and companies with decentralized management, crucial decisions aren't being made only at the highest levels. In fact, in large companies, important decisions are often made several rungs below the very top of the corporate ladder. So we specifically tried to include the decision making at those middle-management levels. Even if we had chosen to look at just the senior executive level (or, conversely, if we had surveyed people further down the corporate ladder), again we strongly believe that we would have found the same five styles of decision makers, although their relative percentages might have been different.

We are planning to investigate those and other related issues in our future work. In fact, our project studying executive decision making is an ongoing effort: We have continued to collect data and are planning to update our results on an annual basis. Another area that we are interested in investigating is whether the relative percentages of the five styles might change with respect to the size of an organization. We suspect, for instance, that large corporations tend to have more Followers, and smaller entrepreneurial firms would likely have more Charismatics and Skeptics. Again, our contention is that different types of organizations tend to encourage and reward certain aspects of decision making, such as risk taking, but we have yet to confirm this quantitatively.

Appendix II

The Twelve Components
of Decision Making

The following charts display how each of the five styles of executives (Charismatics, Thinkers, Skeptics, Followers, and Controllers) rank in terms of the twelve components of decision making, such as risk, responsibility, and competitiveness. Although we have presented the data with respect to the individual attributes, we strongly recommend that you consider the information in totality. For example, Charismatics like bold, innovative ideas, yet they are neutral with respect to the attribute of rebellion (the desire to move beyond the status quo). That, at first, might appear to be contradictory, but consider also how strongly Charismatics desire both risk and responsibility. In other words, Charismatics are risk takers who do want to move beyond the status quo, but they are also responsible decision makers who will pursue innovative ideas only when they make good business sense. That is, they won't buck convention just to be rebellious, whereas Skeptics might be prone to because they seek rebellion and risk, *and* they shun responsibility.

RISK

Strength of Desire in the Buying Experience

SEEK MORE

Average

Charismatics	44
Skeptics	12
-3	Followers
-12	Thinkers
-45	Controllers

AVOID MORE

Error ±2.9 points

© 2003 Miller-Williams Inc. (millwill.com)

Note: The data have been normalized to range from −100 (maximum aversion) to +100 (maximum desire).

RESPONSIBILITY

Strength of Desire in the Buying Experience

SEEK MORE

Average

Charismatics	51
Followers	15
Thinkers	5
-33	Skeptics
-54	Controllers

AVOID MORE

Error ±2.9 points

© 2003 Miller-Williams Inc. (millwill.com)

Note: The data have been normalized to range from −100 (maximum aversion) to +100 (maximum desire).

COMPETITIVENESS

Strength of Desire in the Buying Experience

SEEK MORE

Average

- Charismatics — 29
- Thinkers — 25
- Skeptics — 10
- Followers — -7
- Controllers — -14

AVOID MORE

Error ±2.9 points   © 2003 Miller-Williams Inc. (millwill.com)

Note: The data have been normalized to range from −100 (maximum aversion) to +100 (maximum desire).

REBELLION

Strength of Desire in the Buying Experience

SEEK MORE

Average

- Skeptics — 38
- Controllers — 37
- Thinkers — 9
- Followers — -2
- Charismatics — -8

AVOID MORE

Error ±2.9 points   © 2003 Miller-Williams Inc. (millwill.com)

Note: The data have been normalized to range from −100 (maximum aversion) to +100 (maximum desire).

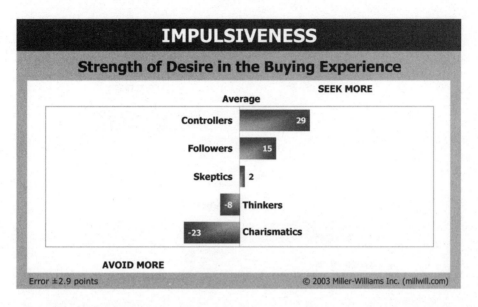

Note: The data have been normalized to range from −100 (maximum aversion) to +100 (maximum desire).

Note: The data have been normalized to range from −100 (maximum aversion) to +100 (maximum desire).

FEAR & UNCERTAINTY

Strength of Desire in the Buying Experience

SEEK MORE
Average

Controllers — 58
Thinkers — 16
Followers — 8
Skeptics — -2
Charismatics — -51

AVOID MORE

Error ±2.9 points   © 2003 Miller-Williams Inc. (millwill.com)

Note: The data have been normalized to range from −100 (maximum aversion) to +100 (maximum desire).

SELF-ABSORPTION

Strength of Desire in the Buying Experience

SEEK MORE
Average

Controllers — 79
Skeptics — 44
Thinkers — 12
Followers — 8
Charismatics — -49

AVOID MORE

Error ±2.9 points   © 2003 Miller-Williams Inc. (millwill.com)

Note: The data have been normalized to range from −100 (maximum aversion) to +100 (maximum desire).

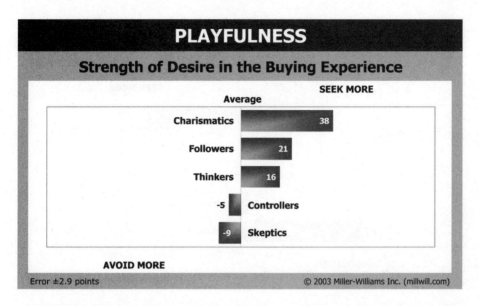

Note: The data have been normalized to range from −100 (maximum aversion) to +100 (maximum desire).

Note: The data have been normalized to range from −100 (maximum aversion) to +100 (maximum desire).

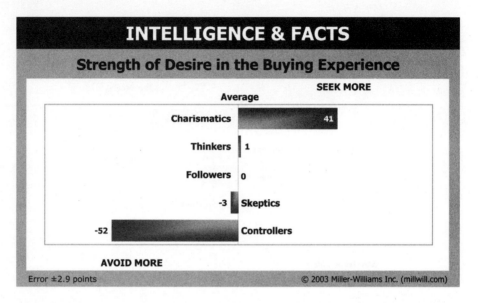

Note: The data have been normalized to range from −100 (maximum aversion) to +100 (maximum desire).

BARGAINS

Strength of Desire in the Buying Experience

SEEK MORE

Average

Followers   31

Charismatics   28

Thinkers   19

-2 Controllers

-5 Skeptics

AVOID MORE

Error ±2.9 points   © 2003 Miller-Williams Inc. (millwill.com)

Note: The data have been normalized to range from −100 (maximum aversion) to +100 (maximum desire).

Notes

Chapter 3

1. "Air Herb's Secret Weapon," *Chief Executive* magazine, July/August 1999.
2. "Can Anyone Replace Herb?" *Fortune*, April 17, 2000.
3. "How Does He Do It?" *Fortune*, May 28, 2001.
4. *Iacocca: An Autobiography*, Lee Iacocca with William Novak (Bantam, 1984).
5. "Jack on Jack," *Harvard Business Review*, February 2002.
6. "The Jack and Herb Show," *Fortune*, January 11, 1999.
7. "The Business of Being Oprah," *Fortune*, April 1, 2002.
8. "Finance Innovator: Richard Branson," Lucy Siegle, *Observer*, March 31, 2002.
9. *Losing My Virginity*, Richard Branson (Times Books, Random House, 1998).
10. *Jack: Straight from the Gut*, Jack Welch with John A. Byrne (Warner Business Books, 2001).
11. Ibid.
12. Ibid.
13. "Jack: The Exit Interview," *Fortune*, September 2001.
14. "Red Baron," *Forbes*, July 3, 2000.
15. *Talking Straight*, Lee Iacocca (Bantam, 1988).
16. "Then Came Branson," *BusinessWeek* (international edition), October 26, 1998.
17. *Iacocca: An Autobiography*, Lee Iacocca with William Novak (Bantam, 1984).
18. Ibid.
19. *Guts*, Robert A. Lutz (John Wiley & Sons, 1998).
20. "How Does He Do It?" *Fortune*, May 28, 2001.
21. "Jack of His Trade," *New Yorker Online Only*, November 5, 2001.
22. "Jack on Jack," Harvard Business Review, February 2002.
23. *Losing My Virginity*, Richard Branson (Times Books, Random House, 1998).
24. "Jack on Jack," *Harvard Business Review*, February 2002.
25. *Jack: Straight from the Gut*, Jack Welch with John A. Byrne (Warner Business Books, 2001).
26. *Iacocca: An Autobiography*, Lee Iacocca with William Novak (Bantam, 1984).
27. "The Chairman of the Board Looks Back," *Fortune*, May 28, 2001.
28. *Jack: Straight from the Gut*, Jack Welch with John A. Byrne (Warner Business Books, 2001).
29. Ibid.
30. "The Business of Being Oprah," *Fortune*, April 1, 2002.
31. "The Jack and Herb Show," *Fortune*, January 11, 1999.
32. *Jack: Straight from the Gut*, Jack Welch with John A. Byrne (Warner Business Books, 2001).
33. "What They Say About Herb," *Fortune*, May 28, 2001.

34. "The Jack and Herb Show," *Fortune*, January 11, 1999.
35. *Losing My Virginity*, Richard Branson (Times Books, Random House, 1998).
36. "The Business of Being Oprah," *Fortune*, April 1, 2002.

Chapter 5

1. "Facetime with Michael Dell," *FastCompany*, March 2001.
2. *The Profit Zone: How Strategic Business Design Will Lead You to Tomorrow's Profits*, Adrian J. Slywotzky and David J. Morrison with Bob Andelman (Times Books, Random House, 1997).
3. *Direct from Dell: Strategies That Revolutionized the Industry*, Michael Dell with Catherine Fredman (HarperBusiness, 1999).
4. "Homespun Wisdom from the 'Oracle of Omaha,'" *BusinessWeek*, July 5, 1999.
5. *Greenspan: The Man Behind the Money*, Justin Martin (Perseus Publishing, 2000).
6. Ibid.
7. "Coke Strikes Back," *Fortune*, June 1, 1981.
8. "Katharine Graham: The Power That Didn't Corrupt," *Ms.*, October 1974.
9. Ibid.
10. "Coke Strikes Back," *Fortune*, June 1, 1981.
11. *For God, Country and Coca-Cola: The Definitive History of the Great American Soft Drink and the Company That Makes It*, Mark Pendergrast (Basic Books, 1993).
12. "Facetime with Michael Dell," *FastCompany*, March 2001.
13. "The Value Machine," *Fortune*, February 19, 2001.
14. Ibid.
15. "The Fountainhead," *New Yorker*, April 24, 2000.
16. "Coke's Man on the Spot," *BusinessWeek*, July 29, 1985.
17. "The Fountainhead," *New Yorker*, April 24, 2000.
18. "How Alan Greenspan Runs the World," *salon.com*, January 10, 2001.
19. Ibid.
20. *Business Masterminds: Bill Gates*, Robert Heller (Dorling Kindersley, 2000).
21. *Business the Bill Gates Way: 10 Secrets of the World's Richest Business Leader*, Des Dearlove (AMACOM, 1999).
22. "Katharine Graham and How She Grew," *McCall's*, September 1971.
23. "Katharine Graham: The Power That Didn't Corrupt," in *Ms.*, October 1974.
24. "The Fountainhead," *New Yorker*, April 24, 2000.
25. "Katharine Graham: New Power in the American Press," *Vogue*, January 1, 1967.
26. "Katharine Graham and How She Grew," *McCall's*, September 1971.
27. *A Good Life: Newspapering and Other Adventures*, Ben Bradlee (Simon & Schuster, 1995).
28. *Personal History*, Katharine Graham (Knopf, 1997).
29. Ibid.
30. Ibid.
31. "Homespun Wisdom from the 'Oracle of Omaha,'" *BusinessWeek*, July 5, 1999.
32. Ibid.
33. "Coke's Man on the Spot," *BusinessWeek*, July 29, 1985.
34. Ibid.
35. Ibid.
36. "Katharine Graham: The Power That Didn't Corrupt," *Ms.*, October 1974.
37. "Katharine Graham, 1917–2001: An American Original," *Newsweek*, July 30, 2001.
38. "The Fountainhead," *New Yorker*, April 24, 2000.
39. *For God, Country and Coca-Cola: The Definitive History of the Great American Soft Drink and the Company That Makes It*, Mark Pendergrast (Basic Books, 1993).
40. *Business the Bill Gates Way: 10 Secrets of the World's Richest Business Leader*, Des Dearlove (AMACOM, 1999).

41. *Direct from Dell: Strategies That Revolutionized the Industry*, Michael Dell with Catherine Fredman (HarperBusiness, 1999).
42. "The Fountainhead," *New Yorker*, April 24, 2000.
43. Ibid.

Chapter 7

1. "The Man Who Would Be Gates," *Vanity Fair*, June 1997.
2. "The Next Richest Man in the World," *Fortune*, November 13, 2000.
3. "Can Larry Beat Bill?" *BusinessWeek*, May 15, 1995.
4. "Confessions of a Control Freak," *Fortune*, September 4, 2000.
5. Ibid.
6. "The Lost Tycoon," Ken Auletta, *New Yorker*, April 23 and 30, 2001.
7. Ibid.
8. Ibid.
9. "The Man Who Would Be Gates," *Vanity Fair*, June 1997.
10. "The Lost Tycoon," Ken Auletta, *New Yorker*, April 23 and 30, 2001.
11. Ibid.
12. Ibid.
13. "The King of Customer," *www.industryweek.com*, February 2002.
14. "Confessions of a Control Freak," *Fortune*, September 4, 2000.
15. Ibid.
16. "The Next Richest Man in the World," *Fortune*, November 13, 2000.
17. Ibid.
18. "The Lost Tycoon," Ken Auletta, *New Yorker*, April 23 and 30, 2001.
19. "Steve Case's Last Stand," *Vanity Fair*, January 2003.
20. Ibid.
21. "The Next Richest Man in the World," *Fortune*, November 13, 2000.
22. "Steve Case's Last Stand," *Vanity Fair*, January 2003.
23. Ibid.
24. "Larry Ellison Is Captain Ahab and Bill Gates Is Moby Dick," *Fortune*, October 28, 1996.
25. "The King of Customer," *www.industryweek.com*, February 2002.
26. "Steve Case's Last Stand," *Vanity Fair*, January 2003.
27. Ibid.
28. "The King of Customer," *www.industryweek.com*, February 2002.
29. "Level 5 Leadership: The Triumph of Humility and Fierce Resolve," Jim Collins, *Harvard Business Review*, January 2001.

Chapter 9

1. "Voices from the Front: Replacing a Legend," *Fortune*, November 18, 2002.
2. "Holding Steady: As Rivals Sputter, Can Southwest Stay on Top?" *BusinessWeek*, February 3, 2002.
3. "The Battle for Hewlett-Packard," *Vanity Fair*, June 2002.
4. "Carly's Last Stand?" *BusinessWeek*, December 24, 2001.
5. "Home Depot: Exit the Builder, Enter the Repairman," *Fortune*, March 19, 2001.
6. "What Worked at GE Isn't Working at Home Depot," *BusinessWeek*, January 27, 2003.
7. Ibid.
8. "Home Depot: Exit the Builder, Enter the Repairman," *Fortune*, March 19, 2001.
9. "Holding Steady: As Rivals Sputter, Can Southwest Stay on Top?" *BusinessWeek*, February 3, 2002.

10. "If You Knew Suzy . . . ," *New York*, May 6, 2002.
11. "Home Depot: Something to Prove," *Fortune*, June 24, 2002.
12. "The Bronfman Saga: From Rags to Riches to . . . ," *Fortune*, November 25, 2002.
13. Ibid.
14. "The Battle for Hewlett-Packard," *Vanity Fair*, June 2002.
15. *Perfect Enough: Carly Fiorina and the Reinvention of Hewlett-Packard*, George Anders (Penguin Putnam, 2003).
16. *Citizen Coors: An American Dynasty*, Dan Baum (HarperCollins, 2000).
17. "Home Depot: Something to Prove," *Fortune*, June 24, 2002.
18. Ibid.
19. "Now for the Hard Part: Carly Fiorina Sold Investors on the HP Merger. To Make It Work, She's Still on the Road," *Fortune*, November 18, 2002.
20. *Good Spirits: The Making of a Businessman*, Edgar M. Bronfman (G. P. Putnam's Sons, 1998).
21. *Backfire: Carly Fiorina's High-Stakes Battle for the Soul of Hewlett-Packard*, Peter Burrows (John Wiley & Sons, 2003).
22. "Now for the Hard Part: Carly Fiorina Sold Investors on the HP Merger. To Make It Work, She's Still on the Road," *Fortune*, November 18, 2002.
23. *Good Spirits: The Making of a Businessman*, Edgar M. Bronfman (G. P. Putnam's Sons, 1998).
24. *Citizen Coors: An American Dynasty*, Dan Baum (HarperCollins, 2000).

Chapter 11

1. *Only the Paranoid Survive*, Andrew S. Grove (Doubleday, 1996).
2. "I Love Martha," *New York*, October 21, 2002.
3. "Blood Feud," *Fortune*, April 14, 1997.
4. *Jose Ignacio Lopez de Arriortua*, Michael H. Moffett and William E. Youngdahl (Thunderbird, The American Graduate School of International Management, 1998).
5. Ibid.
6. "Steinbrenner Reminds Jeter Just Who the Boss Is," *New York Times*, February 20, 2003.
7. "Cracklin' Rosie," *Vanity Fair*, December 2002.
8. "Martha Inc.," *BusinessWeek*, January 17, 2000.
9. "What's Behind Ford's Fall?" *Fortune*, October 29, 2001.
10. *Dallas Times Herald*, March 14, 1974.
11. *Built from Scratch: How a Couple of Regular Guys Grew the Home Depot from Nothing to $30 Billion*, Bernie Marcus and Arthur Blank with Bob Andelman (Crown Business, 1999).
12. *Washington Post*, April 12, 1987.
13. "Jac Nasser Is Car Crazy," *Fortune*, June 22, 1998.
14. "Cracklin' Rosie," *Vanity Fair*, December 2002.
15. Ibid.
16. "Lunch at Martha's," *New Yorker*, February 3, 2002.
17. "I Love Martha," *New York*, October 21, 2002.
18. *New York Post*, April 27, 1986.
19. "Jac Nasser Is Car Crazy," *Fortune*, June 22, 1998.
20. Ibid.
21. "Lunch at Martha's," *New Yorker*, February 3, 2002.
22. Ibid.
23. "Family Feuds Don't Get Nastier Than This," *BusinessWeek*, February 10, 2003.

Chapter 14

1. *The Faber Report*, David Faber with Ken Kurson (Little, Brown, 2002).

Index

About Miller-Williams Inc.

Numerous publications and companies all over the world recognize Miller-Williams Inc. as the leading authority in measuring customer value. Our proprietary, patent-pending methods to conduct research provide accurate and meaningful insights into how customers think and behave. The research behind this book is just one application of how today's most influential corporations use our methods. As of May 2003, we have collected more than 2 million responses in more than twenty industries using these methods.

Most research methods employ a simple, direct questioning technique when conducting interviews. Yet this technique uncovers only a portion of how customers think. To understand their total desires, the Miller-Williams research methods go well beyond surface-level data and techniques.

The most revealing way to discover customers' desires is through the use of metaphors. Using a proven, standard set of constructs, our methods enable customers to communicate their desires by figuratively describing their ideal. The output then applies quantitative, statistical rigor to what is typically available only in small, qualitative studies. This in-depth, comprehensive analysis unveils the common drivers of customer behavior shared by seemingly endless, diverse groups of customers. These groups—for example, the five executive decision styles in this book—provide a simple, concise way to build action plans that work consistently because these commonalities tend not to change quickly. Further, this balances the cost-intensive "one size fits all" approach with the resource/knowledge-intensive "one-to-one" approach to substantially reduce the intensity of both efforts while increasing effectiveness.

To see how companies use our research methods or to view results from other Miller-Williams Inc. studies, visit our Web Site at http://www.millwill.com/ or contact us at 800-790-6070 (U.S.) or info@millwill.com.